The Economic Fabric of Society

The Harbrace Series in Business and Economics
EDITORIAL ADVISORY BOARD

THE
ECONOMIC
FABRIC
OF
SOCIETY

CHARLES L. COLE

California State College at Long Beach

Harcourt, Brace & World, Inc.
New York / Chicago / San Francisco / Atlanta

Library of Congress Catalog Card Number: 69–14398

Printed in the United States of America

PREFACE

This brief history of economic thought is written for students with little or no knowledge of economics. Its specific purposes are several: first, to introduce the student to the economic problem, to what economics is, and to the nature of the economist's work; second, to show the relevance of economic thought to economic affairs by placing the work of the great economists in its historical context; third, to explain, in a manner suitable to an introductory course, the contributions of the great economists to our intellectual heritage and to economic thought in particular; and, fourth, to familiarize the student with a few simple tools of economic analysis.

The book is intended primarily for use in a general introduction to the social sciences. It is there that the vast majority of students have their sole encounter with economics, and it is there that the book must make its contribution to general economic literacy. To that end, I have tried to make it more than a history of economic thought. I have tried to write a book *about* economics—a book that allows the student to sample the discipline's techniques and theories as well as to follow its chronological development. Consequently, I have taken economic problems as they arose, shown how the great economists responded to them, introduced in an uncomplicated way the theoretical methods these men used or developed, and indicated the impact of their work.

The present volume should be useful also as a supplement in the first course in economics. Students in this course are given a thorough grounding in the theory that is necessarily the essence of the discipline. Economics, however, is a peculiarly *reactive* discipline, having developed almost entirely in response to real economic situations and to the weaknesses of existing economic beliefs. For this reason, I feel, economic theory becomes most meaningful to the student when he can see it in the context of the facts it was intended to explain. In other words, he needs to understand the history of economics and of economic thought if he is to find the reality behind the abstract hypotheses of theory. This book may help him toward such an understanding.

CONTENTS

WHAT IS
ECONOMICS?

1

Before you begin to read this chapter, write down somewhere what you think economics is. Having done that, read the chapter and then compare your impression at the end with what you wrote down.

Although economics deals with the most mundane matters—indeed, one of the greatest economists, Alfred Marshall, described economics as "a study of mankind in the ordinary business of life"[1]—I have been tempted to conclude in bleak moments that most people have a somewhat more accurate understanding of such esoteric fields as nuclear physics and topology than of economics. At the same time, few subjects generate more heated argument than economics. Although well-founded controversy is not to be avoided—in fact, it makes life more interesting —much cloudy thinking and hence many useless disputes about economic affairs could be avoided if the economic literacy of our population were greater. Although this book is not intended to make an economist of anyone, it should leave you with no doubts as to what economics and economists are about. I hope, too, that it will give you some understanding of the important implications that economic matters have for private and public policy decisions.

This book is not, however, a text on economic analysis, economic

[1] Alfred Marshall, *Principles of Economics,* 8th ed. (New York: Macmillan, 1948), p. 1.

history, or the development of economic thought, although it draws on all three fields. Its main object is to show how economists have attempted to explain the weaving of the economic fabric of our society and what meaning this process has for us. To do this, we shall first define economics. Then we shall examine the work of the great economists in the light of the historical contexts in which they worked, for one of my main contentions is that economics is essentially a *reactive* science. That is, economics has developed as individual economists have striven with the problems that were the most pressing during their lifetimes. Finally, in order to understand these motivating historical events and their theoretical explanations, we shall develop, as we move along, some modest tools of analysis.

THE STUDY OF ECONOMICS

Will the study of economics do anything for you? Uninformed opinions seem to cluster at opposite poles. One group of optimists fondly hope that the study of economics will make them rich. At the other extreme, a group of cynics doubt that the study of economics will make anyone wealthy or even wise; in proof of their disbelief they ask, "Where are all the rich economics professors?" Neither opinion reflects an understanding of the nature of economics—or of any academic discipline, for that matter. The study of economics is no more likely to make you rich than the study of physical education is likely to enable you to run the four-minute mile. The study of economics is not a royal road to wealth, but it is not a roadblock either.

What Economics Is

It may be easier to discover what economics is if we look first at some things that economics is not.

The study of economics will not teach you how to play the stock market or speculate in commodities. It is not a course in investments. A course in economics will not tell you how to put together a great corporate venture or how to proceed under Chapter X of the Bankruptcy Act. It is a course in neither corporate finance nor corporate law. At a more modest level, economics will not teach you how to live on a budget, balance your checkbook, or stretch your income. It is not the study of personal finance. Economics will not teach you how to become a successful executive. It is not a course in business administration.

Economics will not tell you whether the distribution of income is just—whether, for instance, a cat ought to have a saucer of cream while there is one baby in the world that is suffering from malnutrition. It will not tell you whether profit maximization is a morally sound drive. Economists have no special competency in moralizing. Economics is not ethics. And, despite some appearances, the study of economics does not center upon the examination of reams of financial data, the figuring of probabilities, or the solving of complex equations. Economics is not accounting, statistics, or mathematics.

Although economics may include, touch upon, or be related to these fields, it is not identical with any one of them. Then what is it? Economics is the study of *the* economic problem. If this statement suggests to you that there is only *one* problem for economists to study, you are absolutely right. Now, what is this one economic problem?

To answer this question in the most direct way, ask yourself, "What is *my* economic problem?" Now you doubtless know what economics is. Unless you are a very unusual person, or wealthy, your answer is that you do not have enough wherewithal to satisfy your numerous longings. The means for satisfying your wants are scarce. This is *your* economic problem, and, on a larger scale, it is *the* economic problem. *The means for satisfying the wants of the human race, even in the most affluent societies, are scarce.* In a word, the economic problem is *scarcity*. This is what economics is about. This is what economists study. The level of study makes no difference, whether it is this book or the most difficult treatise used in a graduate course; the student of economics studies scarcity. And it makes no difference what a course in economics is called—elementary economics, money and banking, public-utility economics, or price theory. The focus is always the same—scarcity.

But how do we define scarcity? Is there not "an awful lot of stuff" in the world? Are there not some things that, rather than being scarce, are superabundant? In a good many cases, would we not be better off with less of something instead of more? Although some nations may be on the edge of starvation, are not other nations,—the United States, for example—wealthy? How can we give sufficient precision to a concept such as scarcity to base a whole science upon it? The answer is that man is the measure, that scarcity is relative. In economics, things are scarce only in relation to man's desire for them.

Often perceptive passages from great works of literature are more helpful in understanding the complexities of the world than are textbooks. For example, let us turn to the Bible. Consider Adam and Eve. In the Garden of Eden they lacked nothing; abundance prevailed. Before man fell, the means provided in Eden for satisfying the desires of its inhabitants were greater than their wants. Hence, Adam and Eve had no economic problem; there was no scarcity. Had such abundance continued throughout history, we would number no economists among our population. No one could possibly think up economics in a society of true abundance—a society in which want-satisfiers exceed wants—no matter how sophisticated such a society may become.

The existence of economics and economists thus indicates that we do not live in a society of abundance. As we continue reading in Genesis, we see Adam and Eve expelled from Eden. Man's utopian existence ends, and the economic problem appears. Instead of a profusion of things for immediate consumption, the earth, untended by man, now produces weeds and leaves him shelterless. Nonetheless, Adam and Eve and their descendants have not been condemned to starvation and exposure to the elements; they can still eat and have shelter—but only at a cost!

To live, man must be a consumer; and, in the face of scarcity, if he is to be a consumer, he *must* be a producer. He must work for his living. This is no less true in "affluent" societies, such as the United States is supposed to be, than in so-called primitive societies. No matter how much of everything man may have, whenever he has to produce —when he has to work—the economic problem exists. The resource situation our world confronts is totally unlike that of the Garden of Eden. We have resources, but they are not supplied in what we may call the most "efficient" forms or combinations. Man must alter the world's resources to meet his wants, and this involves a cost. Meeting the economic problem always involves a cost. This is the meaning of scarcity.

There are two basic ways to attack the economic problem. One way is to increase the amount and variety of want-satisfiers. This course is typical of certain societies, particularly those we of the West are most familiar with. Another way of meeting the problem, followed sometimes in some societies, is to reduce the number and intensity of human wants. Ascetic philosophies have arisen that stress the ephemeral nature of material gain. This second response to the economic problem, however, is becoming less and less acceptable to increasing numbers of the world's peoples, thereby intensifying the economic problem in our time. And, whatever his response to scarcity, man is troubled, even plagued, by his wants.

Now let us sum up. The economic problem exists whenever there is scarcity—or, more accurately, that problem *is* scarcity. The whole of economics is founded upon this basic inequality:

$$\text{man's wants} > \text{the means of want satisfaction}$$

Whenever this inequality exists, the economic problem exists, and there is work for economists.

ECONOMICS AS A THEORY OF CHOICE

Economics may be called a theory of choice, as long as the act of choice is mandatory and not voluntary. Economics studies man's forced reaction to the fact of scarcity. It studies only situations in which a choice *must* be made.

Such a statement may seem puzzling or even nonsensical to you. It appears to have nothing to do with the terms economists commonly use, such as prices, costs, investment, commodities, gross national product, and supply and demand. But we shall see later that economic situations do involve all these things and more.

Suppose that there is only one end you can attain. Let us say that all you have to choose from is x. Then you have no choice at all and, hence, no economic problem. You are not forced to choose between x and something else. To put this rather abstract statement most concretely, suppose that x is involuntary death. For none of us is death an economic problem because we have no choice in the matter. No alternative is offered to the ultimate end of the human condition.

Now let us turn from this macabre, but graphic, example to a situation in which alternatives do exist. Assume we are confronted with alternatives x and y. In an economic situation, it must be not only possible but *mandatory* to choose between x and y. Suppose x is shade and y is fruit. By planting an apple tree, then, it would be possible to have both. Since there is therefore no necessity for making a choice, this is not an economic situation, and it poses no economic problem.

On the other hand, if one *must* choose from among alternatives, then an economic situation does exist. Suppose our tree planter, having disposed of his fruit-and-shade problem, must now consider the allocation of the tree's apples. An apple is a versatile fruit that can be eaten raw, cooked and made into apple pie or applesauce, or pressed to make cider. If the tree will not provide its planter with enough apples to yield him all the apple pie, applesauce, and cider that he wants at the same time, he must allocate his apples to these various alternative uses.

Very seldom in an economic situation is the choice between having all x and no y or no x and all y. In a typical economic situation, the choice-maker would like to have so much x and so much y. But (and this is the crucial point) the choice-maker cannot have all the x he would like to have *and* all the y he wants too. It is necessary for him to give up some x in order to have some y. The amount of x that he must sacrifice to gain some y is the *cost* of y.[2] He *can* choose, and he *must* choose. This choice is the act of economizing. It is what "economizing" means.

As with the fruit-shade example above, you can probably think of many situations in which the necessity for choice does not exist—in which you can have all the x you want without having to give up any of it to get some y. And you may be able to think of situations in which you can enjoy as much as you desire of several want-satisfiers without having to forego an increment of any of them. One common example would be the case in which we let want-satisfier x stand for the air we breathe. Under most conditions (of course, you can think of exceptions), we can get all the air we want to breathe free. This means

---

[2] In our usage, "cost" and "sacrifice" are synonyms. Dollars and cents are not involved in our concept of cost. Suppose that x is cider and y is cider vinegar. Suppose also that the apple tree bears enough fruit to produce two gallons of juice, which may be consumed either as cider or as vinegar. Ideally, our grower may prefer to consume all his apples in the form of cider, but he may need to use a gallon of vinegar during the year. Two gallons of cider is a production and a consumption possibility. But the necessity of consuming one gallon of vinegar per year means that the two-gallons-of-cider alternative is only the second-best choice. The preferred alternative is one gallon of cider and one gallon of vinegar. In choosing this particular combination of goods over the second-best alternative (two gallons of cider), the grower-consumer has had to forego one gallon of cider, which will become one gallon of vinegar. The cider foregone is the *cost* of the gallon of vinegar. *Opportunity cost* is the name economists apply to our measurement of the cost of whatever it is we have in terms of those things we must do without to gain the most desired combination of goods.

we do not have to give up any breathable air in order to enjoy another want-satisfier—say, steak. Economics does not deny that such cases of costlessness exist (costless in the sense that we do not have to give up units of one thing in order to have units of something else), but economics is not concerned with them, simply because they are not economic situations. We are interested only in those situations in which we are forced to choose among the alternatives to which we devote our limited resources—which is another way of expressing the fundamental inequality of economics, scarcity. And situations that involve scarcity are far more common than those that do not. If this were not so, the business of living would be much less costly than it is.

Up to now, we have conducted our discussion as if there were only two alternatives, x and y, facing the choice-maker or economizer.[3] As you know, the opportunities for choice facing you as an economizer appear to be infinite. You may be faced with the problem of choosing between a college education, a sports car, a vacation, getting your teeth fixed, betting at the races, to name only a few possibilities. We could easily exhaust several alphabets, and ourselves as well, if we attempted to list symbolically only a few of the alternatives facing an economizer of even moderate means. When we restrict our discussion of a choice situation to the two alternatives x and y, we are not unmindful of the virtually limitless combinations of alternatives that exist in the real world. We usually restrict our discussion of an economic situation to two alternatives for two reasons: First, as we have mentioned, two ends are the minimum number necessary to have an economic situation. Second, the use of more than two alternatives vastly increases the complexity of illustrations and conceptualizations without appreciably advancing our understanding of economics. We can learn all the economics we need to know at this stage with just two alternatives and without the necessity of learning a great deal more mathematics to learn very little more economics. So we are not taking an excessively simple approach when we appear to be oblivious to the countless choices open to an economizer in the real-world economy; much economics can be learned with simple techniques and abstractions.

---

[3] There is a difference between an economizer and an economist. An economizer is a person who economizes, that is, a person who makes a choice. An economist is a person who studies the act of choice itself as well as the events and processes leading up to it and the ramifications proceeding from it.

THE BASIC POSTULATES OF ECONOMICS

Like any discipline, economics rests upon several fundamental postulates. Ours are derived from the basic fact of scarcity. We have asserted that economic situations are far more common than noneconomic situations—so common that we would be pragmatically accurate in contending that scarcity is a universal fact. Scarcity, as the word is used in economics, reflects human nature and the view humanity has of the created order. If scarcity is all-pervasive, it must be because human beings want "an awful lot of things." And if people want "an awful lot of things," it must be because the resources at our disposal do not provide the countless items that all of us want. In other words:

1. Human wants are infinitely expansible.
2. The means for satisfying these wants are limited.

Upon these two statements rests the whole structure of economics. Therefore, let us examine them.

You may object that you know some wants that can be satisfied once and for all and that you know some people who have almost no noticeable acquisitive propensity. Surely there are wants, such as appendix operations, funerals, and births, in which one want fulfillment per person ought to be enough. There are people—ascetics—who take vows of poverty. But these cases do not really violate our first postulate because it does not apply to particular wants or to particular people. It is a statement about wants in the aggregate. And these, we assert, expand without limit.

In the case of an individual, a particular want may be satisfied, but others will take its place. Wants themselves will always exist. The desire of a child for a tricycle yesterday becomes the desire for a used Chevrolet today and tomorrow will be transformed into a wish for an Aston-Martin. Wants feed upon themselves; the very process of want fulfillment creates new wants.

Moreover, when we speak of the infinite expansibility of human wants, we refer not to the wants of any particular person but to the wants of a whole society—what we might call social wants. In order to understand this concept, let us return to an example of what seems to be a clear case of the sufficiency of one want satisfaction per person, the appendix operation. There are competing uses for the things involved in an appendix operation. By this we do not mean that the scalpel used to make an incision in some person's abdomen could have been used to peel an orange. We do mean that, although society wants a multitude of appendix operations, society wants many other things. The steel of which the scalpel is made could have been used in making an automobile; the materials of which the hospital is built could have formed a Las Vegas casino; the surgeon could have become an automotive engineer; and the nurses could have been chorus girls. We could have more automobiles and more entertainment, and at lower prices, were it not for the fact that a significant number of us have trouble with our insides. Because some individuals must have appendix operations, society does not have all the automobiles and entertainment it would like to have. How do we know? Because to have automobiles and entertainment we must pay a price. *The signal that tells us society has less of a good than it desires is that we have to give up something of value in order to get that good.*

The example of the appendix operation is meant to be taken seriously but not literally. We are using a specific instance to generalize. In the real-world economy, we obviously do not pair alternatives; rather, we are forced to decide which of our limited means we shall apply to what limitless ends. Thus, we have arrived at the second postulate, which holds that the means for satisfying human wants are indeed limited. Want-satisfiers, in their basic form, are what economists call *resources*. There are numerous possible uses for every resource of society. In the vast majority of cases, the available amount of any particular resource or combination of resources is not great enough to permit society to put it to every possible use. All these uses therefore compete with one another for resources. The function of the economizing process is to allocate scarce resources to specific ends. This is another definition of economics.

THE LANGUAGE OF ECONOMICS

Economics, like other disciplines, has a vocabulary peculiarly its own. Although many of the terms used in economics are also used in everyday speech, their economic meaning is usually somewhat different from their ordinary usage. However, since their economic meaning is precise and unvarying, if you learn them once you will always know what we are talking about in this book.

Resources

For example, take a word we have already used, "resources." What does the word mean to you? Probably you envision forests, oil fields, steel mills, a sturdy labor force, perhaps even the integrity and education of a people. Doubtless these are resources, and no economist would question that. However, economists have found it helpful to distinguish between resources—to categorize them. Such specific resources as railroads, mines, actors, psychoanalysts, and shovels are usually reduced to their elemental forms—forms that are sufficiently unlike one another so as to have a fairly clear separate identity. How many resources do economists define? Three, usually: land, labor, and capital. The usage of these three terms in economics (they are also known as *factors of production*) comes close to their meaning in ordinary speech; but there is a difference, and that difference is essential in the study of economics.

Land is an old, traditional term in economics; "natural resources" would be a better expression. To economists, land means all the non-human resources that are part of our environment: the land itself, the minerals under the soil, the air around us, the rivers, oceans, snow, and wildlife.

Labor is all human effort, mental as well as physical. This means that the actor and the psychoanalyst are every bit as much "laborers" in the economic sense as the man on the automobile-plant assembly line.

Capital is the most complicated term of the three. Not only does it have widely varying usages in fields other than economics but it may appear to have various meanings within the discipline itself. Upon examination, these differences will be seen to be virtually illusory. For our purposes, we shall use "capital" to mean the produced means of production. Capital consists of those items that are themselves produced and that are used to produce other goods. You may contend that capital is not really an elemental resource but a combination of natural plus human resources, and this is true. But there is an element of arbitrariness in all classifications, and economists have found capital to be sufficiently different from the other two resources that the study of economics is facilitated by treating it as a separate and distinct resource classification. What are some examples of capital? Such diverse items as printing presses, automobile plants, and libraries are all "capital."

In an economy such as we have in the United States, most resources are owned by private individuals or business firms; and since the business firms themselves are owned by private individuals, ultimately, most American resources are owned by private persons. The owners of resources are paid a fee or reward for the use of their property. Economists, as you would expect, have precise terms also for the rewards paid to resource owners for allowing others to use their property:

Rent is the reward paid to owners of "land"—natural resources. (The usage of this term in economics has only a slight connection with the ordinary contract rent paid to landlords.)

Wages comprise the reward going to labor. Just as economists define all human effort as "labor," so they make no distinction between what are commonly called wages, salaries, piece-rates, bonuses, fees, tips, and commissions. If a payment is made to induce a human being to render a service requiring effort on his part, that payment is "wages."

Interest is the name of the return paid to owners of capital. Again, we make no distinction between contract interest, dividends, and royalties. If the payment is made to obtain the use of a piece of capital, it is "interest."

Some economists contend that there is a fourth factor of production (that is, a fourth resource) called *entrepreneurship,* or *enterprise.* The productive contribution of entrepreneurship is seen as the establishment and operation of business firms. The reward of the entrepreneur is *profit.* Many economists omit entrepreneurship from their lists of factors of production because they feel an entrepreneur is really a compound of at least two of the other factors of production: To the extent that he provides the equipment used in his business, he is a capitalist; to the extent that he runs the affairs of the firm, he is a manager—and management, after all, is a form of labor. Thus, the reward "profit" is merely the sum of interest and wages. But economists who see the entrepreneur as a separate factor of production are not dissuaded by this argument. They insist that in taking the risks attendant upon the creation of a new enterprise, in nurturing it, and in pioneering the introduction of new goods and services and new ways of doing things, the entrepreneur is doing something not performed by any combination of landlord, laborer, and capitalist. These economists hold that the *risk-taking* inherent in an economy such as we have in the United States is a unique function and justifies applying the classification "entrepreneur" to those who provide the main driving force in a free-enterprise economy.

The resources and rewards that we have defined are abstractions; they are seldom, if ever, encountered in a pure state in the real world. For example, a farm is not really "land" in the sense we have defined it formally, for the productive farm represents a combination of natural resources (the soil, natural factors affecting the soil's fertility, the climate), labor (the exertions of the farmer and his hired hands), and capital (tractors, fertilizers, barns). And the farmer's actual income is thus a composite of rent, wages, and interest. However, you will discover in later chapters how such abstractions facilitate the study of the economy.

THE VALUE OF GOODS

We have said that resource owners are paid for the use of their resources. Obviously, this indicates that the resources have some value. Why are resources valuable? Not simply because they are scarce but because they are scarce and can be made into goods that people want. Resources are used to produce goods, and that is the sole reason they are valuable.

What are goods? *Goods* are those things, tangible or intangible, that can satisfy human wants either directly or indirectly. Intangible goods are commonly called services and include such items as legal advice, teaching, acting, and preaching. A good may satisfy a want directly— as, for example, when a glass of water quenches thirst—or a good may satisfy a want indirectly—as when a pipe carries water that eventually quenches someone's thirst.

The ability of certain items to satisfy human wants is called *utility*. This is a very old expression, and if you are familiar with the philosophy of Jeremy Bentham and John Stuart Mill—the philosophy known as utilitarianism—you have encountered the word before. Things may possess utility—that is, they may be goods—according to the particular situation. For example, garbage is frequently a nuisance or an "ungood"; it has negative utility or "disutility," and the householder will pay to get rid of it. However, when there are pigs to eat the garbage, the very same refuse contributes to maintaining the supply of pork and thus has utility (it satisfies a human want indirectly). Therefore it would be considered a good.

A good (that which has utility) is not so called because it has any moral value, because it is "good" rather than "bad" in a moral sense. For example, a *bon vivant* would consider champagne "good," whereas a prohibitionist would condemn it as "bad." In economic terms, however, champagne is *a* good because it has utility for someone. Similarly, we can argue about the "goodness" or "badness" of heroin or cosmetics, but we do agree that they both possess some utility: Therefore the economist calls them goods. Economists as economists are not concerned with the legitimacy of human wants. This does not mean that economists as individuals are amoral. It simply means that economics takes all human wants as "givens." Its sphere of inquiry is not that of moral values or ethical judgments. All that is required for a thing to be an economic good is that it be able to satisfy some human want.

Is the possession of utility sufficient to make a good valuable? In the strict usage of economics, it is not. In everyday speech, we might say that air is valuable, but economists would say only that it has utility. Certainly air satisfies a human want, but it is not scarce enough to command anything in exchange for its services. You do not pay anyone for the ordinary air you breathe, nor do airline companies have to buy or rent air as the medium in which to fly their aircraft. Air in its natural state we call a *free good* because it cannot command a price. You can think of other free goods. Economics is not concerned with them—not because economists think that they are unimportant but because they present no problems of choice. The air is there for breathing or flying whether you wish to use it for those purposes or not.

But air and other similarly plentiful goods may not always be free under all conditions. If we do not like air in its natural state because its temperature, humidity, pressure, or purity is somehow unacceptable, the natural state of the air may be altered so that it possesses greater utility. But the process of conferring greater utility on the air involves a cost, and we must therefore pay for such air. Heated, cooled, humidified or dehumidified, pressurized, or purified, such air is scarce and therefore valuable. It is scarce because the means of treating the air are themselves scarce. Air-conditioning equipment is not a free good, and, thus, neither is the air that is treated by it. Such air is valuable, then, not only because it has utility but because it is also scarce. But scarcity alone is not enough to confer value. Old copies of the local supermarket's weekly advertisements may be quite scarce, but if nobody wants them they have no utility (they are not goods), and, hence, they have no value. Thus, we see that there are two components of value—utility *and* scarcity. Economics is concerned solely with *desired scarce goods*—or, as they are often called, *economic* goods.

OPPORTUNITY COSTS AND THE PRODUCTION POSSIBILITIES OF AN ECONOMY

Costs as Sacrifices

We have already come across the idea of "cost" (page 6); now let us examine that concept more closely. What is the sacrifice society must make in order to have economic goods? That sacrifice consists of the other goods society could have had if it had not chosen to have a certain quantity of the goods in question.

You have probably always thought of the cost of something as so many dollars and cents, but costs expressed in terms of money only represent the basic physical reality underlying the production and consumption of goods. Money exists for a number of reasons, including costs. But eliminating money would not eliminate costs. Consider a barter economy. The most basic function of money is to facilitate exchange. Instead of exchanging the goods and services that we produce directly with other people for their goods and services, we exchange what we have to sell for money and then exchange the money for what we want to buy. Thus, we avoid such troublesome problems as finding a dentist, when we have a toothache, who would take a gross of eggs in exchange for his services. Money is immensely useful; no modern economy could exist without it. It is therefore an important area of study in economics, but it often beclouds the real nature of economic processes.

The Production-Possibility Curve

Let us return to our discussion of cost as a sacrifice. We shall now introduce our first graph, and you will see how fortunate we are to be able to depict economic situations with just two alternatives. No one should fear graphs; they are introduced to make concepts easier to understand, not more difficult. They are simply pictures; and as pictures they are often much superior to words. However, to allay any fears, all the graphs in this book are accompanied by a complete verbal explanation. If you attempt to learn what a graph means instead of merely memorizing a senseless pattern of lines, you may, after a while, begin to think like an economist; you may actually prefer graphs to verbal explanations.

Let us suppose that we are dealing with a two-good economy—that is, an economy capable of producing only two goods. (Do not worry about the apparent unreality of this situation; as we have said before, the principle is the same whether we use two variables or many, and it will be easier to grasp if we confine ourselves to two.)

Since we have been talking about alternatives x and y, let us continue to do so. Suppose that our two-good economy produces xylophones (x) and yachts (y). Now look at Figure 1. On the horizontal axis of

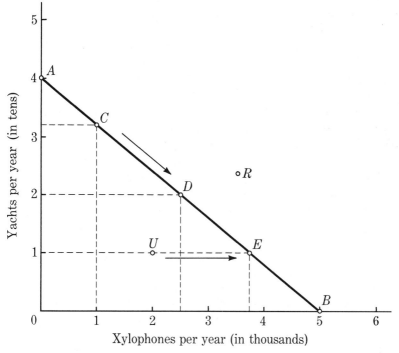

FIGURE 1 *Production Possibilities in a Two-good Economy*

the graph we shall measure the quantity of xylophones the economy is capable of producing, and on the vertical axis we shall measure the quantity of yachts it can produce.

Xylophone production is measured in thousands; that is, each division on the horizontal axis stands for 1,000 xylophones—for example, the division marked 3 stands for the production of 3,000 xylophones. Yacht production, however, is measured in tens, since a great many more resources are required to make one yacht than to make one xylophone. Each division on the vertical axis, then, represents 10 yachts, which means that the third division on the vertical axis stands for 30 yachts.

Let us suppose that if our hypothetical economy were to devote all its resources to the production of yachts, the greatest number of yachts it could possibly produce would be 40. The actual yacht limit would be that determined by the available resources and current yacht-making technology in our hypothetical economy. Let us put a dot at the fourth division mark on the yacht, or y, axis and label it A.

Now, let us take the other extreme. We shall suppose that if our economy were to devote all of its resources to xylophone production it could make 5,000 xylophones; we shall therefore put a dot at 5,000 units on the xylophone, or x, axis and label it B.

Note what we have at this stage of our analysis. Our economy has two basic alternatives before it; it is able to make both xylophones and yachts. We have plotted the two extreme production possibilities: at possibility-point A, the economy can make 40 yachts and no xylophones; at possibility-point B, the economy can produce 5,000 xylophones and no yachts. It is not likely, however, that our economy would wish to choose either of these extreme alternatives. It would probably prefer to have some of both yachts and xylophones. And our economy *can* have some of both goods. The question is: How many of each can it have?

Let us draw a straight line between points A and B. Just as A and B showed the amounts of each good that could be produced when all the resources of the economy were devoted to producing one good and none were used in making the other, any other point on the line segment AB will show how many units each of xylophones and yachts may be produced when resources are applied to the production of both goods. At point C, for example, the economy is producing 1,000 xylophones and 32 yachts; at point D, total output consists of 2,400 xylophones and 20 yachts. Note that we have plotted only four of an infinite number of possible points on AB. You can choose other possible points yourself and read off the composition of the total output (the gross national product) of the economy. Each point on AB is a production possibility open to the economy; hence, economists have given lines of this type the name *production-possibility curves*.[4]

---

[4] A *curve* is simply a line passing through a collection of points lying in a two-dimensional space. The pattern of the points does not alter the definition of a curve. If a line passing through a set of points is straight (mathematicians would

Suppose that one year the economy is producing at point C; its total output, or gross national product, is 1,000 xylophones and 32 yachts. Now suppose that in the next year there is a greater demand for xylophones, such that consumers want 1,400 more instruments—the number of xylophones that is produced at D. Remember that there is no way of increasing xylophone production without impinging upon yacht production. If the members of the economy still want 32 yachts, they cannot have all the yachts they want and all the xylophones they want at the same time. If the demand for xylophones increases relative to the demand for yachts, yacht production *must* suffer. This is so because resources must be taken away from yacht production in order to make more xylophones.

You can see from the graph that in increasing xylophone production from 1,000 to 2,400 units the economy does indeed undergo a sacrifice: Yacht production must be decreased to an output of 20 units. This sacrifice is the cost of producing 1,400 additional xylophones. The actual sacrifice, or cost, to the economy is the 12 yachts it must give up to have 1,400 more xylophones. Economists call this type of cost an *opportunity cost* because it consists of the alternatives foregone by an economy to have whatever output is chosen above all other possible outputs. In order to increase xylophone production by 1,400 units, the members of the economy must give up 12 yachts they could otherwise have had.

Opportunity costs exist in any economy, regardless of the number of goods it produces. The cost of any particular good we consume is all the other items that the resources used in making the chosen product could have made had we not insisted upon having the particular good at hand.

As we conclude our discussion of what economics is about, bear in mind that we have been speaking of costs without any reference to money. Costs have been expressed in units of goods. Money has nothing to do with the existence of the costs of production. Every economy experiences costs because of the inadequacy of its resource base relative to the want patterns of its members. Money merely provides a convenient way to express the sacrifices of goods that an economy must

---

say that the slope of such a line is constant), it is properly called a "linear curve." If a line drawn through a series of points is not straight, it is called a "nonlinear curve." Examples of such curves are circles, ellipses, hyperbolas, and parabolas. Therefore, *any* line, regardless of its shape, is a curve.

make in order to have the particular composition of output that it chooses to have.

SOME THINGS TO THINK ABOUT

We have now barely started our exploration of economics. Our introduction to the production-possibility curve has answered some questions, but it has surely raised many more. If a number of questions occur to you now about implications of the production-possibility curve other than the ones we have discussed, rest assured that they also have occurred to economists. In the ensuing chapters, we shall see how some of the great minds of economics have dealt with them. But let us enumerate briefly some of the questions the production-possibility curve poses before turning to the great economists and their explanations. You may find it interesting to try to work out your own solutions before reading the rest of the book.

To begin: In our discussion of the production-possibility curve, we have taken the various points on the curve as given; that is, we have not inquired why the economy chooses point D instead of point C, how the xylophones and yachts are apportioned among the members of the economy, or how the economy decides what methods to use in xylophone and yacht production. Neither have we inquired what would happen if the economy were producing at a point *inside* the curve, say, at point U, at which the gross national product consists of 2,000 xylophones and 10 yachts. Remember that all points *on* the curve represent the full use of all resources; therefore, any point *inside* the curve must represent a less than full use—the unemployment—of resources. Would an economy ever allow itself to produce at U? Examine the diagram and think about the problem. What would be the cost in terms of yachts if the production of xylophones were expanded from point U to point E?

Similarly, have you wondered why the production of xylophones and yachts could not be carried on *outside* the curve, say, at a point such as R? The simple answer is, of course, that to produce at R would require *more* than *full* use of the economy's resources, which is impossible. Every point on the curve represents the full use of all resources. Therefore, given the resource base and the economically practical ways of using these resources (technology), production must be conducted on or within the limits of the curve. But is point R forever closed to the economy? Is there no way of making R a feasible production-possibility point? To put it another way, must the production possibilities of the economy invariably be bounded by AB? Draw a new line, $A'B'$, through R and parallel to AB. Why could not $A'B'$ become a production-possibility curve? Notice how the members of the economy could be better off if the production-possibility curve were to become $A'B'$. Although it is easy to *draw* a new production-possibility curve to the right of any existing curve, in practice it may be quite difficult for an economy to move from AB to $A'B'$. One of the great features of the American economy has been precisely its ability to keep moving its production-possibility curve ever outward. And the amelioration of the misery of many of the world's peoples, and perhaps peace itself, will depend on our continued ability not only to move our production-possibility curve outward but to help the so-called underdeveloped nations of the world move their production-possibility curves outward too. Can you think of forces that might move an actual production-possibility curve to the right? We will return to this question in Chapter 3. The movement of an actual production-possibility frontier ("frontier" is a better word when we are considering an actual multigood economy) is called *economic growth*. Although we have noted that the American economy has had considerable success in moving its production-possibility frontier outward, there have been numerous instances in our economic history when, for reasons yet to be explored, we have not managed to operate on our production-possibility frontier, operating instead at some point such as U.

In the following chapters, we shall see how economists have dealt with these problems and what impact their solutions have had on our lives. We can summarize these problems into five major questions— questions that *any* economy *must* answer, be it the United States, the Soviet Union, or an aborigine village in Australia.

1. *What goods* are to be produced?
2. *For whom* are these goods to be produced?
3. *How* are the chosen goods produced?
4. How does an economy achieve the *full employment* of its resources, so that it does not have to forego unnecessarily any of the output that it could have?

5. How does an economy *grow* and *develop*? How does it expand its range of production possibilities?

In this chapter, our emphasis has been on the one fact that creates all of these questions—scarcity. In the chapters to come, we shall see how certain men—economists—have attempted to explain man's encounter with that basic fact.

EARLY
ECONOMIC
THINKERS

2

The major premise of this book is that economics is a *reactive* science. For the most part, it has developed in response to the particular, often acute, needs of a given time. The specific subcategories of the economic problem that face a community at any point in time are worked through by economists of that time and become part of the subject matter of economics. For example, it is improbable that an economist, in deciding what research to conduct, would say to himself, "Today I shall study the problem of a nation's loss of gold," if at the time a gold flow out of a particular nation was causing no severe problem. If, on the other hand, a major nation was experiencing a gold outflow that posed serious domestic and international problems, it is altogether likely that a great number of economists would have the situation under study.

Let us see how our premise that economics is a reactive science is supported by some notable examples of the evolution of economic thought.

"ECONOMIC THOUGHT" AND "ECONOMICS"

Many economists celebrate Adam Smith (1723–90) as the father of their discipline, and some hail him as the greatest of all economists.

But many writers of antiquity, the Middle Ages, and the centuries preceding Smith discussed economic matters. You may have noticed that there is considerable economic content in the Bible. This is also true of the writings of Aristotle and of the early Church fathers, of medieval and Renaissance philosophers, ministers of finance, and noblemen, and, later, of early businessmen. Some of these authors, especially the more ancient ones, discussed economic matters much as other writers devised models of the solar system before there was a science of astronomy, or declared that the elements were earth, fire, air, and water before there was a science of chemistry, or stated that "nature abhors a vacuum" before there was a science of physics. Just as there was *thinking* about natural phenomena before the development of the natural sciences, so there was economic *thought* before there was economics.

Economic thought includes "economics," but the reverse is not the case. What makes some economic thought economics? The same thing that makes a science of any area of inquiry. When economic thought becomes organized and systematized, when it is stated in testable hypotheses framed by rigorous logic and based upon premises derived from empirical observations, then we can say that it is economics.

Not too long ago in the history of the human race, people believed that economic matters were not important, and, to an extent, they were correct, for there were no real economies—no systems for economizing—despite the fact that all throughout history the vast majority of men have borne the weight of the economic problem in a real, and usually urgent, way.

For example, economic life in Europe became stagnant following the collapse of the Roman Empire and the rise of Islam. The power of the Islamic rulers transformed the Mediterranean, the *mare nostrum* of the Romans, into a Moslem sea and forced the Europeans, in order to survive, to gather in small, tightly knit, self-sufficient, well-fortified communities. Until the twelfth century, when trade began to revive in Europe, relatively little economic activity existed between, or even within, the feudal states. Self-sufficiency was the rule for households and for the larger communities in which men lived. Manufacture, if indeed it may be called that, was conducted by craftsmen. Trade was carried on almost entirely by barter. Although occasionally there were spectacular instances of commerce between nations, for the most part individuals in one community lived in isolation from those in other communities.

ARISTOTLE AND HIS INTELLECTUAL PROGENY

Aristotle's Economic Thought

Of all the figures of antiquity who have influenced men's minds over the centuries, surely Aristotle is one of the most commanding. Although a great champion of the human mind and spirit, Aristotle exerted an effect upon economic activity and economic thought that was enormously inhibitory. He held that trade is "unnatural" and money barren. Each object of human desire, said Aristotle, has both a "natural" and an "unnatural" use. For example, the natural use of a shoe is to be worn on the foot of its owner; its unnatural use is as an object of exchange. Aristotle did not mean to rule out all exchange, since obviously men cannot be entirely self-sufficient. Goods must be exchanged for other goods; the shoemaker must trade his shoes for bread. But Aristotle asserted that the involvement of men and goods in the exchange process should be discouraged. The artificial uses of goods never should be allowed to overshadow their natural uses; men should not try to derive their livelihood solely by selling or trading goods or services manufactured by others. Buyers and sellers should exchange *equivalent values*. Such an exchange is just, and the transaction is a natural one. Aristotle measured values in terms of the intensity of the wants of the community. Suppose a cobbler can make a pair of shoes in the same amount of time and with the same exertion that it takes a potter to make a vase. This does not mean, said Aristotle, that a pair of shoes should exchange for a vase. If the product of the potter's art is more highly prized by the community than the cobbler's work, the cobbler will have to sell more than one pair of shoes to earn enough money to buy one vase. In such a transaction, equivalent values are exchanged; the potter has not gained at the expense of the cobbler. Both shoes and vases exchange at their "natural" prices.

"Unnaturalness' in commerce becomes a possibility when a third party, the merchant, insinuates himself into the transaction. If the merchant is to gain anything for himself, he must create a spread between the price a producer is willing to accept and the price a consumer will agree to pay. This spread is his profit. The values exchanged through the merchant intermediary are not equivalent. The merchant has made shoes and vases objects of exchange and not of use. Thus, in Aristotle's eyes, the merchant's function and his income are unnatural.

Aristotle was willing to concede that the merchant did have some place in the simple economy he knew, and he was agreeable to allowing the intermediary a profit so that he might fulfill his function. But to Aristotle, the merchant's function remained unnatural, and the philosopher admonished his followers to keep the role of the merchant small and his reward as innocuous as practicable. This teaching that commercial activities are not altogether wholesome was to be one of the basic premises of economic thought in the Middle Ages.

Another long-lived Aristotelian doctrine was the philosopher's disapproval of usury. Today, "usury" means lending money at an illegally high rate of interest. To Aristotle, the term meant lending at any rate of interest at all. This meant that a lender should expect nothing in return for his loan beyond the amount of the loan itself.

What was the rationale for this doctrine? Simply that money (or gold, which was the same thing) is "barren." Money cannot reproduce itself. Put it in a box, and when you open the box a year later it will not have increased in amount. How, then, can a borrower justifiably be expected to return more to the lender (interest, or usury) than he has borrowed? Today, we wonder at Aristotle's naïveté. Even more, we wonder at his inconsistency, for the philosopher held it perfectly legitimate for the owner of a horse to charge anyone who borrowed the animal a "rental" fee. What is the difference between lending someone a horse and lending him the money to buy a horse? How valid is the distinction made between the "rental fee" of a certain horse and the "interest" charged on a certain sum of money used to buy a horse?

Scholastic Economic Thought

The major impact on Western civilization of Aristotle's distaste for usury came through the early Church fathers and through the greatest of the scholastic philosophers, St. Thomas Aquinas. Scholasticism, a philosophy deeply related to the spirit of the Middle Ages, infused the basic teachings of Christ and the Apostles with Aristotelian philosophy. There are many areas of agreement between Christian doctrine and Aristotelian philosophy. In particular, the scholastics saw a seeming compatibility of Aristotle's work with the discourses on the economic aspects of life found in the Scriptures. In both, riches and rich men appear to be deprecated; commerce seems to be viewed as something less than a worthy activity; and, assuredly, taking advantage of one's fellow men is strongly condemned.

In his monumental *Summa Theologica,* Aquinas addressed himself to all phases of life. In economic affairs, Aquinas insisted that every transaction must result in justice for all parties. His prescription became the basis of the Church's famous rule of a "just price." Indeed, if one word can epitomize the position of the medieval Church on economic matters, the word is justice.

But what is "justice"? This is one of the most ancient of questions, and it is commonly answered by saying that justice is what is due a man. This answer, however, merely substitutes one question for another. How did the Church answer in practice the question, "What is justice?" It declared that a "just price" and a "just wage" were, in effect, *customary* payments. They were payments that enabled the recipient to live in his "appointed station" in life.

How did usury (interest) fit into this scheme? Welding together precedents he found in the Bible and Aristotle, Aquinas condemned usury as an unjust price. Christ, in Luke's Gospel, indicates that one ought to lend expecting no return. Aristotle taught that money is barren and that it is therefore an unnatural transaction for a man to lend a sum to another expecting at some future date a return greater than the principal amount. Aquinas amplified Aristotle's view. Money, he said, is not a thing of value in itself. It was created to facilitate exchange, not to be an object of exchange. To both Aristotle and Aquinas, money was solely a *pure* medium of exchange. As such, it could not command a price. Something that is not a good has no value. When one sells a good, his rights of ownership are terminated; but when one lends money, he sells only the *use* of it. The sum itself will be returned at some agreed-upon future date. If interest is added to the amount the borrower must return to the lender, the borrower is forced to pay for the money, and money, not being a good—not being a thing of value in itself—may not be sold. To compel another to pay for that which does not exist certainly is an injustice. If money is really a pure medium of exchange, then Aristotle and Aquinas do have logic on their side. If their premise is wrong, then the logic of their argument is immaterial. But correct premise or not, Aquinas' teaching provided the philosophic justification for the Church's prohibtion of usury.

One might wonder how European commercial activity revived and flourished after the close of the eleventh century when the still-powerful universal Church frowned upon moneylending. The answer is that the Church doctors themselves rationalized the Church's rules against usury.

To a great extent, the Church remained opposed to interest charges on loans made to individuals for consumption purposes. These loans often were a matter of survival to the borrowers, and the very slight chance most people had to earn more than their daily subsistence almost precluded their earning enough over the amount of the loan itself to pay interest. Besides, the Church viewed charity as a Christian duty; to lend to one's needy brother expecting to profit from his need was a plain violation of Christian morality. But, in the case of loans that were made for business purposes, the Church evolved a host of exceptions to its proscription. Thus, even before the Church's dominance over the temporal facets of life began to wane, it is probable that almost no commercial activity was seriously hindered by its anti-usury tenets.

In all fairness, let us note that from the Church's point of view its rule against usury made good sense for at least two reasons, one spiritual and one economic. Spiritually, life in the Middle Ages was "otherworldly." Men's minds seldom were without thoughts of the life to come; in fact, the next life may often have been more real to them than their earthly existence. Each person, the Church taught, was placed on earth for a specific purpose—to rule, to administer the sacraments, to plow fields, to make shoes, to wage war; and economic affairs must be so ordered that each individual can fulfill his God-appointed station in life. What if some people fared better in this life than others? Life is short; eternity is long. In the life to come, the Church taught, justice would prevail and all men would be rewarded perfectly.

The economically sound reason for the Church's position in the early Middle Ages was that the period was a static one; methods of agriculture and manufacture changed imperceptibly, and there was very little progressive augmentation of their productive capacity. Thus, the price customarily paid could well have been an economically sound price. Without anyone's realizing it, perhaps the forces of supply and demand hammered out the "just price" as in an ordinary market economy; and, with virtually no change in economic relationships over decades, the insistence of the Church that prices be those customarily charged can perhaps be justified as economically appropriate.[1]

The generally anticommercial position of the Church also made sense

---

[1] The precise meaning of the terms "supply" and "demand" will be considered in Chapter 6.

from the standpoint of practical politics, for the power of the Church was best maintained in a static society that emphasized tradition over innovation, the spiritual over the material, and religious belief over secular inquiry. With the flowering of the opposite tendencies that contributed to, and emanated from, the growth of trade, the immense political power of the Church began to wane. The Church's provincialism could not survive the spirit of inquiry that contact with other peoples and ideas fostered. Its political power was effectively challenged by national monarchs who were ambitious for *national* power and wealth, and its spiritual power was shaken by an increasingly well-schooled, nonclerical group of thinkers.

We turn now to an era dominated by hopes for increasing the wealth of nations—although, despite the use of so famous a phrase, we have not yet reached the age of Adam Smith.

THE MERCANTILISTS

Competition between national sovereigns preceded widespread competition between businessmen. In the major European nations, each national ruler was bent upon discovering the principles and practices that would make his nation the wealthiest and most powerful on earth. The principles and practices these rulers adopted are collectively called *mercantilism,* and, broadly defined, mercantilism is a philosophy of national power. (I say *is* because it has not completely disappeared. Elements of mercantilism continue to appear from time to time in the international activities of nations.)

The earliest published tract presenting mercantilistic ideas appeared in the early 1600's; the last significant writer on the mercantile system, Sir James Stewart, published his exposition in 1767. Mercantilism itself, however, was not confined to the period between these two dates. The plundering of the New World's gold by the Spanish conquistadors was a very early and significant practice of mercantilism. France was a thoroughly mercantilistic state under the programs of Jean Baptiste Colbert, who served Louis XIV as French finance minister from 1661 to 1683. England practiced mercantilism for about two centuries, beginning in the early 1600's. Her eventual abandonment of the system was, as we shall see, one of the most dramatic events in Western economic history.

Although we now wonder at some of the incongruous policies of the mercantilists, the development of mercantilistic thought represents a deliberate attempt to formulate economic policy on the basis of what was then considered rational economic calculation and to use economic policy to further the objectives of the state. We may say, then, that mercantilism was the embryonic stage in the development of *political economy*—that branch of economic thought which attempts to prescribe economically advantageous courses of national conduct. The development of political economy was a necessary prelude to the fashioning of economics, or economic analysis, itself.

Mercantilism probably represents the first important employment of economic advisers to heads of state. Whether such individuals can be regarded as precursors of our President's Council of Economic Advisers is a moot question turning upon whether you believe the members of the Council to be economists or *political* economists. Certainly, most mercantilist advisers were political economists, since their focus, for the most part, was on prescription and not analysis.

The development of trade in goods and ideas, which led to the simultaneous rise in power of economically linked nation-states and the decline in the influence of the Church, led also to the evolution of a money economy. The role of money in the development of economic analysis is a fascinating study in paradox. On the one hand, the development of the monetary economy produced by the growth of economic activity led to the establishment of economic systems; and this in turn eventually gave birth to the science of economics. On the other hand, economic thinkers have often been confused by the place of money in the economic system, granting it either too much or too little importance. Quite frequently the true nature of economic problems was obscured by a preoccupation with money; and, conversely, as we shall see later, the failure of many economists to give monetary problems due consideration resulted in an economics entirely unable to cope with the Great Depression of the 1930's. Thus, money is variously regarded in the history of economic analysis: Sometimes it is overemphasized; at other times it is almost forgotten.

The mercantilists were among the first economic thinkers to be overly impressed with the role of money in the national economy. Yet, because they were also among the first to think seriously about money, they originated some useful contributions to economic thought.

Premises of Mercantilism

The most fundamental tenet of mercantilism is that wealth—a store of tangible goods—is power. Therefore, the proper economic course for a nation that seeks power is to become wealthy—to accumulate a stock of things of value. The mercantilists, as we have noted, were also money-minded; thus, their second basic tenet was that a nation's wealth was best held in the form of money (rather than goods). Since nearly all money of consequence was some form of gold or silver, this meant that the mercantilists favored the collection and hoarding of a stock of bullion in the national treasury. Simply put, the ultimate aim of foreign policy for many mercantilists was to pursue whatever tactics would maximize the inflow of gold and then, once the gold was secured in the treasury, minimize the outflow from the nation's coffers.

Generally, there were two methods by which a nation could induce a gold inflow. The first was by some form of theft, and the second was through foreign trade. The first route was that of imperialism and colonialism. It led Spain to search the world for the yellow metal and to relieve the Aztec nation, among others, of its stores of gold. A subsidiary form of theft was practiced by other nations, such as England, which, upon observing the Spanish ships heavily laden with ill-gotten gold, employed pirates (an honorable occupation for those appointed by the Crown) to lighten the Spanish vessels.

The essence of the second method, that of profitable foreign trade, is precisely conveyed in a phrase closely identified with mercantilism, the "favorable balance of trade." We have in this concept of a balance of trade a seminal contribution by the mercantilists to economic analysis: the definition of a measurable economic indicator. True, the mercantilists were not quite sure how the balance of trade could be measured accurately—indeed, some of them made too large a problem of its measurement—but the *concept* of the balance of trade provided an economic magnitude that could be used to gauge certain aspects of a nation's economic performance.

A *balance of trade* is the difference between the value of a country's exports and the value of its imports. If exports exceed imports—if a country sells more to foreign nations than it buys from them—the balance-of-trade figure is positive, or, in mercantilist language, "favorable"; if imports exceed exports, it is negative, or "unfavorable."

Although the mercantilists presented so many diverse viewpoints that we really cannot talk about mercantilist thought as if it were a cohesive body of economic doctrine, the fundamental instrument of mercantilist policy was the continual pursuit of a favorable balance of trade. Why was this so?

Essentially, foreign trade is a barter situation. A nation exports items of which it has a surplus,[2] exchanging them for goods of which it has a deficiency. If a country is able to export goods of a greater total value than it chooses to receive in exchange, it can require those nations to whom it exports to settle their debts in gold rather than in goods.

To pursue such a policy over a long period of time, a mercantilist nation must regulate strictly all aspects of its economic life. Thus, mercantilism often has been identified with gross interferences with private liberties. To acquire gold, theft aside, a nation must sell much abroad and buy little. To ensure this, a mercantilist government must restrict severely the purchases of its citizens. It must prevent its residents, as far as is possible, from obtaining goods made in foreign lands; that is, it must minimize imports. More than this, it must suppress the consumption of domestically produced goods so that as much of its own production as possible can be sold to foreigners. In France, under the influence of Colbert, regulations were minutely detailed, even specifying the number of buttons the members of each social class could wear on their clothing.

The economic doctrines of mercantilism had definite political implications. (You know of one far-reaching effect on the politics of the American colonies.) In his classic *England's Treasure by Forraigne Trade,* posthumously published in 1664, Sir Thomas Mun, now generally regarded as a highly enlightened mecantilist writer, pointed out that a nation should not refrain from buying *all* goods abroad; rather, it should seek actively to import raw materials or bulk goods to use in domestic manufacture. These manufacturing operations could be extensive, but they might be negligible, amounting to nothing more than unloading raw materials from the colonies at an English dock to reload them on another ship bound for a foreign port (after suitably marking up the price of the goods, of course). The nation could then re-export the initially imported goods, selling them at a price higher than that which it had originally paid. The difference, hopefully manifested in

[2] In the sense the word is used here, a nation is said to have a "surplus" of a certain good if it can sell the good at a higher price abroad than at home.

a gold inflow, could be kept in the state treasury. What better way to ensure the fulfillment of Mun's prescription than by colonizing, thereby simultaneously providing a source of raw materials for the mother country and a ready market abroad for the same materials after they had undergone processing?

An Appraisal of Mercantilist Doctrines

Any overall appraisal of the work of the mercantilists as a group is likely to be unsatisfactory, since among them one finds the most simplistic and blatantly nationalistic advocates of state power as well as some truly sophisticated economic minds. As a start, however, let us examine the most famous of the mercantilist doctrines, the relentless quest for a continuing favorable balance of trade and the equating of gold with power. Are there any elements of rationality in these doctrines? (When economists speak of "rationality," they mean conduct that will bring an economizer closer to his desired goal of obtaining all he wants of one good while giving up as little as possible of other goods to get it.) We want to know whether the mercantilists' definition of wealth and their prescriptions for getting and holding it brought their respective nations the power their rulers wanted. What did the mercantilists propose to do with their stores of gold? Were they right or wrong in repudiating Aristotle and Aquinas, both of whom taught that gold is barren?

Man tends to invest gold with a kind of mystique and often thinks of it as something good in itself. But what can be done with gold? Is a gold hoard really the route to national power? And what price did the mercantilist nations pay to get gold?

Unlike the great moral teachers Aristotle and Aquinas, the mercantilists were expansive. They did not hesitate to employ war as an instrument of national policy. As a result, their nations were embroiled in frequent and costly wars—especially costly because the mercantilist states often employed the subjects of foreign sovereigns to do their fighting. These mercenary soldiers engaged in war in behalf of the highest bidder. Their main motivation was monetary, and they wanted to be paid in gold—the money that was universally acceptable. Gold also found ready use in buying arms and supplies from other nations when a warring power was undergoing a siege. Since the mercenaries, the arms makers, and the suppliers were paid out of the public treasury with the universal money, the gold hoard of a mercantilist nation was its war chest. In addition, the mercantilists believed that an increase in the amount of gold in a country would stimulate production—a belief we will examine in the next section.

But mercantilist nations did pay for their gold hoard. They gave up a host of valuable things (their exports) that their own citizens could otherwise have had. This is evidenced by the severe restrictions on consumption mercantilist rulers imposed on their subjects. Mercantilist nations exported textiles, spices, books, medicines, tools, and other valuable goods, many of which their own citizens would have liked to buy, in exchange for bricks and coins of gold. Who was better off? The citizens of the nations that had traded gold for these items or the citizens who received gold in exchange for the goods made by the sweat of their brows?

One could argue that the gold-receiving nation might eventually conquer the goods-receiving nation; this is a mercantilistic point of view. But we must again ask: Is gold the true source of national economic power? A country gets the things it exchanges for gold by manufacturing them. And this capacity for *producing* things of value is the real source of economic power. But manufacturing requires plants and equipment and a labor force. In addition, an *increase* in economic power over the years necessitates an increase in productive capacity—more plants and equipment and perhaps more laborers. If a nation devotes itself to exchanging for gold as great a part as possible of its items of current manufacture, instead of setting aside a substantial part of its output for the replacement and enlargement of productive capacity, the time will come when that nation will find itself with less and less goods to trade to foreigners for gold and, therefore, less and less economic power.

If you find this idea somewhat puzzling, go back to the preceding chapter and study the production-possibility curve. Put "exchangeable goods" on one axis and "plants and equipment" on the other, and see what happens as production is increasingly concentrated on "exchangeable goods." After you have done this, remember that the plants and equipment produced today will manufacture the exchangeable goods of tomorrow. Consider, therefore, how movement *along* today's production-possibility curve in the direction of more plants and equipment sets in operation the very forces that will push tomorrow's production-possibility curve outward.

Furthermore, in a world of mercantilist nations, can every country maintain a favorable balance of trade? For example, in a two-country world, can nation *A* sell more to nation *B* than it buys from nation *B* while *B* does exactly the same thing to *A*? Of course not! Thus, all nations cannot simultaneously fulfill the favorable-balance-of-trade tenets of the mercantilists. Actually, this is not really a shortcoming of mercantilist analysis, for the mercantilists were, above all, nationalists, and their prescriptions were for *their own* nations to follow. Indeed, an English mercantilist would devoutly hope that France would find it impossible to follow mercantilist principles.

However, a related and more significant question is whether a nation that does achieve a favorable balance of trade during a certain span of time can expect to maintain that situation indefinitely. Some mercantilists apparently thought so until that notion was upset by David Hume. The great but controversial Scottish philosopher was also a fine, though usually neglected economist. He pointed out that as long as a nation maintains a favorable balance of trade, it continues to receive an inflow of gold, thereby altering the relationship between the amount of gold and the total nongold wealth of the country. Wealth in the form of gold becomes ever more plentiful relative to other forms of wealth. As the gold stock increases, the metal becomes less valuable relative to the nongold items. As a result, prices will rise in the goods-exporting nation. And that nation will tend to demand greater amounts of gold for the same quantities of the goods that they sell to foreigners.[3] In the goods-receiving nation, the reverse happens. As the supply of gold decreases, the remaining gold becomes more valuable relative to the nongold forms of wealth, and the prices of the latter, in terms of gold (money), will fall.

What is the result? How long will prices continue to rise in the gold-receiving nation and to fall in the goods-receiving country? The process will continue until it becomes cheaper to buy goods in the goods-receiving nation. Eventually, the country receiving gold will find that it is cheaper to buy goods from the nation to whom they have been selling goods, while the former goods-receiving country will find that it is better off buying and using its own goods than giving gold in exchange for the (now more expensive) goods of another nation's manufacture. Ultimately, the flow of gold will be reversed, and with it the trading position of the two nations. Thus, as Hume pointed out, a

[3] Gold literally was money—the everyday medium of exchange—in mercantilist days, and to demand an increased amount of gold for the same quantity of a good was the same thing as increasing its price.

favorable balance of trade for any one nation is necessarily a transitory phenomenon, and the quest for a permanently favorable balance of trade is the pursuit of a will-o'-the-wisp.

Mercantilist Monetary Theory

Since the mercantilists were so money-minded, they naturally enough developed the rudiments of a monetary theory. Many of them were not unmindful of at least part of Hume's theory of the self-reversing gold flow in international trade; they realized that the greater the amount of money (gold) in a nation, the higher would be the general level of prices. Today we would say that the mercantilists were expressing a form of what has been called the *quantity theory of the value of money*. The simplest form of the quantity theory of money, which is all that the mercantilists developed, states that there is a direct relationship between the amount of money in circulation in a nation and the general price level. (By *general price level*, we mean the average of the prices of all goods and services.) As the nation puts more money into circulation, whether by printing additional currency or by increasing its gold inflow, the prices of all goods and services tend to rise together. This comes about simply because money becomes more plentiful relative to the things bought with money. The modern term for this phenomenon is *inflation*.

Today we generally regard inflation as undesirable. We know that we are experiencing inflation when, in everyday speech, we hear that the cost of living is rising. The mercantilists disliked inflation as much as we do. After all, if prices, including wages, rise in the gold-receiving nation, the costs of producing export goods will rise; and the nation will find its net proceeds from foreign trade diminishing.

With this understanding of the relationship between money and prices, how could the mercantilists refuse to modify their doctrine of the wisdom of maintaining a constantly favorable balance of trade with its consequent gold inflow?

We are again confronted with a paradox. The mercantilists' answer was a blend of naïveté and sophistication. Although they accepted a direct causal connection between the amount of money in national circulation and the general level of prices, the mercantilists also believed that money would stimulate the actual volume of trade—that the production of goods and services would increase as the result of an influx of money. That is, the mercantilists saw a direct causal relationship not only between the quantity of gold in a country and the general price level but also between the inflow of gold and the level of production. In terms of the production-possibility curve, they believed that an inflow of gold would push the curve itself outward. Since the mercantilists continued their advocacy of measures to ensure a gold inflow, we must conclude that they believed that the influence of "new" money on production would at least compensate for any rise in prices an increase in the gold supply might bring.

What was their reasoning? They realized that if increases in production kept step with increases in the money supply, the general price level would not rise. Increases in output require additions to productive capacity, which the manufacturer usually borrows money to finance. Borrowing is encouraged by low interest rates. Perceiving the interest rate as the "price of money," some mercantilists concluded that if interest rates were kept low (by the constant increase in the supply of gold), this would encourage borrowing by merchants to finance a greater volume of production and, hence, of trade.

We said earlier that the mercantilists' monetary theory was a blend of naïveté and sophistication. Actually, their naïveté was far greater than their sophistication. They really did not understand how, and under what conditions, an increase in the money supply increases economic activity. They only *believed* that there was a causal connection; they were never able to offer a satisfactory proof of their contention. Unless production does increase concomitantly with increases in the money supply, inflation will result. Why should an increase in the supply of money necessarily call forth greater production? After all, is not money merely a medium of exchange? Does it not sound somehow "magical" that merely by printing more money the general level of material well-being can be increased? Some later economists thought so and rejected the mercantilists' belief that the flow of causation is from an increase in the money supply to an increase in the physical output of goods and services. Still later economists were to reverse this position and to find some use for the idea that there *is* a connection between money-flows and product-flows; but this time, the causal relationship would be more clearly established.

The Demise of Mercantilism

One of the most serious weaknesses of mercantilism was its adherents' obsession with trade to the point of neglecting production.

Commercial activity *is* important, and individuals, as well as nations, can benefit greatly therefrom. But trade can only take place if there is something *to* trade. As we have pointed out, there must be better reasons for trade than the accumulation of gold in a national storehouse, since the ability to *create* wealth, not the mere possession of money, is the real source of economic power.

The death of mercantilism came from both internal and external sources. The more enlightened mercantilists, such as Thomas Mun (1571–1641) and Sir William Petty (1623–87), knew that economic activities other than pure trade were important to national wealth. Mun saw that national wealth consisted of more than gold: He included in his definition of wealth those items that could be used to produce a return over and above their costs—for example, the fish swimming in British waters. Petty began the development of rudimentary theories of rent and interest in the mid-1600's. He was unusual in that, unlike the great majority of mercantilist writers, he was something of a theoretician.

From without, the challenge to mercantilism came from the inexorable change of the economic order. It is often said that the reactions of the French physiocrats and Adam Smith against the mercantilists sped the decline of the system. Although physiocracy and Smithian economics certainly helped to defeat the mercantilists, glimmers of the Industrial Revolution were already evident in their time, especially in England. Thus, the island kingdom was straying from mercantilist ideas and practices even before Smith wrote his explanation of the British economic system.

THE PHYSIOCRATS

In eighteenth-century France, which was noted for its thoroughgoing mercantilism, a group of thinkers reacted against the severe strictures of the mercantilists. These men, called physiocrats, centered their economic theories around production, rather than trade. Physiocracy—a word meaning "the rule of nature"—was an attempt to show that nature is the sole source of national wealth. In trying to demonstrate this proposition, the physiocrats helped to prepare the way for a more tenable explanation of how wealth is created.

They began with the plausible assumption that the way to increase national wealth is to increase the national output each year. How does an economy get an incremental gain in output each year? The physio-crats believed that the only source of such an increase was nature. Only by working *directly* with nature could man finish the year with more than he started. Their reasoning was simple: Nature is the source of everything that exists; man, by himself, makes nothing. He only changes the form of those things that nature provides.

In what pursuits can man work in direct partnership with nature? The physiocrats believed they had the obvious answer in what they called the extractive industries: farming, fishing, forestry, mining, and the like. The physiocrats deemed these industries alone to be produc-tive and all other areas of work unproductive, no matter how useful or wanted such services might be.

The physiocrats divided society into three classes: "cultivators," "proprietors," and those who were "sterile." For practical purposes, we could say that they believed there were only two classes, the productive class (cultivators, miners, and so forth) and the unproductive class (everybody else). These terms were not meant to confer encomiums or cast opprobrium on individuals. Many physiocrats might well have been included in the sterile class themselves, for this group included lawyers, physicians, philosophers, priests, artists, and statesmen. The terms "productive" and "sterile" were purely technical, and the physiocrats did not deny that the work of the members of the "unproductive" classes could be useful. The sterility of an occupation meant only that its practitioners contributed nothing to the output of a nation above the value of their own labors.

The case was different in agriculture, they thought, for although the farmer prepares the ground, sows the seeds, tends the plants, and harvests the grain—all human exertions (labor); nature is the source of the original fertility of the soil and sends sunlight and rain for the nurture of plants and insects for their pollination. Nature does not have to be paid for these services. Is not the grain harvested from the soil each year more valuable than the seeds sown at planting time? By working with nature, man gets back from the soil a crop of greater value than the value of all the things he puts into it. This increase the physiocrats called the "net product," and they supposed that it was obtainable only in those industries in which man could form a direct partnership with nature.

The physiocrats, like the mercantilists earlier and Adam Smith later, were searching for a way to increase the wealth of nations. They thought that they had found it in the extractive industries, since, according to their beliefs, only men who worked in direct partnership with nature could produce an output greater than the inputs, including their labor. In all other occupations, the value of the product equaled only the value of the labor in it plus the value of the other inputs; and, since no greater value was produced by the members of the unproductive classes, no addition to national wealth could be attributed to people such as artisans, merchants, and chimney sweeps.

Since the physiocrats thought that the extractive industries were the sole route to increased national wealth, it is not surprising that they favored the expansion of agriculture relative to other industries. But they did not exalt the farmer above other workers; he was no better than anyone else; nature, not the cultivator, was the source of the surplus or net product.

Under the sway of the mercantilists and a succession of vainglorious French kings, the burden of enormous taxes fell largely on the French peasant. Those most able to pay taxes—the Church, clerics, the nobility —were exempt from taxation as a matter of class privilege.

Happily, the physiocrats also believed that they had found the only theoretically correct solution to the problem of taxation. If agriculture alone could produce a surplus, then only agriculture could support a tax. Thus, the physiocrats urged that national expenditures be paid out of a single tax levied solely on landholders. Although the peasants actually work with nature, the surplus ultimately accrues to the landlords, so they are the only proper subjects for taxation. The members of the other classes (proprietary and sterile) create no net revenue, and, therefore, they generate no income; they are, in essence, only exchanging equivalent values.

Despite some shortcomings, the physiocrats have left us a durable heritage, for they believed rightly that man could join with nature to increase the wealth of nations. But they also thought that such a cooperative effort took place on nature's terms. They posited a "natural order" in life that man transgressed at his peril. No manmade laws, no government could prevail against *"le ordre naturel."* The only consequence of interference would be to lessen nature's cooperation and thereby reduce the contribution made by nature to the increase of the national product. The physiocrats therefore inveighed against any kind of intervention in the economy—governmental or otherwise. But they were emphatically not anarchistic. They believed in and supported the existing French governmental institutions, including the monarchy with its history of luxurious profligacy. They were convinced of the supremacy of reason—of action in accord with the natural law. The physiocrats devoutly believed that men were reasonable creatures, who, if they knew what the natural law was, would act in accord with it. Thus, enlightenment of king and subjects was the goal and method of the physiocrats in achieving the perfectly functioning economy.

Since the time of the physiocrats, numerous individuals, although not sharing the French thinkers' faith in reason, have preached the unwisdom of governmental intervention in economic affairs. They are advocates of *laissez faire* economics. They believe that there is something natural—something right—in the way a self-regulating economy works. In their view a self-regulating economy is the only proper economic system. This belief in *laissez faire*—and the expression itself—began with the physiocrats. Literally, it means, "let things alone." Although the classical economists, especially after Adam Smith, viewed the relationship between man and nature in a vastly different way than did the physiocrats, they also viewed the ideal economy as self-regulating and rejected government intervention and direction. Physiocracy and classical economics together, then, form the foundation of the tradition of *laissez faire* thinking.

Physiocratic Economic Analysis: The Circular Flow of Income

It is possible to argue that analytic economics started with *some* physiocrats. One of the most remarkable Physiocrats was François Quesnay (1694–1774), court physician to Madame de Pompadour and Louis XV. Inspired by William Harvey's description of the circulation of the blood in the human body, Quesnay attempted to trace the flow of economic activity in the nation. It was a great accomplishment even to recognize that an economy is a flow and an even greater insight to perceive it as a circular flow. Quesnay worked out a flow chart of the economic system as described by physiocratic doctrine, which he called the *Tableau Economique* (the "Economic Table"). Briefly, Quesnay was attempting to show the process of wealth creation in the physiocratic model of the economy: how the net product arises; how it is distributed among the three classes of society; and how, at the end of the year, the economy, with more product than it had at the start of the year, is ready to begin the process once again.

We shall not delve any deeper into the intricacies of the Economic Table, for it is of interest only to advanced students of the history of economic thought. We mention it here, however, because it is the precursor of our own much simpler and more meaningful depiction of the economy as a circular flow, which we shall now examine.

It is essential to the correct understanding of economics always to remember the simple fact that economic activity flows as through a circular pipeline. Unfortunately, many absurdities are committed by ordinary citizens, legislators, and journalists either because they do not know or because they choose to ignore this fact.

The circular-flow theory is based on the almost banal truism that for every expenditure there must be an income. No one can spend money without someone else's receiving it. The picture of the simple circular flow in Figure 2 shows this idea graphically. Depictions of

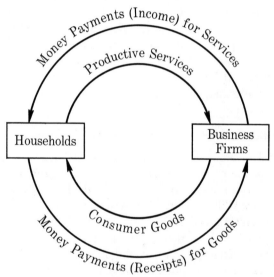

FIGURE 2 *The Economy as a Circular Flow*

the circular flow may range from simple line drawings to illustrations resembling mazes. Our figure splits the economy into two sectors: households and business firms.

Households are both the ultimate consumers of the final goods produced by business firms and the original source of all the productive services used by business firms to produce the total output (gross national product) of the economy. That all goods and services produced by business firms are ultimately consumed by individuals is true despite the fact that some business firms make goods solely for the use of other business firms. For example, the manufacturer of stamping presses for General Motors does sell his output to individuals, although indirectly. Over time, the value of the stamping presses passes into the value of the automobiles that General Motors dealers sell to the general public, since the company must eventually recover from its customers the cost of its plant and equipment. In other words, the output that is sold directly to its ultimate consumers (what we call *final output*) actually includes the value of all the other output that was used in its production. So, the output shown in our diagram (final output), which goes directly from business firms to households, includes the value of the economy's total output (gross national product).

In a free economy such as ours, households supply productive services to business firms, for individuals are the ultimate owners of their labor skills (including managerial and professional talent), as well as of natural resources and of the funds wanted by business to buy capital equipment. Business firms combine the productive services—labor, raw materials, funds—offered by individuals to make the goods demanded by households.

The inner circuit on the diagram is called a "real" flow; it consists of *actual* goods and services. The outer circuit in the diagram is the *monetary* flow. It expresses in monetary terms, the *value* of the goods and services entering into the inner flow between the two sectors. The money flow *reflects* the real flow. By itself, a flow of money between the two sectors would be meaningless. On the other hand, the real flow would be quite possible, although severely impeded in a modern economy, if money were not used. Money is a medium of exchange; goods and services can be exchanged directly for each other, but the use of money as an intermediary obviates such situations as the owner of stock in a rubber company being paid dividends in tires.

The inner circuit is thus the basic flow. In essence, the exchange process between housholds and business firms is the exchange of productive services for consumer goods and services. In practice, however, the exchange process of the monetary economy consists of business firms' making money payments to households in exchange for the productive services provided by the latter. Thus, the expenses of business firms are the personal incomes of the members of households. Households, in turn, use the funds that they have received to buy products from firms. Once again, expenditures become incomes, as the costs of living of individuals become the income of business firms.

You may object that we have left out two important elements of the modern economy: banks and government. Undeniably, these institutions are important, and we will consider their respective influences in later chapters; but their inclusion here would not alter the basic concept of the economy as a circular flow.

Because our model of the economic flow is a closed circle, must the level of economic activity stay the same year after year? For example, say that business firms turn out $700 billion worth of goods and services and consumers buy that output. Then business firms have the wherewithal to produce another $700 billion worth of goods and services (although perhaps of different composition), and the $700 billion that they paid to households for their productive services enables the households to buy that $700 billion worth of output. Does this process continue *ad infinitum*? You know from your own experience that it does not. Why not?

You might think the answer has to do with profits—that when consumers pour $700 billion into the circular flow as household expenditures, business firms extract, say, $100 billion in profit, so that as a result, only $600 billion worth of actual output emerges from the business sector to enter the real portion of the circular flow. But this is *not* the answer. Remember that we may do one of two things. We may regard profit as included in the factoral payments as interest and wages (see pp. 10–11), in which case the diagram immediately disposes of any supposed inequivalency in the top and bottom flows, or, if we want to regard entrepreneurship as a fourth factor of production, we can simply add that function to the factoral services provided by households and then add "Profit" to the outer ring on the lower half of the diagram. In either case, profit neither contradicts nor explains the changing level of economic activity. The problem we are considering is of much greater consequence than the arbitrary but useful names economists have given to productive services and the rewards going to their owners.

Before we are through, we shall explore the problems of unemployment and growth, but for now, we shall return to the thinkers who made a science of economic thought.

By the middle of the eighteenth century, mercantilism and physiocracy were moribund. British "classical" economics was becoming the popular form of economic thought. However, the demise of the mercantilists and the physiocrats and the rise to dominance of the British classical economists cannot be said to have come about solely because of the superiority of the Englishmen's theorizing. Rather, the primacy of the British classicals was thrust upon them by the amazing performance of the British economy in the late 1700's. The immense and growing power of Britain apparently meant that whatever she was doing, it certainly was right. The British nation was becoming an economic giant; Englishmen and the rest of the astonished world demanded an explanation. Its explainers, some of whom we shall meet in Chapters 3 and 4, became giants themselves.

ADAM SMITH:
FATHER OF
ECONOMICS

3

Accounts of the Industrial Revolution commonly follow two patterns: one is a recital of the intricacies of a number of dreary-sounding textile-making machines; the other is an often vivid portrayal of the human degradation that accompanied the early stages in the evolution of the factory system. Each of these pictures is accurate—as far as it goes. But both, even taken together, are incomplete, for they miss the crucial fact that the Industrial Revolution was a major *liberating* force in human affairs. The Industrial Revolution *was* painful, but the wholesale individual and social disorientation that accompanied it only showed its profound influence and immense power. That men did not focus that enormous power too well is simply another manifestation of mankind's regrettable tendency to lag socially and culturally behind its own technology.

THE UNKNOWABLE REVOLUTION

Men did not understand the Industrial Revolution very well while it was happening, and, not understanding it, they could not control it. Neither had they known what to do when the earlier Agricultural Revolution so increased agricultural productivity that fewer farm workers were needed. As a result of this earlier revolution, great numbers of farm workers left the land for the cities, where the Industrial

Revolution later created giant factories in which the new urban dwellers could work. Men accustomed to the fresh air and open spaces of the British midlands lost their sense of personal worth crowded together in the grime and sordidness of industrial London, and it would be a long and painful time before they regained their status as human beings.

The Entrepreneur

The tremendous productivity unleashed by the Industrial Revolution was soon felt, especially in Britain, where the outpouring of inventions was torrential. Inventions, however, are not enough to produce economic expansion. A nation may have superb technical competence, but unless inventions are utilized in the economic process they will make no contribution to material progress. The act of applying inventions to economizing is called *innovation,* and the individuals who perform this act are called *innovators, enterprisers,* or *entrepreneurs.*

The entrepreneur is the individual who sees the economic potentialities of a new product, raw material, or process and who applies them in business, hoping to make a profit. He may not make a profit. Uncertainty and risk-bearing are the entrepreneur's lot; society rewards him with profits if his guesses are right and penalizes him with losses if they are wrong. The economic motivation for entrepreneurial activity is the hope of profits. The legal foundation of entrepreneurship is private property. The institution of private property is essentially the right of a person to do with his possessions whatever he wishes.

Late-eighteenth-century Britain was the scene of hitherto unparalleled economic activity. A number of factors that had been developing combined at that time to place Britain in what some economists call "the takeoff position"; that is, the almost simultaneous fruition of a number of powerful forces enabled the island kingdom to make a tremendous economic leap forward.

What were some of the reasons for Britain's amazing economic upsurge? One of the most obvious was the great stream of inventions pouring forth from the considerable number of technical minds with which Britain seems to have been blessed. The chronological sequence of these inventions was fortunate. Agriculture was the first beneficiary of the new technology. This fact accomplished two interrelated things: First, the new tools and techniques of British agriculture enabled fewer farmers to feed a growing nonagricultural population; and, second, agricultural technology released workers from the farms, making available a labor force soon to be required by the developing industrial technology.

New developments in technology are a necessary, but insufficient, prerequisite to economic development. Some of the new inventions must be *applied* to the productive process in the form of capital equipment. Manufacturers must also be able to purchase the new equipment. This usually calls for borrowing, which, in turn, requires saving on the part of someone so that there are funds available to be borrowed. And even if people are willing and able to save a portion of their incomes, there must be some way of attracting loanable funds into the industrial sector and marshaling them so that the small contributions of many persons can be combined to make the usually considerable expenditures required for the purchase of large-scale pieces of capital equipment. The power to attract loanable funds is manifested in the interest rate. English manufacturers were willing to promise those individuals lending them funds a return sufficiently high to induce a large number of would-be consumers to forego the pleasures of immediate consumption. The evolving financial institutions—banks, underwriters, and brokerage firms—assembled these funds from various sources and channeled them into the firms bidding the highest interest rate for them.

At about the same time, new forms of business organization were developing—forms that were particularly suited to accumulating and disbursing the great sums necessary to building large-scale industrial enterprises. These firms—joint-stock companies—are the ancestors of the modern corporation. The advantages of today's corporate form of business organization include both the ability to split ownership interests in the firm into small units (so that funds can be obtained from small savers) and the limitation of the liability of those who buy ownership interests to the amount they have invested.

Probably, the technological, managerial, and financial aspects of the Industrial Revolution would not have been realized had it not been for the evolving tradition of British political democracy, especially as it was reflected in the common law. A large part of the common law deals with the rights of private property; another major division of the common law is concerned with contractual agreements. Precise, clear, definite, yet flexible property and contract laws are vital to free commercial activity. Britain possessed all the prerequisites for a high level of economic activity—political democracy, private property, technological advances, the common law—by the middle of the eighteenth century; these prerequisites had evolved gradually, although not without some strife and drama.

The Industrial Revolution did more than bring about the triumph of technology. It destroyed the old order in Britain, beginning an era of social mobility that was to distinguish Britain from the moribund European states and was eventually to be a hallmark of life in the United States. The burgeoning technology was essential to, but was not alone a sufficient cause of, the Industrial Revolution; it needed implementation to make Britain a great economic power. For the potentialities of inventions to be released into the circular flow of economic activity, someone must believe in possible gains from using new techniques, materials, and products. This person is the entrepreneur.

Observable Success: Hidden Reasons

In the late eighteenth century, the success of Britain's economic system was readily apparent. By the standards of the day, Britain was affluent—although her wealth was distributed in such a way that most Englishmen were not themselves affluent. With economic success came political power. Britain was becoming the unquestioned leader among world powers, a position she was to hold until well into the twentieth century. Surely, she was the envy of, and a conundrum to, her European neighbors. But if Britain was a puzzle to the European powers, she was also something of a mystery to herself.

Here was a nation following neither the tenets of mercantilism nor those of physiocracy. Indeed, she was apparently pursuing no conscious plan at all and yet was enjoying unprecedented prosperity and growth. The traditional sources of power had been severely weakened; the members of the old power structure seemed to have been displaced. Who was replacing them? No one was quite sure. It was true that the merchant and manufacturing class was growing in power, but were its members really replacing Britain's traditional leaders—the princes, landowners, clerics, statesmen, and intellectuals? Even if, by some chance, this might be so, what was the businessmen's plan for governing? How could they possibly implement their plan if they had one? Yet the evidence was incontrovertible and embarrassing: A nation that had given up the power-conscious policies of mercantilism, that had displaced the leaders and prophets of the old order, and that had allowed disorganized profit-seekers to gain ascendancy in an atmosphere of political liberalism was beginning to shake the world.

Economic success was the fact. What men, particularly Englishmen, wanted was an explanation. In other words, the time was ripe for an economic theory and a theorist; the theory that emerged was economic liberalism and the theorist was Adam Smith.

ADAM SMITH: THE BACKGROUND

The Life of Adam Smith

Adam Smith (1723–90) did not know that he was a political economist; to himself and his peers he was a moral philosopher. Moral philosophy, in the eighteenth century, was the repository of various separable branches of thought that today have become distinct disciplines, among them economics, jurisprudence, sociology, political science, public administration, and business management. Adam Smith was a professor of this wide field of inquiry at the University of Glasgow.

Smith was a fairly well-traveled Scot and was well acquainted with the French physiocrats owing to his position (1764–66) as private tutor and traveling companion to the young Duke of Buccleuch. Not only did his continental travels influence his later thinking but the reasonably adequate lifetime pension provided for him by Buccleuch enabled him to do his reflecting and writing in a manner that would please any scholar.

Adam Smith, moral philosopher, is unquestionably one of the greatest, and perhaps the greatest, of all economists. Like many great men, Smith met the needs of his time. The English nation, indeed the whole civilized world, wanted to know how the presumably undirected British economy could function so magnificently. Smith gave them the answer in one of the world's two major documents bearing the date 1776, *An Inquiry into the Nature and Causes of the Wealth of Nations.*

Smith's book, usually called simply *The Wealth of Nations,* is a gospel in the true meaning of the word, for it is "good news." It is an explanation of how a society respecting individual and property rights and employing no central authority to guide economic affairs could develop the greatest economy in the world.

What is *The Wealth of Nations* about? Despite the literary style of the period, which called for long titles, the wording is precise. Smith had written an explanation—a theory—of the growth of national wealth. Today we would call it a text on economic development.

The Influences Affecting Smith

Among the forces influencing Smith as he inquired into the causes of the wealth of nations were his education in moral philosophy, the economic doctrines of mercantilism and physiocracy, and the rising economic and political fortunes of English businessmen. Smith came to the field of economics as a rather ordinary moral philosopher; he left it as a great economist. Yet the influence of moral philosophy upon him was so decisive that it is worthwhile to examine his experiences in this now extinct discipline.

FRANCIS HUTCHESON. Smith's teacher and predecessor in the chair of moral philosophy at Glasgow was Francis Hutcheson, a deeply religious yet quite unorthodox Protestant Ulsterman. Hutcheson was a sentimental moral philosopher and so, for a time, was Adam Smith. "Sentimental" as used here does not mean "romantic" or "maudlin" but denotes the desire of such moral philosophers to study human sentiments or value judgments. One of Hutcheson's major works is *An Inquiry into the Original of Our Ideas of Beauty and Virtue.* From the title, you could reasonably conclude that this was a volume about esthetics and morals, and you would be correct. But what have esthetics and morals to do with economics? The link may be tenuous, to say the least, but a closer examination of Hutcheson's philosophy may clarify some points about Smith's economics.

In the development of his system of moral philosophy, Hutcheson promulgated what he called the concept of "the guiding hand." He tried to explain how things could work together for good despite the apparent inability of countless numbers of independent individuals to predict the ramifications of their actions. Since society is not completely chaotic, Hutcheson reasoned, in some intuitive way men must make morally sound decisions leading to socially desirable results that they had not consciously intended. Hutcheson concluded that these instinctual decisions came through divine intervention—the guiding hand—in human affairs. If you know anything about Adam Smith, you probably see a similarity between these ideas and Smith's famous theoretical construct, "the *invisible* hand." But there is also a major difference. Smith, in *The Wealth of Nations,* set about to show that a socially desirable end emerging from the uncoordinated, self-interested actions of individuals could be explained without reference to divine intervention. Hutcheson's guiding hand was providential, whereas there was nothing mystical about Smith's invisible hand. The latter is, as we shall discover shortly, nothing other than a euphemism for what economists now call "perfect competition."

Let us consider two important concepts that Hutcheson and Smith shared in reaching their different conclusions: the principles of benevolence and self-interest. They believed that men are governed to a great extent by their self-interests. But this "instinct" of self-interest is not necessarily bad; both Hutcheson and Smith held that it is not synonymous with avarice and selfishness but is rather the individual's concern for his own preservation and fulfillment as a human being. Besides, they believed that this self-interest is tempered by the "instinct" of benevolence, which causes men to want to perform good actions toward each other.

DAVID HUME. Another notable philosopher who affected Smith's career was David Hume (1711–76). Hume was a greater philosopher than Smith—at least his reputation at the time was greater. Since, however, Hume was a convinced atheist, when the chair of moral philosophy at the University of Glasgow became vacant, Smith received the prestigious appointment. Had Hume's beliefs, or lack of them, not rendered him unemployable at the University, the world might never have heard of Adam Smith.

Hume's approach to philosophy, although not his atheism, so impressed Smith that Smith revised the ideas about the ethical system he had inherited from his old master, Hutcheson. Smith set forth his new ideas in *The Theory of Moral Sentiments,* a book that concerns us for two reasons. First, it contains Smith's promise to write *The Wealth of Nations* at some future date. Second, it contains four parts, one of which, called, in typical Smithianese, "The Political Regulations which do not deal with Justice and Jurisprudence, but are Calculated to Increase the Riches, Power, and Prosperity of the State," Smith later expanded and published as *An Inquiry into the Nature and Causes of the Wealth of Nations.*

Hume, like Smith, also wrote on economic matters; today we consider Hume as having been a first-rate, if rather disorganized, economist. His ideas and Smith's were markedly similar. If Hume had clarified and systematized his economic writings and had he been able to make himself acceptable to the University of Glasgow, he and Smith might have shared the honored place in the history of economic thought that today belongs to the latter alone.

THE "FABLE OF THE BEES."   One final, and perhaps unusual, figure who influenced Smith was Bernard de Mandeville, whose 1714 verse *The Fable of the Bees: Or Private Vices, Publick Benefits* suggested that the prosperity of society depends upon "vice" and not virtue.[1] By "vice" Mandeville meant not that the well-being of society depended upon the depraved conduct of individuals but only the innocuous (though distasteful) idea that society is propelled forward materially as men attempt to satisfy their desires for wealth, luxury, ostentation, and comfort. Mandeville was really doing nothing more than continuing the Hobbesian view of self-interest as plain selfishness. Smith reacted vigorously against this view, for he considered self-interest to be a *natural,* divinely implanted, instinct for survival and self-fulfillment as a human being. This conception of self-interest justified Smith's argument that, for the most part, the drives behind human wants are virtuous.

Today, some would say that Mandeville's verse is rather silly, but this would be selling it short. Smith himself rather grudgingly found something worthwhile in the *Fable.* In choosing a hive of bees as a model of society, Mandeville stated the circular-flow idea earlier and more forcefully than did Quesnay in his *Tableau Economique,* for a beehive is one of the most interdependent of all communities. More than simply seeing the economy as a circular flow, Mandeville stressed the importance of spending in maintaining prosperity: Like bees in a hive, we also are members of a highly interdependent society, in which each must tend to his special tasks and trade the fruits of his efforts uninterruptedly with others for societal well-being. Mandeville, in a crude way, was arguing for what we would call today a high level of aggregate effective demand. Despite his disagreement with many of Mandeville's conclusions Smith readily accepted the concept of the interdependence of economic units, amplifying it in his famous "divi-

---

[1] Mandeville had expressed the same idea nine years earlier in a cheap pamphlet, *The Grumbling Hive.* Owing to its lack of clarity, it was not nearly as popular with the public as the later revision, which was accompanied by a detailed commentary explaining the verse to its readers.

sion-of-labor" principle, which we will discuss shortly. Smith, and subsequently other perceptive economists, knew that spending is the *sine qua non* of a high level of economic activity. But he broke with Mandeville over the objects of expenditure, contending that in a self-regulating economy (the subject of Smithian theory), the demands of all men for worthwhile goods and services would be sufficient to keep the economy operating at a high level. He thus negated the Mandevillian thesis that the self-indulgent, socially useless, expenditures of the idle rich were necessary to absorb completely the national output.

In Mandeville, we once again have encountered a man who seems to have been ahead of his time. Although the classical economists, with the exception of Thomas Malthus, never feared a deficiency of aggregate demand, the specter of a lack of generalized purchasing power was to haunt men as their economies became more advanced. But Mandeville was not really concerned with depressions; he could not have been, since the economies of his day were not advanced enough to have them. Other than his stress upon the interrelatedness of economic units, he did not make and was not really trying to make a theoretical contribution to economics; he was simply arguing the philosophical, not the economic, case for a highly egoistic interpretation of self-interest.

The Economic Background

In the late eighteenth century, the unleashing of great productive forces in England was apparent to the Western world. What was obscure was how this enormous power was being directed. That there was some guiding force was evidenced by the incontrovertible success of whatever it was that passed for the British economic system. Obviously, the British were not practicing the tenets of mercantilism or physiocracy. The passion for gold had waned. The British were becoming progressively less interested in agriculture as the chief national enterprise. Imported grain cost the British less than that which they grew at home. The physiocratic proposition that only the extractive industries added to national wealth was palpably false. British wealth increased as Englishmen deserted field for factory.

By their new affluence and influence, businessmen were gaining political power at the expense of the nobility and landed gentry. Nothing could be more natural in a land that had enshrined personal liberty and property rights in its common law than that self-interested, pros-

perous, and highly motivated tradesmen would refuse to allow interference in business affairs from a class whose position was founded
solely on inherited wealth in land. The factory owners and shopkeepers
were forcing change on the old economic interests and systems; and the
new economic system, which was their creation and which had yet to
be given a name and dignified by a theory, was compounding its successes. A nation singlemindedly pursuing the banalities of manufacture
and trade, without any central guidance from a class born with a presumably divine right to rule, was becoming the world's greatest power.
England—a nation of shopkeepers—had somehow stumbled upon the
most direct road yet found to national wealth. In the late 1700's, moreover, she had barely started up that road; she was yet to generate the
wealth that would finance an empire *and* provide much of the capital
investment needed by the young United States of America.

Despite the greatness of Smith's contribution, let us be clear that
Adam Smith did not create that free-market economy; it already existed. Although he did not understand it, the English businessman had
discovered the true philosopher's stone. Smith discovered *how* the
system functioned—he was its theoretician, expositor, missionary, and
biographer.

Smith's Approach to Economics

The Wealth of Nations is a great book. But the heavy encrustation
of honor that time has laid upon it must be ruthlessly chipped away,
so that Smith's contribution can be seen in its historical context.

Lacking the refined tools of today's economic analysis, Smith was
unable to demonstrate rigorously how the British economy worked.
This does not mean that he was wrong (even though he was sometimes
confused). Smith was a brilliant inferential economist, and he had an
intuitive understanding of the workings of the British economy,
which he was able to convey to his readers.

When it was published in 1776 *The Wealth of Nations* was not regarded purely as a textbook on political economy. And Smith did not
intend it to be. He wrote it to sell, which meant that it had to speak
clearly to an audience outside the groves of Academe. It did. The people who read Smith understood him, perhaps because they, too, had
an intuitive understanding of how the British economy worked. More
probably, however, Smith's readers, principally the members of the

new entrepreneurial class, desired an academician's endorsement of their activities. By explaining the socially useful functions of business and businessmen, the great Scottish intellectual gave the entrepreneurial class self-esteem and a certain dignity. That *The Wealth of Nations* was itself a successful item of commerce indicates that it satisfied a basic psychological need of its purchasers.

SMITHIAN PSYCHOLOGICAL AND SOCIAL PREMISES

The Role of Self-Interest

The first question Adam Smith had to answer was this: What was the basis of the increase of wealth in England? It was obviously not direction by the head of a mercantilist state bent on national power, nor was it the desire of the people to serve the state. The force moving England toward wealth more efficiently than any other national economic mainspring was pure self-interest. "It is not from the benevolence of the butcher, the brewer, or the baker that we expect our dinner," wrote Smith, "but from regard to their own self-interest."

THE MAXIMIZING PRINCIPLE. So that we may be on common ground with Adam Smith, we shall adopt his definition of the expression "self-interest." Although the definition of self-interest is a philosophical concept, Smith incorporated his definition into his economics. He had a definite model of man in mind when he constructed his economics. The self-interest of Smithian philosophy became the maximizing principle of Smithian (and other) economics.

Smith's model man knows better than anyone else what is good for him. As a consumer, he will act so as to get the greatest possible utility from the combinations of goods and services available to him, given his limited income. As a producer, he tries to obtain the greatest possible profit, given the demand for the goods he makes and the costs of producing those goods. Smith's man is mature, rational, and intelligent. To those who think differently and who would assume the burden of directing the economic activities of others, Smith wrote:

> Every individual it is evident, can in his local situation judge better than any statesman or lawgiver can do for him. The statesman who should attempt to direct private people in what manner they ought to employ their capital, would not only load himself with a most unnecessary atten-

tion but assume an authority which could be safely trusted, not only to no single person, but to no council or senate whatever.

THE "SYSTEM OF NATURAL LIBERTY." Smith, an inheritor of moral philosophy and physiocracy, believed that the economy would function best if human beings were allowed to employ, with the least possible hindrance, the drives implanted in them by nature—hence he characterized the economic system described in *The Wealth of Nations* as one of "natural liberty." Today we call this system "eighteenth-century economic liberalism."

Although Smith believed, as did the physiocrats before him, that the natural order exists independently of the will of man and that, for his own benefit, man ought to conform to that order, he did not feel that a society following the "simple system of natural liberty" would be a utopia. He claimed nothing more for the system of natural liberty than that it was the context in which personal freedom and social welfare would most likely be consistently maximized, subject to the constraints one places on the other. *The Wealth of Nations* is not just another volume in the series of optimistic but groundless eighteenth-century treatises on social harmony. The optimal mixture of social welfare and personal freedom of which Smith wrote was based upon his assumptions about the nature of the men and the society he knew. As Smith put it:

> All systems of either preference or restraint, therefore thus being completely taken away, the obvious and simple system of natural liberty establishes itself of its own accord. Every man, as long as he does not violate the laws of justice, is left perfectly free to pursue his own interest in his own way, and to bring both his industry and his capital into competition with those of any other man, or order of men. The sovereign is completely discharged from a duty, in the attempting to perform which he must always be exposed to innumerable delusions, and for the proper performance of which no human wisdom or knowledge could ever be sufficient . . . .

To say that the quotation above encapsulates Adam Smith's theory may be reckless, but this passage reveals so much about Smithian economics that it deserves careful analysis. Smith tells us that the system of natural liberty will work if each man pursuing his own interest "does not violate the laws of justice." This prohibition is important. The system of natural liberty will work, if at all, only in a society whose laws reflect a basic moral code in which it is expected that bargains will be kept. The legal, moral, and social climate *is* important to the functioning of an economy. When each transaction becomes an adventure, when haggling over price is the custom, when shaving quality and quantity is the mark of a clever tradesman, when promises are made to be broken, when bribery becomes an accepted cost of business—in short, when transactors cannot generally rely on each other's word—a significant level of economic activity is impossible. Without casting aspersions on those nations that are poor—for there are many varied and complex reasons for underdevelopment—it is safe to say that in the nations that *are* numbered among the economically advanced the level of morality essential to regular business activity is widely accepted. Despite the presence of some dishonest men among them, the bulk of the populace of the developed nations expect to meet their contractual obligations. One great obstacle to the economic development of many backward nations today is the complete unfamiliarity of many peoples with the essentiality of a critical minimum level of business ethics, a concept exemplified in the Western principle of the inviolability of contracts.

To an important, if limited, extent, some harmonizing and channeling of individual interests toward socially desirable ends is done by an institution Smith is often erroneously supposed to have abhorred—government. Smith delineated two inescapable functions of government. First, he did not expect private enterprise to undertake those activities that, although conferring utility, could not either recompense their producer properly or be charged to their consumer. Thus he declared that the state must be responsible for national defense and provide certain essential, but privately unprofitable, services such as building and maintaining roads, and keeping public records of vital statistics.

Second, and most important, the teacher of jurisprudence held the paramount function of the state to be the administration of justice. In this sphere, government does not hinder but helps self-interested businessmen who "do not violate the laws of justice." Government discourages the activities of the relatively few individuals who will not live by the canons of moral conduct concretized in the common law.

When we talk about Smithian economics as laissez faire economics, we must understand that Smith intended government to take a negligible part in the purely economic decisions of private transactors. Except in well-defined areas, government must not tell consumers what they may buy or firms what they may make and how they should make it. These decisions are made in the market. But government does have a function in the economy—to help make the market a viable context in which independent decisions can coalesce into the social good. The relationship of government to the market is to ensure a framework within which rational individuals who are *contributors* to the economy can expect reasonable performance from one another. Thus, actions inconsistent with rational decision-making may properly be proscribed by government. Mislabeling, short weighing, specious claims for goods, counterfeiting, and all practices that impair the ability of producers and consumers to act rationally call for government intervention. Those who steal, embezzle, perpetrate frauds, or supply merchandise harmful to either soul or body may be removed by government from the society of those who adhere to "the laws of justice."

Before we leave the subject of Smith's interpretation of laissez faire, let us note that he had a less than sanguine opinion of the activities of some members of the business community. On the character of businessmen, Smith remarked:

> People of the same trade seldom meet together, even for merriment and diversion, but the conversation ends in a conspiracy against the public, or in some contrivance to raise prices. It is impossible indeed to prevent such meetings, by any law which either could be executed, or would be consistent with law and justice. But though the law cannot hinder people of the same trade from sometimes assembling together, it ought to do nothing to facilitate such assemblies; much less render them necessary.

Of private property in the form of land, Smith wrote: "As soon as the land of any country has all become private property, the landlords, like all other men, love to reap where they never sowed . . . ." Of the laboringman, he said: "The property which every man has in his own labour, as it is the original foundation of all other property, so it is the most sacred and inviolable." And of the contest between consumers and producers, Smith declared: "Consumption is the sole end and purpose of all production; and the interest of the producer ought to be attended to, only so far as it may be necessary for promoting that of the consumer." Adam Smith may be the patron saint of economists, but it is not so apparent that he ought to occupy the same position with respect to businessmen.

THE INVISIBLE HAND

When you think about it, does it not seem somewhat preposterous that we should expect our dinner to result from the self-interest of the butcher, brewer, and baker? Many persons in the eighteenth century thought that expectation absurd, and some advocates of central planning still think so, although perhaps for reasons better than those of the educated man of the late 1700's. Even if we restrict ourselves to the idea of self-gain in the Smithian sense, will not the natural short-sightedness of human beings lead to an irrational composition and distribution of the gross national product? How could Smith argue that the sum of individual Englishmen's private well-being would be the well-being of all England? Why was the English economy not a chaos instead of a system?

Smith called his answer to these questions the "invisible hand." [2] Suppose, said Smith, an individual desires by his industry to further only himself and,

> by directing that industry in such a manner as its produce may be of the greatest value, he intends only his own gain, and he is in this, as in many other cases, led by an invisible hand to promote an end which was no part of his intention. Nor is it always the worse for society that it was not part of it. By pursuing his own interest he frequently promotes that of the society more effectually than when he really intends to promote it.

Smith is esteemed as a great economist not because he invented clever expressions like "the invisible hand" but because, without the refined tools of later economists, he correctly deduced the operation of a free-market economy. More than a hundred years were to pass before economic analysis developed to a point where economists could prove rigorously Smith's propositions about the market economy—namely, that the economy, made up of seemingly independent, totally unco-ordinated, wholly self-interested individuals, produces at the lowest possible costs those things that consumers most value.

---

[2] The term is unfortunate from the point of view of economists, even if such catchwords do help sell books, for it conveys the idea that the invisible hand is an actual *thing*. It would be more accurate to speak of the invisible-hand *doctrine* or *process*.

We have noted before that the phenomenon about which the economist Smith theorized and which the writer Smith called "the invisible hand" today goes by the colorless, and somewhat confusing, name of *perfect competition*. Let's look at this concept. Economic competition generally exists in a market. A market does not have a location. For example, although the New York Stock Exchange building is at the intersection of Broad and Wall Streets in New York City, the "stock market"—the market for securities *listed* on the "Big Board"—is nationwide or even worldwide. It is surprisingly difficult to define a market precisely, for, despite its ordinary-sounding name, it is a highly abstract concept. More than anything else, a market is a situation in which buyers and sellers may compare their respective offers to buy and sell and, on the basis of these comparisons, consummate or reject proffered bargains. In a competitive market situation, no party has enough economic power to force another to comply with his specific terms, so buyers and sellers are both perfectly free to reject offers and to make counter-offers. But the market *situation* is more than the obvious confrontation of buyers and sellers; buyers also vie with other buyers, and sellers compete with one another, each economic unit following the principle of maximization (p. 55).

Competition is said to be *perfect* when, among other things, no economic unit—household or firm—is large enough in relation to the market to affect prices. Collusion between economic units (for example, for the purpose of fixing prices) is ruled out in the Smithian model, since the joint action of several economic units against other economic units is the antithesis of competitive behavior. What Smith was describing was an economy made up of *atomistic* firms and consumers.

For a firm, by itself, to be unable to affect the prices of the goods it sells requires not only that the firm be small in relation to the market but that it be powerless to give its products a special quality, real or imagined, which might cause consumers to show a preference (and therefore be willing to pay more) for the goods of one producer over those of another. The perfect competitor's goods are homogeneous; one producer's output is a perfect substitute for the product of any other firm making the same good. Consumers do not care from whom they buy. For example, a bushel of wheat of a certain grade is interchangeable with any one of ten thousand other bushels of wheat of the same grade. Wheat buyers do not have the slightest interest in knowing which farmer grew the grain. Therefore, it would be pointless for any one farmer to advertise his grain. He would be adding to his costs without being able either to sell more or to get more money for what he sells.

If the buyers of some products are not as knowledgeable about the things they buy as wheat buyers are about wheat, a producer may, by some promotional scheme, make buyers *believe* that his product is different from and superior to that of all other producers, whether it is in fact different or not. The ethics of the matter is not a question here. What is of consequence is that a real or imagined superiority attributed by consumers to a product gives its producer an advantage over other producers selling similar goods. Competition between goods on the basis of quality, advertising, service, and snob-appeal is called *nonprice competition*. Smith made little room for competition of this sort in his model economy, hypothesizing instead that competition was expressed by pressures on prices.

The last element of perfect competition we shall consider is *mobility*. All competitors are free from "artificial" restrictions upon their entry into or their exit from the market. By "artificial" is meant any restrictive elements other than those imposed by the nature of the productive process itself. For example, if a wheat farmer becomes disillusioned about the prospects for wheat, he can, if he wishes, grow onions. The only limitations on his making such a transfer are those imposed by nature. He will have to harvest his wheat, clear the land, learn about onion growing, plant the onions, weed, water, and till the soil, and wait a while before his onions are ready for the vegetable market. But no one *tells* him that he cannot leave wheat farming for onion growing. No governmental approval is necessary. No union of onion growers can keep him out, make him wait his turn, or compel him to pay dues. The enterpriser makes his decisions and carries them out free from any "coercive" interference.

In sum, then, the elements of perfect competition are, by definition:

1. Small economic units—buyers and sellers must be so small in relation to the market that no one economic unit, by itself, can exert any influence upon the market behavior of any other economic unit.

2. Homogeneous products—all units of a given good, from whatever producer, must appear identical to consumers.

3. Market knowledge—market participants must have a high degree

of knowledge not only about the composition of the good being traded but about possible differences in prices between geographic regions and in different seasons of the year and about changing technologies and consumer tastes. (This requisite is probably the least frequently realized component of the various elements of perfect competition.)

4. Mobility—all resources must be free to move to whatever use will pay their owners the highest reward.

This kind of competition is, according to Smith, the great safeguard against the antisocial application of economic self-interest. This is the core of his invisible-hand doctrine. No one economic unit, by itself, possesses enough power to hurt any other unit, at least as far as economic behavior is concerned. The small size of economic units relative to the markets in which they operate is a powerful equalizing force. Self-interested, anonymous, and equal competitors bid against one another in the market. Consumers try to get the most for the least, and sellers try to give up the least for the most. Everybody is out for himself. The baker is not motivated by a desire to keep his consumers from starving, and his customers are not interested in his survival as a baker. Is this immoral? chaotic? Not according to Smith. The perfectly competitive context orders the individualistic actions of producers and consumers into a purposive and beneficial social action. The competitive market—the invisible hand—tells producers what goods consumers want, how many of each class of good should be made, and how they should be made, and determines who gets them. In short, the market mechanism answers the questions that any economic system must answer (see p. 19); and, Smith asserted, it responds more successfully than could a system directed by the wisest and most benevolent despots. The Smithian criterion of "success" is the maximization of the total income of the economy. To Smith, the success of the economy directed by the invisible hand was its efficiency in providing society with the greatest quantity of sought-after goods at the lowest reasonable costs. Smith, and the classical economists who followed him, had a striking, albeit simple, index of economic well-being; it was simply this: "More goods for more people at the lowest costs."

The Invisible Hand Made Visible

We must not allow Smith's pithy phrase to delude us into believing that we cannot see how a perfectly competitive market operates. In Chapter 6, we shall make the process *graphically* visible when we encounter the tools of demand and supply analysis; for now we shall, as did Smith, use a word picture.

The Model

The market is an impersonal arena for competitive forces. This situation sounds about as grim and divisive as the gladiatorial combats that the Romans staged in the Colosseum. Economically, men are pitted against other men, each trying to do the best for himself with little or no thought for other human beings individually or for the whole of society. The market seems to be a battleground, and economizing appears to be war. This is what many well-intentioned people have concluded in deploring the competitive nature of the free-market economy. We know Smith's answer to this contention: The good of all is served better by competition and self-interest than by each member of the economy's conscious striving for the social good.

Let us begin our examination of Smith's thesis with his remark that the self-interest, not the benevolence, of the baker, the brewer, and the butcher is responsible for our dinner. How is our individual well-being harmonized with social well-being? To answer this question, we can employ our customary two-alternative case, selecting for the procedure two of the goods Smith named.

Brewing and baking are especially well suited to our illustration in that many of the same resources are required to produce them. It is reasonable to assume that in eighteenth-century England these two industries would be in fairly direct competition for resources and sales and that their customers would be in competition with one another for two goods such as ale and bread. If you object to these concrete commodities, you can convert them into abstract goods simply by calling the two alternatives *a* and *b*.

At the opening of our drama, the economy is at a certain point on its production-possibility curve. We are assuming that resources are fully employed throughout our example and that the economy is in equilibrium. *Equilibrium* means that there is no tendency to change. In the absence of a change in consumer tastes or in the costs of production, there will be no movement away from the initial point on the production-possibility curve.

We now disturb the tranquillity of our system by bringing on stage some disequilibrating forces. This is quite realistic; all modern economies are subjected to continual pressures; disequilibrating forces are the rule. Let us suppose that a temperance leader has achieved marked success in convincing people that they ought to imbibe less and that, to fill up the void in their stomachs formerly occupied by ale, consumers eat more bread. Today, economists would say that there have been *changes in the demands* for the two goods; the demand for ale has decreased, and the demand for bread has increased. The brewers find out about the decrease in the demand for ale when they notice that unsold kegs of ale are beginning to accumulate at the breweries. The bakers are apprised of the increase in the demand for bread when they find that they cannot keep loaves moving into and out of the ovens fast enough. This situation is summarized by saying that there is a *surplus* of ale and a *shortage* of bread. No producer wants to make goods destined for a permanent inventory, so each brewer who is experiencing an unwanted accumulation of ale will cut back production and will therefore hire fewer resources. Similarly, bakers, seeing that they can sell more bread if only they can bake it, will hire more resources—flour, yeast, and workmen—to give their customers as much as they want. If the economy remains at the full-employment level (a situation postulated by classical economists for reasons to be explained in the next chapter), the resources formerly used by brewers will be hired by bakers. The grain formerly destined for mash will go to the mills. The cooper who formerly made ale kegs will make flour barrels. Thus, consumers direct not only the activities of brewers and bakers but also the actions of those who supply the producers of consumer goods.

Now let us look at the competition between the buyers and sellers of a single good. Suppose that an innkeeper comes into the ale market for some supplies. He wants to buy his ale from a brewer at the lowest price he can and hopes to resell it to his guests at the highest possible price. This is considered responsible business behavior or at least accepted business behavior, even though it may seem that the innkeeper wants to take unconscionable advantage of both the brewers and his own customers. But if there is an innkeeper who feels this way, there is a brewer to match him. So, we have an innkeeper and a brewer who have come to the ale market, an innkeeper who would like to buy ale at a price as close to zero as possible and a brewer who would like to charge an infinitely large price. These two—buyer and seller—compromise in order for the transaction to take place. The innkeeper pays more than nothing for the ale, and the brewer receives something less than an infinite number of pounds and shillings.[3]

But we have abstracted too much; this is not really the situation in the market. The market does not consist of one innkeeper and one brewer; it comprises a great number of each—a host of ale buyers competing with each other to get the available ale; a host of brewers competing with each other to sell that ale; and buyers together and sellers together, each group competing against the other across the market. But the result is not chaos; it is the efficient allocation of society's resources to their most urgent uses at clearly established prices—prices that tend to a level no greater than the costs of producing the traded goods. No computer, no dictator, no committee of experts is needed to solve the countless number of highly complex simultaneous equations that must be solved in a functioning economy. Regardless of the number of participants, regardless of the number of goods, regardless of the number of equations representing the interaction of goods, prices, buyers, and sellers, the market mechanism directs the economy with an efficiency that cannot be matched by any other guidance system. It does so by coordinating the single, unrelated economic actions of millions of self-interested individuals into a socially desirable end.

We have seen how the invisible hand works to determine what goods are produced, in what quantities they are produced, and at what price they are sold. Let us now see how it dictates the methods of production. When we say that producers attempt to maximize their net revenues (the excess of total revenues over costs), we are also saying that they try to minimize the costs of producing the output they choose to make. In minimizing costs, producers are forced to be efficient, and efficiency—getting the most units of salable product out of the fewest units of the least costly resources, given a certain standard of quality—is widely accepted as a desirable social objective. What compels producers to use the most economically efficient methods of production?

Suppose that one brewer is careless in making his ale and has to use more malt than the other brewers do. He does not worry because he contemplates charging a higher price for his ale. Upon his entry into

[3] In Chapter 6 we shall see how the theory of market price is made *determinate*—that is, how we can say what the price of ale is in shillings or dollars instead of contenting ourselves with the knowledge that the actual price is some figure between zero and infinity.

the market, his plans are demolished. No innkeeper is interested in buying overpriced ale from a careless brewer because any tavern owner can get all the ale he wants from more efficient and, hence, lower-cost competitors. The careless brewer will find that he has an inventory of unwanted ale on his hands. Rather than lose the whole value of his inventory by allowing it to remain unsold, he will try to recoup some of the expenses he incurred in making his ale by cutting his price down to that of his competitors, even though this price is too low to allow him the profit earned by his competitors.

In order to understand the choices now open to this inefficient brewer, let us examine how profit aids the working of the invisible hand. In a perfectly competitive equilibrium, the price of a good (in this case ale) is maintained at the level that yields the amount of profit, or net revenue, that just keeps the existing producers satisfied to remain in the market. This amount of profit is "normal" profit.

Let us see how the price level is maintained. If the price is higher and the profit is therefore larger than "normal," new businessmen will enter the field to get some of the higher-than-normal profit. (Remember the requirement of perfectly free entry and exit.) But the added amount of the good these new businessmen produce sets in motion the very forces that drive the price back to its competitive level and profit back to normal. If, on the other hand, the price falls below its competitive level, yielding lower-than-normal profit, some of the existing producers will leave the market in search of normal profit elsewhere. This in turn creates forces that drive price and profit back up. In both cases, the market automatically works toward the price at which long-run competitive equilibrium—that is, a situation in which producers are neither entering nor leaving the field—will be achieved.

If the net revenue is unsatisfactory to a particular producer because of his own high costs, he will be inclined to leave the field. This is the situation confronting our inefficient brewer. Once he has disposed of his existing high-cost ale at the going price (which, as we have seen, he does not do voluntarily), he has two courses open to him. He can either go back to the brewery and straighten out his brewing practices, so that he can meet the competition of his rivals, or, if he cannot operate efficiently, he must go out of business since he will not accept below-normal returns on a long-term basis. Whichever path he chooses, the forces of competition ensure that society will have its ale brewed

—indeed all of its goods will be produced—by firms using the lowest-cost methods of production.

We have remaining the final question of classical economic theory: How does the economy determine who gets what amounts of ale and bread—or, more accurately, what principle determines the division of the gross national product? The answer is productivity. Those who contribute the most to the economy may also take the most out of it. Suppose you are a teamster driving a brewery wagon when the popular fervor of the temperance movement causes the demand for ale to decrease. Your job and your wage are not as secure as they were before the movement began. Just as there is a tendency for the ale supply to become excessive until brewers cut their production, there is a tendency for brewery resources, including draymen, to become superfluous. Some drivers will probably be laid off. If you are one of the most unfortunate brewery employees, you will be fired. Being unemployed, you will be totally unproductive; and, being unproductive, you will receive no wage. So far as the economy is concerned, you are making no contribution to it, and thus you cannot take anything out of it. You may be able to live on savings for a while, but eventually you will starve unless someone who is sufficiently productive to earn more than is necessary for his own survival is willing to share with you. In short, as long as you are unemployed you must look to charity, not to the economic system, for your sustenance.

But suppose you are a drayman fortunate enough not to have been fired yet. Probably your wage rate will be under pressure. There will be a surplus of draymen. Brewers will be motivated to reduce whatever costs of production they can, and your wage is a cost your employer may find easy to reduce when there are a number of former drivers who would rather work at a reduced wage than starve. Suppose you do accept a pay cut. Now you cannot share in as much of the nation's output as you did before. You have become a less productive member of the economy, so it rewards you with less of its goods. To say that you have become less productive does not mean that you have become a poorer driver; it means that the members of the economy value your services less than they did before abstinence became popular. Personal qualities are not involved; the market is impersonal.

Many people object to the free-market system precisely because of the way in which it answers the "for whom" question. To put the matter in appropriate language, their objection is to the *distribution of income* under the competitive system. Either they object to rewarding people on the basis of their productivity, or they object to the way that productivity is measured. For example, they may bring up the point we mentioned— that the driver really remains as productive as always, that his performance as a driver has not deteriorated. Those who dislike the productivity system of rewards may contend that it is reprehensible for a person to lose his job because of, or have his wage depend on, the passing whims of consumers. Thus, they would interfere with the economy to prevent it from answering the "for whom" question in the way that it does.

But classical economics had an answer for these people. If resources continue to be fully employed,[4] consumers, in competing with each other to get more bread, will drive up its price. Bakers, in endeavoring to meet the increased demand for their product, must hire additional resources. Where will the new resources come from? From the brewing industry, which now has surplus resources. Therefore, if you do not wish to accept the judgment of the economy that you are less productive and that you are to receive less goods, you will leave your dray at the brewery and become a driver of bakery wagons. By so doing you will be able to consume as much as ever of the national product, and, in addition, consumers will have the amounts of ale and bread that they really desire.

But what about the other brewery draymen? In the long run, will wages be high in the baking industry and low in brewing, assuming people do not once again change their consumption habits? Not in a perfectly competitive system. For a while, until bakers can meet the greater demand for bread and brewers can bring their labor force into a proper relationship with the lower demand for ale, there may be an upward pressure on wages in the baking industry and a downward force on wages in the brewing business. But, assuming that consumers continue to want both ale and bread, eventually work of essentially the same nature must be compensated equally in both industries. If wages were to keep rising in the baking industry, eventually all the brewery workers would drift into baking; but this is inconsistent with the de-

---

[4] The classical economists after Adam Smith worked out an explanation of why the economy could not operate for long at less than full employment, and Smith himself, as we shall see, glimpsed this principle. For now, we shall accept this hypothesis on faith; we shall examine it in Chapter 4.

mand of consumers for the products of both industries. Bakers cannot afford to continue raising wages and hiring people, and breweries cannot afford to continue reducing wages and losing workers. In the long run, the flow of workers out of brewing and into baking will cease when an equivalence in wages is established in both industries for similar jobs. There might, of course, always be *some* differences in wages, but these would be only *compensating differences*. For example, if the work of drivers in the two industries is the same except that brewery drivers must lift heavier loads, then we would expect the wages for brewery drivers to be higher than those for bakery drivers to compensate the former for the more difficult nature of their work.

In a going economy, adjustments are not likely to happen in the seesaw fashion depicted here. It is unusual for consumers' buying patterns to change rapidly, although in some cases—fashion goods, for example—this may occur. The going economy is constantly making fine adjustments, constantly moving to an equilibrium position that is itself constantly changing. As a result, most people gravitate into one line of work or another believing that they have made a purely autonomous choice, never realizing how much their decision depended upon the pervasive wishes of sovereign consumers.

We have described how the invisible hand works. You may think that you do not like it. You may wish to join those who object to the way it distributes incomes, on the grounds, for instance, that to attribute the enormous income of, say, an entertainer or an oil-field owner to his enormous "productivity" is specious. But is an income distribution based on this rather doubtful "productivity" of the oil-field owner or the television personality strictly in keeping with the premises of the invisible hand? Smith would have said that the inordinately large incomes of such people are created by the *possession* of some *thing*—talent, licensure, real or personal property, beauty, or charisma, for example—and that these incomes are composed, in part, of *monopoly* gains! If an individual's share of the national income seems disproportionately large compared to his productive contribution, it may be that his monopoly power over a unique asset biases the distribution of income in his favor. Lopsided income distributions owing to the possession of monopoly power are not made by the invisible hand, since the premises of Smith's model specify that one economic unit does not have enough power to harm another economic unit. In other words, monopoly is an aberration in the Smithian system. If you disapprove of including in personal incomes a portion that represents monopoly gains, you can probably think of countermeasures that would not cripple the invisible hand.

Another argument you might advance against the free-market is that certain goods ought not to be produced. Someone might object to our own example, feeling that ale should not be produced at all. In this case, the objection can take one of two forms: You can object either to the *system* or to the *preferences* of individuals. If you object to the system, then your attack is directed against the principle of consumer sovereignty. You must advocate in its place some form of centralized control over consumers' demands, so that they will not get things that (someone decrees) they should not have, even though they may want them. The Prohibition law of the 1920's is an example of governmental interference with the principle of consumer sovereignty.

If, on the other hand, you accept consumer sovereignty but deplore ale drinking, the only course open to you is to try to change consumers' preference patterns through some kind of educational program. This is the approach used in the attempt to reduce the consumption of cigarettes.

These objections involve value judgments. They involve economic matters, but they are not questions that economics itself can answer. Although Smith's economic theory does rest heavily on the principle of consumer sovereignty, he did not hold that the economic system he was explaining was one of perfect justice and morality. All he contended was that, given man's nature and the social objectives of the British people, this was the most effective—that is, the most efficient —system of economizing man had yet devised.

The Validity of Smith's Model

Judging the validity of Smith's model in the light of our present economic experience would produce a spurious verdict. We must assess his model in its late-eighteenth-century setting, for the functioning of the British economy at that time was the subject of his theory.

How well were the competitive conditions of our brewer-baker drama met in Smith's time? Not perfectly, but sufficiently for the economy to work much the way Smith said it would. The most sophisticated of theories are only approximations of the real world, which they have to be, since men can only understand the real world in bits and pieces.

For the most part, eighteenth-century business firms were small. England, generally, was a nation of small entrepreneurs. There were several reasons for this. First, the exigencies of using power supplied by water wheels and steam engines, with the consequent inefficiencies in power transmission, severely limited the size of manufacturing plants. Second, the legal concept of the corporation, that form of business organization which alone allows firms to grow to the great size of the giants of modern American industry, had not yet fully evolved. Third, the supporting financial institutions—the commercial banks, underwriters, private banks, brokers, and stock exchanges—that must exist to supply funds to corporations were in such a rudimentary state that large-scale economic organization was impossible for that reason alone. Fourth, the communications media and scientific-management procedures now so common, and so essential to the operation of today's business firms, were absent.

Although consumers may have preferred some particular goods and services to others, the ability of either buyers or sellers to differentiate goods was probably much less than it is now. This would be particularly true of goods sold to the majority of consumers. The members of the upper class may, for example, have had a favorite tailor whose appeal was more a matter of personality than anything else; but for most people price was usually the major desideratum influencing a purchase. Brand names, distinctive wrappings, "Madison Avenue" advertising were unknown. Many goods were sold in bulk; hence, a consumer could not know and did not care if a piece of worsted came from any one of a hundred mills.

Mobility of both firms and laborers was greater than it is today. Skills were not highly specialized. Adam Smith himself is an example of this on a high professional level. He was a professor of moral philosophy teaching political economy, ethics, public administration, and jurisprudence, among other things. Similarly, if one could "cypher," there was really no reason why one could not keep books, operate an inn, clerk in a retail establishment, or teach school. Although it might have been fairly difficult for a stonemason to become a physician, the level of training required for the professions was appallingly low. Entrance to the professions, trades, and business was largely unhampered by unions, professional societies, trade associations, and long years of formal education. The smallness of most business establishments meant that obtaining the capital necessary to open a new business would not be the barrier it often is today. Thus, there is a high degree of plausibility in the assumptions of Smith's theory.

THE WEALTH OF A NATION

> The annual labour of every nation is the fund which originally supplies it with all the necessaries and conveniences of life which it annually consumes, and which consist always in the immediate produce of that labour, or in what is purchased with that produce from other nations.

With these words, *The Wealth of Nations* begins, and we see immediately that Smith means to separate himself from the doctrines of the mercantilists and physiocrats. Work, not trade or the extractive industries, is the path to wealth; and wealth is not bullion alone. This is the genesis of the classical concepts of productivity and wealth. The reading of this quotation out of context—indeed, even the reading of much of Smith's treatise—may suggest that he committed the same error as the physiocrats in thinking of labor as the source of the wealth of a nation. True, Smith did stress the importance of labor in the productive process, but even a cursory reading of *The Wealth of Nations* reveals that he considered land and "stock" (what we now call capital) to be productive. Smith's introduction is an example of his gaining dramatic effect at the expense of accuracy; he paid the penalty for this indulgence in subsequent pages, where he was forced to amend his vigorous opening statement. What Smith wanted to do and succeeded in doing was to show the reader immediately that he was going to encounter a wholly new economic theory. The prospective buyer of *The Wealth of Nations* could see quickly that the author was disavowing the mercantile and physiocratic systems.

Smith completely redefined wealth. *All* tangible goods, he said, constitute the wealth of a nation. Gold is not to be excluded, but any item of value is clearly part of the store of wealth. Most important is the way in which national wealth is advanced. Having placed fundamental reliance on the power of human labor to augment national wealth, Smith gave two prescriptions for wealth building: the *division of labor* and *parsimony*.

In Chapter I of Book I, Smith takes his reader on a visit to a pin factory. Here Smith vividly presents the case for the nascent Industrial Revolution and simultaneously exposes the moribund craftsman system.

In the pin factory, we find no pin-maker, only workers, perhaps scores of them. Let Smith guide us:

> One man draws out the wire, another straights it, a third cuts it, a fourth points it, a fifth grinds it at the top for receiving the head; to make the head requires two or three distinct operations; to put it on, is a peculiar business, to whiten the pins is another; it is even a trade by itself to put them into the paper; and the important business of making a pin is, in this manner, divided into about eighteen distinct operations. . . .

The astounding aspect of the division of labor is not that the practice enhances the productivity of *craftsmen* but that a group of unskilled or semiskilled laborers gathered in a factory, with the manufacturing process suitably divided among them, can outproduce by far the same number of independent skilled pin-makers who perform all of the pin-making operations themselves. By themselves, it is probable that not one of these unskilled laborers could produce a single pin in a day; but, combined in a factory, the average product of each laborer (the total daily output of the factory divided by the number of workers) will be greater than the daily output of a skilled pin-maker.

Today, we are so familiar with the reasons for the high productivity of unskilled and semiskilled workers that we need only remind ourselves of a few. When a complex job is broken down into a number of simple operations each worker gains great facility at one simple task, finally reaching a level at which he performs the operation almost automatically. No time is lost in shifting from one set of tools to another or from one location to another.

Smith profoundly believed in the benefits to all men of applying the principal of the division of labor. The more *extensive* and the more *intensive* the division of labor is, the higher will be the standard of living in a given country.[5] One of Smith's famous sayings is that the division of labor is limited "by the extent of the market." The larger the market to be served, the greater can be the division of labor and the higher will be the standard of living for all the members of the economy. The simple implication of this statement is that Smith favored the expansion of markets. This is no doubt true. But the more important, and less obvious, principle he was enunciating involves what

---

[5] By "extensive" we mean how widespread the division of labor is. The division of labor becomes more "intensive" as the number of steps into which a given process is broken down is increased.

economists today call "economies of scale" or "economies of mass production." As firms grow larger, output will increase by a greater percentage than does the number of factors of production employed by the firm. For example, suppose a London pin-maker—owing to the increasing popularity of pins, the growing population of London, the improved local and national transportation system—finds that he could sell many more pins if he could make them. So he doubles the scale of his plant, increasing the machinery, the square footage, and the labor force twofold. If Smith's assumption is correct, the output of pins will *more* than double.

The benefits of the division of labor and the economies of scale lead us to the second of Smith's wealth-producing principles, parsimony. Smith's idea of the division of labor is quite simple; he did not realize all the potential benefits of parsimony.[6] The employer, having gathered a large number of relatively unskilled workers under one roof, can train each one to perform a simple, repetitive task. By properly planning and coordinating their jobs, a skilled manager can combine the efforts of the workmen in a unified productive activity. The result of specialization and management enables hired workers to produce an output greater than the total product of the same number of independent craftsmen. In this case, the simple division of labor itself has accounted for most of the increase in worker productivity. The role of parsimony is small. The capitalist-employer furnishes a place to work, provides management, pays wages to the workers, and possibly furnishes some simple tools. All this requires that the capitalist-employer be "parsimonious"—that he save. By refraining from using all his income for immediate consumption, he is able to provide the context necessary for the application of the division-of-labor principle.

But parsimony can raise output to a greater amount than that accounted for by simple specialization. This Smith did not see. A factory can be more than a big shop. The productivity of workers can be enhanced beyond the level that specialization by itself allows. In a plant turning out a large output, a large number of workers assigned to

<hr/>

[6] Lest we be inclined to think that Adam Smith had all the answers, we must note that there were a number of aspects of the economizing process about which he was unsure or even wrong. For example, his discussion of value is so confused that we shall skip it altogether, deferring any inquiries into the matter until Chapter 4. Smith was not particularly astute in his discussion of the role of parsimony, nor were most of the other classical economists. Nevertheless, Smith gave the concept more consideration than any earlier economic thinkers.

specialized tasks in a unified productive process can effectively make use of specialized equipment that a single man could neither afford nor make efficient use of. *Machines* can raise the average productivity of workers beyond the increase attributable to specialization. Indeed, machines can permit further specialization by releasing men from serving as energy sources, thereby allowing human beings to work at tasks machines cannot perform.

Smith did not pay much attention to the great productivity of capital, possibly because the benefits of the simple division-of-labor principle were still so spectacular in his time and because most of the truly revolutionary items of capital equipment had not yet been invented.

It is in the provision of capital that the benefits of parsimony, which Smith praised but rather dimly perceived, are most apparent. Spending money for a machine to make other goods means that someone must forego the pleasure of the immediate consumption of some consumer goods. One reason craftsmen operate on a small scale is that they cannot generate enough income from their work to buy anything more than their daily subsistence and the simplest tools. If this is true of craftsmen, it is even more true of unskilled laborers. But, if a would-be employer can find a group of people who can spare a little of their incomes to lend to him, he can pool their funds to buy costly equipment. These lenders—capitalists—*save* a portion of their incomes and lend it to the employer, who *invests* the proceeds in plant and equipment. To economists, "investment" means *the actual purchase of capital* by business firms. (It has nothing to do with the purchase of stocks and bonds by those who, in popular usage, are called investors.)

Saving is not particularly pleasant for most people. Thrift, or parsimony as Smith called it, is an often hard-won character trait. Saving means doing without want-satisfiers. The mature person will save something to provide for unforeseen contingencies or for a future purchase requiring an expenditure that he cannot finance out of his current income. But it takes more than simple virtue and maturity to induce a person to abstain from current consumption and lend his savings to another. The rational lender demands interest. Interest is usually expressed as a rate. If the interest rate is 5 percent per annum, a person lending another $100 today will receive back $105 at the end of the year. Classical economists believed that interest is paid to overcome the *time preference* of consumers. People would rather have a good now than later; but, if you promise a consumer greater purchasing power tomorrow than he has today by promising to return to him a sum greater than that lent, you may be able to turn a would-be consumer into a lender.

The borrower is able to pay back a sum greater than that which he borrowed because capital has a "net productivity." The employer-borrower, his employees, and his raw materials can, in combination with the capital equipment purchased with borrowed funds, produce an output of greater total value than they could without the machine. As long as a machine more than pays for its original cost, the interest charges on the money advanced to buy it, and its costs of operation, the employer will find it worthwhile to obtain loanable funds for its purchase by promising to pay interest on them.

Although Smith was more perceptive than either the mercantilists or physiocrats in correctly concluding that a stock of capital goods is an especially desirable form of national wealth, he and most other classical economists considered capital as taking the form of a "wages fund" out of which workers were paid. The greater the productivity of an economy, the greater is the division of labor and the more roundabout, or time-consuming, is the productive process. A considerable period may elapse between the performance of a laborer's work and the time by which enough of the final product is sold to pay him. For example, it will be a long time before a mill being built by a stonemason will have produced enough cloth to pay him, the other stonemasons, and all the workers whose diffuse labors finally result in bolts of cloth. In the meantime, stonemasons must eat. They must be paid before the cloth is sold or even made. Their rewards come from the wages fund, which is furnished by lenders, whose postponed desire for the immediate consumption of goods (once their subsistence requirements have been fulfilled) is appeased by the promise of interest.

In real terms, the wages fund is the stock of "wage goods"—the items workers consume for their subsistence. But the stock exists because the lenders do not draw upon it. They have foregone the consumption of goods they could have had now in exchange for the promise of having more goods to consume in the future. Whether we express what has happened in real or monetary terms, the lenders have *saved*.

Social Harmony

Now we have the elements of what is called Smithian optimism. The invisible hand is not the whole story.

Saving is not an antisocial act and does not constitute a leakage from the circular flow of income. Saving is transformed into investment when businessmen borrow funds to form capital. Thus, nothing is lost; what is saved is spent. What consumers do not spend on goods will be spent as wages or on equipment. No one will lose his job because of thrift. Indeed, the productive capacity of the economy will grow as the proceeds of thrift are applied to the increase of productive capacity.

Happily, in the Smithian system, the interests of capitalists and those of the working class are not antithetical. The greater the output, the more people can save. The more people can save, the greater will be the size of the wages fund; the greater the wages fund, the more money is available for wages; and the greater the level of employment, the greater will be the national output. All things have at least a tendency to work together for good.

The second-greatest obstacle to increasing the wealth of nations, following interference with the self-regulating processes of the economy, said Smith, is prodigality. Merely maintaining the circular flow by consuming luxury goods and services will not increase wealth. Channeling resources away from the wages fund and from capital goods is inimical to wealth-building. Not only was Mandeville's ethics vicious, his economics was faulty. In the Smithian system, what is good for the individual is good for the nation, and we can interpret "good" in both a moral and an economic sense.

ADAM SMITH: AN APPRECIATION

Adam Smith was a great economist; his theories, taken in context, need no defense, and much of both the approbation and the adverse criticism directed toward Smith today is specious. If Smith is frequently misinterpreted, it is the fault of those of his disciples who were more impressed by their master's argument than he himself was. He cannot reasonably be expected to have anticipated changes that would invalidate some of the assumptions of his theory. Smith was writing at the outset of the Industrial Revolution, when there were few examples of capital in the form of costly pieces of equipment. As we have noted, Smith thought of capital as a wages fund, and thus he considered increases in the stock of capital mutually beneficial to capitalists and workers. It was not until the flood-tide of inventions began to be applied in a wholesale way to British manufacturing processes and capital came to be viewed in some quarters as being labor-displacing that it became a matter for concern as a possible source of conflict between workers and their employers. In fact, in Chapter 4, we shall see that the classical economists believed the conflict of economic interests to be between landowners and all other members of society.

In studying the economics of his own time, Smith did not apply his reasoning to obviously inappropriate cases. He did not believe that competition as he described it did, in fact, obtain in every segment of the British economy. He was, for instance, somewhat troubled by the state of the workers. It seemed to him self-evident that a single worker or several unorganized laborers facing an employer—a man of property and influence—are not in a competitive situation. The disproportionate economic strengths of an employer and a worker place the latter at a severe disadvantage in bargaining. The employer, being able to practice parsimony, has funds to tide him over a nonproductive period. But the worker uses all of his funds to live; if he spends a short period away from the productive process, he will starve. Thus, the worker has a powerful incentive to strike a bargain immediately, while the employer can afford to press the worker for more favorable terms. Smith could not accommodate his theory to this situation; it appeared to him that here he could not maintain that the free market worked. But, rather than being a weakness in his analysis, Smith's troubled thinking is one of his strengths, for he saw more clearly than many of the protagonists of "Smithian economics" that when competition does not prevail, economic liberalism will not work. The invisible hand is crippled.

The important lesson to be drawn here is that true Smithian economics deals with *competitive* economies. It is *not* meant to describe an economy at all comprised of such entities as General Motors Corporation, the American Telephone and Telegraph Company, the Tennessee Valley Authority, the Interstate Commerce Commission, the United Auto Workers, the Pentagon, and a national government that uses fiscal and monetary policies to pursue predetermined goals.

Whether we feel that *The Wealth of Nations* has great relevance today or none at all, in the late eighteenth century it spoke clearly to the most important people in the most powerful nation. Smith's most avid readers—the entrepreneurs—were the chief actors in his book. To them, *The Wealth of Nations* was not a textbook on economics; it was a justification of their own existence. Now they understood how they—the manufacturers and shopkeepers—and not princes, statesmen, warriors, scholars, and churchmen, were the source of the wealth of nations.

MALTHUS AND RICARDO: BUILDERS OF CLASSICAL ECONOMICS

4

Thomas Malthus and David Ricardo continued and expanded the tradition that Adam Smith had begun. After Smith, the learning that had once been part of moral philosophy became what we now call classical economics. We consider Malthus and Ricardo together in this chapter, not only because they were contemporaries but because it is illuminating to contrast the methods and conclusions of the two.

MALTHUS AND RICARDO: A CONTRAST

A graduate of Cambridge in 1785, the Reverend Thomas Robert Malthus (1766–1834) was a priest of the Church of England. Although he was a most admirable cleric, he did not long perform the customary duties of the office of clergyman, owing to his interest in economics. He practiced the abstinence he preached by not marrying until he was thirty-eight-years old. In 1805 Malthus became a professor of history and political economy at Haileybury College. (Note that, in distinction to Smith, Malthus actually held a chair of political economy.) The British East India Company had founded the college as a training school. Its graduates were to secure the far-flung empire won largely by the commercial endeavors of Adam Smith's businessmen.

Born in London, David Ricardo (1772–1823) learned the principles of business from his prosperous broker father. At twenty-one, becoming increasingly restive under paternal discipline, he left his father's house and the Jewish religion to marry a Quaker girl, whereupon the elder Ricardo disinherited him. Although young David was now penniless, the business training he had absorbed from his father was put to good use. His father's old business associates, having been impressed by the younger Ricardo's acumen and integrity, lent him funds to start his own business. David abundantly fulfilled his sponsors' expectations—so much so that within five years, still a young man, he had become independently wealthy. At the time of his death his practical economic skill, combined with several fortunate opportunities, had made him one of the wealthiest men in Europe.

Ricardo's involvement with economic theory began one day at the fashionable resort town of Bath, when he chanced to pick up a copy of *The Wealth of Nations.* Smith's masterpiece appealed to the practical businessman in him; after that encounter, Ricardo could not leave economics alone. Now wealthy, he retired from business to devote himself wholly to the study of the system in which he had prospered.

Both Malthus and Ricardo were men of noble character. Despite the great differences in their backgrounds, their scholarly methods, and in some of their conclusions, they were firm friends.

The approach of each to the study of economics belied his background. Malthus, the Cambridge-educated clergyman and college professor, was an empiricist. He based his work upon the statistical data then available and upon the experience gained from his wide and frequent sojourns on the Continent. But he did not consider this factual background sufficient, and he was convinced that the progress of economics was hampered by inadequate statistics. More and better data was essential.

Strangely, Ricardo, the successful businessman, was a strict theorist; indeed, he was one of the greatest deductive reasoners of all time.

THE MALTHUSIAN PRINCIPLE OF POPULATION

In *The Wealth of Nations,* bachelor Adam Smith had written: "A half-starved Highland woman, frequently bears more than twenty children, while a pampered lady is often incapable of bearing any, and is generally exhausted by two or three." Smith apparently believed in the often observed positive correlation between poverty and childbearing;

but, at the same time, he noted that poverty is not conducive to the survival of the children whose birth it seems to favor.

The Origin of Malthus' Essay

Although demography, the systematic study of population, did not develop until many years later, the people of the late eighteenth century were interested in speculation about the future growth of population. One of the most notable, and far-fetched, projections was made by another clergyman, William Godwin (1756–1836). Godwin was optimistic about the future perfectibility of mankind. A strange man, he was the second husband of the ardent feminist Mary Wollstonecraft. Although his intended wife had convinced Godwin that the marriage ceremony was especially degrading to women, for some reason they set aside their convictions and endured the ceremony. Nevertheless, neither of the Godwins was impressed with the sanctity of marriage, although William Godwin, unlike Malthus, did not always practice what he preached. When his daughter, also named Mary, in apparent compliance with her father's advanced morals, ran away to Switzerland with the poet Percy Bysshe Shelley, Goodwin suddenly became a properly furious traditional father. However, Mary Shelley came to have a greater claim to fame than mere amorous adventures with romantic young poets—the authorship of *Frankenstein*.

In 1798 one of the best-selling volumes in English bookshops was *An Inquiry Concerning Political Justice and Influences on Morals and Happiness*. Its author was William Godwin. Godwin's thesis was an extension of an idea propounded by John Locke in his *Essay Concerning Human Understanding:* "Man is perfectible or in other words is susceptible of perpetual improvement."

The immediate cause of all human troubles, Godwin declared, was poor social institutions, with government the worst offender. If only human beings could understand themselves better, they would be able to rectify the ills of current society and advance to a plane of perfection. The route to better self-understanding, Godwin held, was education. Properly conducted, education would lead to such a great understanding of nature that mankind would become immortal. There would be no problem of overcrowding our planet, however, Godwin reassured his readers. Although there would be no natural decrease in the population by deaths, there would be no increase by births. Godwin expected human beings to lose their reproductive powers once they had attained the highest stage of development. The result would be a static society, and mankind's chief joy would be the constant pursuit of learning.

Why have we made this excursion into the work of an eccentric eighteenth-century clergyman? Because his odd discourse was the proximate cause of Thomas Malthus' development of his famous principle of population. Daniel Malthus, Thomas' father, read Godwin's book, became converted to its author's viewpoint, and enthusiastically commended it to his son. Like many young men today, Thomas thought many of his father's ideas absurd, and he told his parent how, in his opinion, Godwin's writings were nonsense. The open-minded Daniel was so impressed with the reasons for his son's adverse reaction to Godwin that he persuaded Thomas to commit his argument to paper. Thomas wrote his rebuttal under the ambitious title *An Essay on the Principle of Population, as it Affects the Future Improvement of Society, with Remarks on the Speculations of Mr. Godwin, M. Condorcet, and Other Writers.* He published the book anonymously in 1798. It was such an enormous success that he wrote another version, which was published in 1803. Perhaps thinking that its lengthy title had stimulated the sales of his previous book, he called this one *An Essay on the Principle of Population: or a View of its Past and Present Effects on Human Happiness; with An Inquiry into Our Prospects Respecting the Future Removal or Mitigation of the Evils which it Occasions.* Malthus' *Essay* completely ruined Godwin.

Malthus: The Empiricist

Malthus believed in using factual data to support his arguments. Therefore he did not simply write down his oral refutation of Godwin or content himself with looking for logical flaws in Godwin's thesis. He searched for statistical evidence to support his population principle. Among his "laboratories" were England, Wales, and the newly emergent United States of America. Malthus observed that the population in England had been increasing rapidly, from about 5.8 million in 1700 to 12 million one and a quarter centuries later. Family size was also increasing, and Malthus believed that the key to this expansion was the Poor Laws.

The Poor Laws were a relief measure. Malthus argued that relief payments prevented economic factors from restricting the size of families because married couples produced more children than they would have produced had they been forced to live on whatever income the family could earn.

Malthus' Premises

Malthus' argument rests upon two fundamental premises. In his own words:

> I think I may fairly make two postulata. First, that food is necessary to the existence of man. Secondly, that the passion between the sexes is necessary and will remain nearly in its present state.
>
> Assuming, then, my postulata as granted, I say, that the power of population is indefinitely greater than the power in the earth to produce subsistence for man

The preceding paragraph presents the essential idea of the Malthusian thesis—the power of the population to increase.

The Progressions

Malthus, like Smith, knew how to write best sellers. He gave dramatic impact to his commonsense-sounding postulates by using two sets of progressions. These progressions are certainly the most famous and probably the least understood part of his *Essay*. It is widely believed that a shorthand expression of the Malthusian population principle is: "Population increases in a *geometric* progression, while the food supply increases in an *arithmetic* progression." Malthus was a shrewd practical psychologist as well as a persuasive empirical economist. His example has the force of today's literary and advertising catchwords; it helped to make his *Essay* the book of the hour—but not without a price. Like other glib and simplistic renderings of a complex thesis, it has tended to induce in generations of readers the belief that this is all Malthus had to say.

Since Malthus' progressions are so famous, let us see where they lead. An arithmetic progression consists of a sequence of numbers of which each number after the first is larger than the preceding number by a constant *common difference*. Thus, the sequence 2–4–6–8–10–12 is an arithmetic progression. Each number after two is obtained by adding the preceding number to the common difference two. A geometric progression consists of a sequence of numbers in which each number after the first is obtained by multiplying the preceding number by a constant number, the *common ratio*. Thus, the sequence 2–4–8–16–32–

64–128–256–512–1024 is a geometric progression. Each number after two is obtained by multiplying the preceding number by the common ratio two.

These are the two rather startling illustrations that Malthus used to jolt his readers into seeing the devastating implications of his rather unexciting postulates. The enormous rate of increase implied by Malthus' use of a geometric progression may be elusive without an illustration. Suppose that you, having been successful in life, are asked to contribute to the alumni fund of your college in recognition of that institution's part in your present success. Suppose also that your college has in its employ an ambitious alumni-affairs director who offers you the following easy-payment plan, which sounds quite reasonable—so reasonable, in fact, that you fear the costs of bookkeeping will exceed the value of your contribution.

The plan is this: You are asked to contribute weekly over a one-year period. You start with an embarrassingly low contribution and slowly accelerate. You simply give one penny the first week, two cents the second week, four cents the third week, eight cents the fourth week, and so on.

It may sound as if the college would go broke by depending on such miserly contributions. But let's look at what actually happens. Your *last weekly* payment for the year would be 2^{51} cents. How much is that in dollars? About $22 trillion. Your *total payments* for the year would be about $45 trillion.

This example makes it clear why if human beings add to their numbers at anything like this rate, they will surely overpower the arithmetic rate of increase in the food supply. Could Malthus really have said anything like that?

What Malthus Really Said

The rapid growth of the American population led Malthus to conclude that *unless* the increase of population in the former colonies were checked, the population of the United States would double every twenty-five years. Thus it was reasonable for him to predict that the American population *could* increase at a geometric rate.

Although some of mankind still lives today with the Malthusian specter of overpopulation, the grim prophecies inferable from Malthus' *Essay* have not been realized in the Western world. What has happened? For one thing, Malthus did not mean his geometric and arithmetic progressions to be a definitive statement of how the population and food supply would necessarily change in relation to each other. Rather, his stark and dramatic statement of the Malthusian principle enabled him to achieve his main purpose in the first edition of his *Essay;* he got people to read it. After the first edition, Malthus softened his statement; but what he then lost in impact he made up in scholarly respectibility.

The Malthusian principle in its more reasoned form is a simple idea, which is summed up most accurately in Malthus' words: "It is the constant tendency in all animated life to increase beyond the nourishment prepared for it." All that Malthus is saying is that there is a *tendency* for the rate of population growth to outstrip the rate of increase in the means of subsistence. As the population grows, given increments in population size will come more quickly. The same idea is involved in an across-the-board salary increase of, say, 5 percent. Those at the top of the pay scale will get a greater *absolute* increase than those at the bottom, although the *percentage* rate of increase is the same for all. Thus, we would expect that a population of 10 million would grow to 11 million sooner than a population of 1 million would grow to 2 million.[1]

Does the fact that there is not now standing room only vitiate Malthus' principle? No, because in his full statement Malthus said that the tendency of the increase in population to overwhelm the increase in the food supply would be defeated by certain checks.

In his first *Essay,* Malthus had two different classifications for these checks. One grouping was that of vice and misery. "Vice" was Malthus' expression for checks to population growth that he, or the conventions of his time, considered to be antisocial or immoral, such as abortion, infanticide, and contraception. "Misery" was the term he applied to checks originating with nature and social conditions, such as famine, pestilence, and war.

Malthus had an alternative classification that is more acceptable to economists in that it avoids value judgments. This grouping classified the checks as either preventive or positive. Preventive checks limit the birth rate; they inhibit additions to the population. Positive checks in-

---

[1] We shall defer our examination of the empirical basis of Malthus' observations about the way the food supply increases until we have discussed the theoretical work of David Ricardo, for Ricardo's work will help us to extract more meaning from this important part of Malthus' principle.

crease the death rate; they reduce the numbers of the existing population.

In the second (1803) edition of his *Essay,* Malthus added another check to the preventive category, his famous "moral restraint." Moral restraint was the sole check that he did not place in his vice-and-misery classification. To Malthus, the phrase meant the postponement of marriage and the avoidance of extramarital gratification—or, simply, continence. He did not intend moral restraint to include contraception.[2]

Malthus, in his complete statement, held that regardless of the tendency of the population to outrun the increase of the means of subsistence, population growth *will* be checked. Man may adopt a rational course of action to restrict the increase of his kind. Failing that, he must either resort to immorality or submit to nature's limitation of his numbers, and both of these solutions involve most unattractive ways of suppressing population growth.

The first part of Malthus' thesis concerning the rate of population growth was based upon data showing a steady increase in the populations of Western Europe and North America. The other part of his thesis—that natural checks would offset the tendency for population to increase—was seemingly demonstrated by several events prior to and concurrent with Malthus' time. One-half of the population of Europe died from the bubonic plague between 1346 and 1350. The Thirty Years' War of the 1600's decimated whole cities. At other times, disease, malnutrition, and unsanitary conditions moved constantly and sometimes devastatingly to restrict population growth. Malthus did indeed perceive the population expansion-contraction pattern that bears his name.

The Impact of the Essay

When Thomas Carlyle read the *Essay,* it suggested to him that it might have been better if some members of the human race had not been born and that many people can expect little better than to live their lives on the edge of subsistence. As a result, he called economics "the dismal science," an unfortunate appellation that has plagued the

---

[2] Later thinkers, particularly John Stuart Mill, were to urge the inclusion of contraception in the general category of moral restraint. Today, advocates of contraceptive measures, especially those who favor limiting the growth of whole populations, are called neo-Malthusians. In fact, however, it is to Mill, not to Malthus, that the neo-Malthusians can trace their beginnings.

discipline ever since. Over the years, Malthus' *Essay* has stirred controversy; it has encountered scurrilous attacks and unthinking acceptance. It has offended the sensibilities of both religious people and atheists. One of the earliest instances of its influence was when Prime Minister William Pitt withdrew the government's bill for an extension of the Poor Laws out of respect, as Pitt said, "for the opinions of Parson Malthus." Malthus found a friendly audience in the members of the English upper classes, since the *Essay* provided scholarly support for their commonsense and comfortable belief that the poor are the cause of their own poverty. One contemporary of Malthus was able to see humor in the situation. His fellow Anglican clergyman the witty Reverend Sydney Smith recounts a visit: "Philosopher Malthus came here last week. I got an agreeable party for him of unmarried people. There was only one lady who had had a child; but he is a good natured man, and if there are no appearances of approaching fertility is civil to every lady."

Has the *Essay* any relevance today? In the areas of the world that Malthus used for evidence, although there is now concern for the future, the populations do not press on the means of subsistence. What about the areas Malthus did not consider? In Asia and Latin America the populations do press on the resource base, and people do die, even if slowly, of starvation. Do these observations render the Malthusian principle invalid?

What has happened in the areas that served Malthus as laboratories? Two things: Birth rates have fallen and technology has kept well ahead of population growth. The dramatic inventiveness of American agricultural scientists and engineers has enabled an ever-diminishing number of farmers to supply an ever-increasing nonagricultural population with a surfeit of food. And, even though other resources have been trenched upon, technological advances have extended the resource base. In the steel industry, for example, new methods have made it economically feasible to process hitherto unprofitable low-grade ore, so, in effect, we have been discovering new resources while using up the old. At the same time, the pressure on iron ore as a resource base has been relieved by the extensive development of cement, glass, aluminum, and plastics as substitutes for steel.

The underdeveloped regions of the world have suffered, in part, from the uneven application of Western technology. In many cases, the condition of the people in these areas has actually worsened since

Malthus wrote his *Essay*. In the poor countries, medical science has had a marked impact in severely reducing the effectiveness of the Malthusian positive checks. The preventive checks, however, remain as weak as they were in Malthus' time. Moral sensibilities, pride, the expense and difficulty of application have precluded the use of scientific developments that could act as preventive checks. At the same time, the population-offsetting benefits of the nonmedical sciences have not been realized in the underdeveloped areas. These areas, with higher birth rates than the West, now approach the West's infant-mortality rate; but lack the technology that has improved Western living standards. They face an ever-increasing ratio of resource-users to resource supplies. The reasons the underdeveloped areas are so deficient industrially and the results of studies on how to overcome these deficiences are too complex and numerous to discuss here. We leave our analysis of Malthus' *Essay* with a bleak outlook. Until their birth rates are significantly lowered and their rate of technological innovation considerably advanced, the peoples of the underdeveloped regions of the world will continue to see the Malthusian specter all too clearly.

DAVID RICARDO

An examination of the work of David Ricardo affords us a unique experience, for in observing his process of theory-building we can see the development and procedure of economic analysis in a microcosm. The work of no other economist shows so clearly the relationship between the concrete and the abstract. Deductive reasoning was a powerful tool when Ricardo wielded it, and it is a mainstay of economic analysis today. But, as our visit to Ricardian economics will show us, economists do not construct abstractions for their own sake; they search for practical solutions to practical problems. The reactive nature of economics is also epitomized in the work of this peerless abstract thinker.

Contemporary conditions sent Ricardo questing for an explanation, and, although explanation may be its own reward, Ricardo and his intellectual descendants did not rest with theorizing but placed themselves and their work at the disposal of policy-makers. In trying to answer the problems besetting his times, Ricardo deduced the basis of international trade, clearly enunciated the law of diminishing returns, worked out a theory of income shares, and combined a number of isolated hypotheses into a coherent system.

The setting for Ricardo's work was the growing conflict of interests between the old landed aristocrats and the new urban class, the latter consisting of two distinct groups, employers and employees. The famous "stately homes of England" that delight tourists today are tangible monuments to those conditions Ricardo sought to explain and modify. The wealth of the aristocrats came from their ownership of British soil. The social and economic positions of the hereditary nobility and gentry were impregnable until the Industrial Revolution, in creating a new urban class, introduced stresses that finally shattered the old order. Statesmen needed guidance in those days of change, and Ricardo tried to draw a map for them.

The Corn Laws

A summary of Britain's experience with the Corn Laws will help us to summarize the situations that were Ricardo's stimuli.

In the nineteenth century, agriculture, as it always has been, was a chancy occupation. Then, as now, agriculturalists saw themselves at the mercy of two despotic forces: nature and the market. Also as at present, they sought relief in the form of legislation. In response to the considerable power of the landowners, Parliament attempted to stabilize grain prices by enacting the Corn Laws.

The principal mechanism of the Corn Laws was a sliding scale of import duties and export subsidies. The basic idea is implicit in today's agricultural price-support programs. It is necessary to have in mind an "ideal" price—a price at which grain *ought* to be sold. The object of governmental regulations is then to keep the *actual* price as close to the ideal price as possible.

Suppose that one year nature was unkind and the English harvests were poor. Grain would be scarce, so its price would rise unless additional supplies were imported. An influx of foreign grain would tend to keep the price at the "ideal" level. To encourage the importation of foreign grain, England would lower her import duty. The worse the domestic harvest, the lower the duty would be. If in another year nature was bountiful and the harvest approached a glut, the price of domestic grain would tend to fall. Seemingly, the impending price drop could be halted by getting rid of a portion of the bumper crop. To facilitate the exit of the grain, the government would grant a subsidy to grain merchants to encourage them to ship more grain out of the country. The greater the glut, the higher the subsidy would be. In other words, when a glut of domestic grain threatened British landowners with low prices, the government would pay grain exporters to ship the grain out of the country. The exporters would receive the foreign-market price for the grain plus the amount of the British government's subsidy. The greater the glut, and, hence, the greater the threat to British grain prices, the higher would be the subsidy and the more incentive exporters would have to get the grain out of Britain and into foreign markets.

The Corn Laws, whether they made sense at one time or not, eventually became an economic millstone to the island kingdom; they evolved into a virtually permanent import duty on grain. In apparent fulfillment of the predictions of Parson Malthus, the British population continued to grow until Englishmen ate up all the grain that Englishmen grew. By 1850, Britain had to import one-fourth of her grain to keep alive. But the pressure of the politically powerful landed aristocracy had transformed the Corn Laws from an agricultural price-stability program into a private tax for the benefit of landowners. The sliding scale moved, if at all, only in an upward direction.

The discriminatory nature of the Corn Laws polarized the classes. Favoring the Corn Laws, of course, were the landed aristocrats, while employers and employees, usually at loggerheads, were united in their opposition to them. Why? For the workers, the Corn Laws meant higher food costs. For their employers, the laws meant higher wage costs, since the cost of subsistence accounted for most of the wage bill.

Economic history seems to demonstrate that people will tolerate a great deal of economic chicanery as long as times are prosperous, but when business conditions are depressed they are much more insistent upon economic probity. Thus, when at the end of the exhausting Napoleonic Wars there was a bountiful harvest that sent the landowners to Parliament demanding more protection for their grain, the urban public—employers and workers—challenged the demand of the aristocracy. The nation looked for light, and one of the chief illuminators was David Ricardo.

Value: The Failure of the Classicals

In trying to build economic thought into a discipline, the early economists, deeply impressed by progress in the natural sciences, felt it necessary to develop measurable magnitudes. One of their strongest, and least successful, efforts was their attempt to explain value. *Value* is the power of a good to command another good in exchange, and price is merely the monetary expression of value. But expressing the value of a given good in terms of how many units of everything else it may be exchanged for is not an explanation of how it came by that value in the first place. The classicals' preoccupation with value is shown in their rather frentic writings on the subject, which suggest that they felt economics could not move ahead until the problem of value was solved. For example, Adam Smith, in *The Wealth of Nations,* employed so many different theories of value that it is difficult to tell which he accepted or whether, perhaps, he felt that different cases each require a special theory of value. Even worse, a number of his theories are inconsistent with each other.

Classical value theory is diffuse. Yet, although continual qualifications must be made, it is possible to subsume it under a general heading. Essentially, the classicals were *cost-of-production theorists;* that is, they held that the cost of production of a good determines its value. Inasmuch as the basic resource used in transforming nature's gifts into consumable goods is human labor, the cost of that labor is the (major) cost of production. Therefore, the most rudimentary form of the cost-of-production theory is the so-called labor theory of value.

An unadorned *labor theory of value* holds that goods exchange at a ratio commensurate with the amount of labor required for their production. Thus, if one hundred ball-point pens can be exchanged for one typewriter, a strict labor theory of value would lead us to the conclusion that it took one hundred times as much labor to build the typewriter as it did to make one pen. This strict labor theory of value is illustrated by a parable in *The Wealth of Nations.* Smith speculated that in a primitive society of hunters, if killing a beaver required twice the labor necessary to kill a deer, then one beaver would be worth two deer.

Labor theories of value are thoroughly discredited today. It is readily apparent that there is something lacking in them. Why is not one of my paintings worth fifty times as much as one of Grandma Moses', when I put fifty times as many hours in on my canvas as Grandma did on hers? Why is a bottle of wine of a certain year more valuable than wine of the same type and brand of another year, when equivalent amounts of labor were involved in their production?

Finally, another question severely troubled the classicals: Why are many frivolities more valuable than some life-sustainers? This puzzle has a name, the "diamond-water paradox," owing to Smith's tortuous reasoning in attempting to explain why a bauble has such great value compared to water. Men can live without diamonds; life is impossible without water. To find some way around these problems (they were not confronted), the classicals devised the troublesome concepts of "value in use" and "value in exchange." These ideas allowed them to conclude that water has use value and diamonds have little use value, while in the case of exchange value, the situation is reversed. Obviously, the mere invention of categories does not explain how a thing comes to possess either "value in use" or "value in exchange." The classicals did not appreciate the potential of the value-in-use category as an economic tool, for they did not know how to use it. Instead, they concentrated on value in exchange, basically holding that labor is the source of this kind of value.

There are many labor theories of value. Their number eloquently reflects the classicals' confusion. Smith, in looking for a yardstick with which to measure value, contended that only labor was an unvarying unit. Ricardo saw that this was not so, since it is evident that the value of labor fluctuates as much as the value of anything else. In this observation, Ricardo had the germ of an idea that could have led to the demise of the labor theory, because the classicals' enunciation of the labor theory is clearly a case of the "chicken-or-the-egg" conundrum. One can say that the labor expended on a good makes the good valuable, but what makes the labor valuable? The classicals, dissatisfied though they were, chose not to abandon the labor theory. After all, it is hard to give up even an unsatisfactory possession if one has nothing better to take its place.

The major flaw in the labor theory of value, insofar as the classicals were concerned, was its difficulty in explaining the value of goods produced with the aid of machines. Rare items whose value increases as time passes, such as Shakespearean first editions and Rembrandts, were largely dismissed as a special case. The classicals were almost exclusively interested in explaining the value of goods of current manufacture—the reproducible goods of everyday commerce.

Ricardo wrestled with the labor theory of value all his life, making many modifications in it, but he knew that he had no generally satisfactory explanation of value. The labor theory of value was a source of embarrassment to all the perceptive economists who were forced to use it. Karl Marx, as we shall see in Chapter 5, worked himself into an inconsistency by his insistence upon making it an important part of his economic theory. Economists who were defenders of the role of capitalists and entrepreneurs in the market economy were troubled by an obvious implication of the theory—to wit, that if labor is the source of all value, then only labor has a right to the output of the economy.

Actually, Ricardo need not have been bothered by his own use of the labor theory, although he may have felt the deficiencies of economics personally. In his development of a *system* of economics, the problem of value was not of great moment. Ricardo settled for taking initial values as given; that is, at the start of his analysis, values were assigned to goods without explaining how they came to possess these values. From this point, the Ricardian system attempted to explain *changes* in these initial values. Initially, a ton of wheat may have the value of one printing press, but, at a subsequent time, a ton of wheat may be worth two printing presses. Ricardo thought the change in value was susceptible of explanation by a modified version of the labor theory of value. Yet even in this Ricardo's work is little marred by the deficiencies we have noted, for the Ricardian system is a theory of production and distribution. Changes in the values of goods were of consequence to him only as far as they bore upon his central thesis.

The Ricardian System

THE THEORY OF DIFFERENTIAL RENT. Ricardo's theory of rent is the core of his system. The development of the economy and the behavior of the other income shares depend upon the course of land rents.

A belief in the natural superiority of agriculture in national wealth-building was the crux of physiocracy. In thinking about the turmoil over the Corn Laws, Ricardo concluded that the physiocratic belief in the beneficence of nature was wrong. He took the opposite stance: Nature is niggardly; she rewards man poorly in return for his labor upon the soil. Ricardo agreed with the physiocrats that the land produces a surplus; but he showed that, contrary to the physiocratic view, this surplus is not healthy; it is a detrimental return that eats up, instead of adding to, the wealth of society. He called this surplus "rent."

As noted in Chapter 1, rent includes the payments made to owners of natural resources; but, more generally, rent is a surplus in the sense that it is an unnecessary payment. The other income shares—wages, interest, and normal profits—that are paid to the owners of labor power, capital, and entrepreneurial ability, respectively, *must* be paid, or these resource owners will not make the services of their productive factors available to the economy. They are *incentive* payments. Rent is not like these income shares; its payment or nonpayment has no bearing on the availability of resource services to the economy. Consider a pool of oil in the ground. That pool of oil exists whether any payment is made for it or not. Nature will neither add to nor withhold her endowment of resources contingent upon any payment or lack of payment. In other words, although we must pay laborers and capitalists to get the oil out of the earth, no payment is necessary to have the oil pool itself.

Although no payment is necessary to produce the oil pool, it is possible to derive an income from the ownership of an oil pool. This income is rent. A rental payment, in other words, recognizes property rights, but it does not induce anyone to create a resource.

Although the clearest case of rent involves payments for the use of natural resources, any income can contain pure economic rent. Rent is generally defined as an *economically* (as distinguished from a legally or morally) unnecessary payment. Therefore, anyone receives rent when he would offer society his services for less than society is willing to pay him. For instance, a noted singer at one time offered his services to New York nightclubs and radio stations for ferry and subway fare. Today, a single appearance in a Las Vegas casino may earn him an income of five figures. The demand for his services has become such that the competition between nightclub impresarios has forced his price astoundingly high. The portion of his income that he must have or leave the world unsung to is a true incentive payment; it is his wage. The remainder, which produces no more songs, but merely reflects the intense competition for his nightclub appearances and the high value that society places on his vocal services, is rent.

What Ricardo was saying in his day that was interesting to employers and employees was that a considerable part of the price of food, specifically that part paid to the owners of the land on which the food was grown, is rent. It is an unnecessary payment. Increasing it would not increase the amount of land available for food production.

Ricardo's reasoning rests on three assumptions. First, Ricardo shared Malthus' view that the supply of basic resource needed for the raising of food, the land mass of the British Isles, is rigidly fixed. Second, Ricardo assumed that the soil is not of homogeneous fertility; different land areas vary considerably in their power to sustain crops. Third,

Ricardo held that the soil possesses an original fertility that can be maintained if the cultivator works the soil properly.

Ricardo's basic proposition is the second—that a nation's various land areas do not have the same natural fertility. In actuality, there may be countless grades of land, so we shall begin the process of abstraction by assuming that the whole of the British Isles is made up of three types of land: "best," "good," and "poor." Let us also assume that parcels of each type of land are randomly distributed over the United Kingdom.

We want to make a comparison between the costs of cultivating each type of land. To do this, we shall approximate Ricardo's deductive method. First, we must compare the yield from uniformly sized parcels of the three types of land. Therefore, we want to know the yield of a specific crop from, say, an acre or a square mile of land. It does not make any difference what the size is, as long as the area is the same for each type of land. Second, since we want to know the yield per unit of land, we must avoid obtaining results that are influenced by differences in the amount of fertilizer used, the number of laborers employed, or the quantity of seed sown. In other words, for scientific validity, we must hold all the variables constant except one; that one is the natural fertility of the soil. This method has come to be known as "partial-equilibrium analysis." It is a mainstay of economic analysis today. (If you are familiar with calculus, you will recognize that it is the equivalent of the procedure of partial differentiation.) We are not "cheating" or abstracting too much from reality by using this technique, because what we want to know is the change brought about by a specific factor and none other. The rather intimidating expression "partial-equilibrium analysis" can be summed up in the simple phrase "other things being equal." Other things being equal, we want to know how the differences in the fertility of the three types of soil affect the costs of cultivation.

To keep other things equal, we must specify that uniform "packages" of all nonland resources be applied to equal areas of different grades of land. Therefore, we shall put into each "package" the same quantity of seeds, tools, fertilizer and labor time. Each element in the package is of equal quality. We shall now measure the wheat yield per acre on each of the three types of land. The results are summarized in Table 1.

Our figures are hypothetical, of course, but they do represent the

TABLE 1   *The Ricardian Theory of Rent Creation*

Total yield per year (in bushels of wheat per acre)			TIME PERIOD	Rent per year (in bushels of wheat per acre)		
BEST	GOOD	POOR		BEST	GOOD	POOR
10	—	—	I	0	—	—
10	8	—	II	2	0	—
10	8	2	III	8	6	0

commonsense conclusion that the best grade of land will yield more wheat per acre than will the good land, and the good land will yield more wheat per acre than will the poor land, when equal quantities of nonland resources are applied to them. Disregard the "time period" and "rent" columns for now, and note that in response to our package of resources, the best land produces 10 bushels of wheat; good land produces 8 bushels; and poor land produces 2 bushels. Since the nonland resources applied to each are identical, variations in soil fertility must account for the differences in yields.

If we knew the resource prices, the differences in the costs of cultivation could be determined from the table. Obviously, in order to bring the yield up from, say, 8 bushels on good land to 10 bushels, the number obtained from the best land, would require the application of more nonland resources. Since more seed, fertilizer, and labor would cost more, the most fertile land is the least costly to farm.

Now let us use the time periods in Table 1 to see how Ricardo deduced the surplus nature of rent. Here Ricardo, who differed with Malthus on many points, incorporated the Malthusian principle of population into his theory. Time period I is the age when the product of the best land alone could sustain the British population. Good land and poor land would not be used since their costs of cultivation exceed that of the best land. Given the demand for wheat, it will be worthwhile for someone to farm only the best land. In response to the application of our specified package of resources, this type of land will produce 10 bushels of wheat per acre per year. A farmer would be irrational to attempt to raise wheat on land of an inferior grade, for it would reward him with a smaller crop for his outlay than would an acre of the best land (or he would have to lay out more for the same crop). Therefore, as long as the population is small enough to be sustained by the amount of wheat that can be grown on the best land, no one will cultivate parcels of inferior soil.

As yet we have said nothing about rent because there is none. The owners of the parcels of the best land are compensated for their efforts and the expenses of cultivation by the revenues they receive from the sale of their crops. This revenue consists solely of wages for their work (which may be either actual field labor or supervision) and interest on capital (seed, tools, and wage advances to hired hands). If the land-owners do not receive these payments, they will not farm their land, and society will go hungry. The payments made for wheat are *incentive* payments; they are true social costs of production.

Now let us introduce, as did Ricardo, the operation of the Malthusian process. The population expands until wheat grown on the best land is insufficient to feed the people. Now parcels of the second-best (good) land must be cultivated. Good land yields only 80 percent of the product of the best land for the same amount of resources applied. A would-be cultivator will notice this and see that, rather than farming the good land, it would be to his advantage to go instead to an owner of a parcel of the best land and offer him some of the crop as a rental pay-ment in exchange for being allowed to expend his money and energy on the higher-yielding land.[3] For example, a farmer faced with the necessity of cultivating good land would find it worthwhile to offer the owner of the best land, say, .1 of a bushel of wheat per acre per year. Since 10 bushels can be raised on an acre of the best land in one year, the prospective tenant would be left with 9.9 bushels for himself. This is 1.9 bushels better than he could do if he farmed his own good land. Rent has therefore come into existence. The .1 of a bushel of wheat per acre per year that the prospective tenant offers to the owner of the best land is rent. The owner of the best land need do nothing to receive it other than allowing someone else to farm his land.

Table 1 indicates, however, that the rent of the best land in period II is not .1 of a bushel but 2 bushels per acre per year. This is caused by the ever-present force of competition. In period II, the good land *must* be cultivated to feed the population. The yield on good land is 8 bushels per acre per year. Therefore, it is worthwhile for a tenant to

[3] In the days of English tenant farming, it was common for the tenant to pay his landlord in actual product. The rental may be converted into a money pay-ment simply by multiplying the number of bushels taken by the landlord by the market price of a bushel.

offer anything up to and including 2 bushels per acre per year in exchange for the privilege of cultivating the higher-yielding soil. If Farmer White offers .1 of a bushel per acre per year, then Farmer Black will offer .2 of a bushel, since he would still be 1.8 bushels better off each year for each acre cultivated than he would be if he cultivated good land. Similarly, Farmer Green would rather pay .3 of a bushel per acre per year to an owner of the best land than cultivate his own good soil. The bidding will continue up to a rent of 2 bushels per acre per year, because at a rent of anything less than 2 bushels of wheat the tenant is better off utilizing his labor and capital on someone else's best land than he is working his own merely good acreage. When the rent reaches the 2-bushel figure, farmers are indifferent to whether they farm their own land or that belonging to another. The yield to the cultivator is the same in either case: 8 bushels of wheat per acre per year.

In Ricardo's example, not only has the economic phenomenon of rent come into existence but the foundation of a new social class has been laid. Now the owners of the best land can continue to cultivate their land, realizing 2 bushels an acre more than their labor and capital alone would entitle them to. Or, what is more likely (providing they own enough best land), they can retire from active farming and do nothing, living on the rental income that they have done nothing to earn. Thus the rental payment is unusual; rather than inducing its recipients to perform a service, as is the case with wages and interest, it enables them to withdraw from productive enterprise. To paraphrase Adam Smith, the owners of the best land can indeed reap where they have never sown. Simple *ownership* of land has become a way to wealth. A landed class—the future aristocracy—has been born.

The process of rent-formation and the enlargement and enrichment of the landed class continues as the population grows. In period III, the population has increased so much that the best and good lands will not support enough crops to feed the people. Now the economy must have recourse to the parcels of poor land. In response to the same amount of resources applied to the other two types of land, poor land yields only 2 bushels of wheat per acre per year. The process described in period II repeats itself. Owners of poor land now enter farming; owners of good land can join the landed class; and owners of the best land become richer. Now it is worthwhile for cultivators to offer landowners the difference between the amount of wheat that can be raised on an acre of poor land and that which can be raised on good and best land respectively. Thus owners of good land will be offered up to 6 bushels of wheat per acre per year, and owners of best land can demand 8 bushels. Poor land is now no-rent land. It is at the so-called margin of cultivation. Its cultivation is just worthwhile. But it, too, could bear rent if the population were to grow to a size that would cause land of a still more inferior grade to be cultivated. Then not only would the poor land produce a rent for its owners but the rents on the better parcels of land would rise even higher.

The rent tenants must pay to owners is a true cost to the tenants. Like all other costs of doing business, the rent must be borne by the ultimate consumer. Consumers as a whole—society—must pay rent to owners of land better than the marginal grade.

The rent society must pay is a surplus in the sense that it is not an incentive payment; in fact, it permits the landowners to live on the efforts of others. The creation of land rent, as Ricardo describes it, is a social process caused by the ever-increasing pressure of population on a fixed supply of land. The land is provided by nature. No price need be paid for its services. Land parcels of all qualities will yield their respective outputs per units of resources applied regardless of the amounts of rent they command. This is not true of other resources that are not fixed in supply. Laborers must be paid to work in the fields or they will not offer their services. Capitalists will not loan funds to cultivators unless they receive interest on their loans. The farmer himself will not be interested in undertaking the risk and effort of cultivation unless he derives a recompense that he regards as adequate. All these people *must* be paid or they will not participate in food production.

But landowners are in a different position. If rent were not paid, the land, with its inherent productive capabilities, would still be usable. There is no *economic* reason for rent. Only the legal institution of private property in land makes it possible for the landlord to exact a tribute from society without doing anything. (Our discussion, however, has nothing to do with the *ethics* of land ownership. We pay no attention whether it is desirable, by any standards, that rent be paid; ours is purely an economic analysis of rent.)

Suppose that once the nation is in period II, when the good land must be cultivated, the rent of 2 bushels per acre per year is taxed away from the owners of the best land. Will the country lose any wheat? No, because the owners of best land will find themselves in the same situation as the owners of good land. With a tax on the produce of best land, the expenses and exertions devoted to both grades of land now yield the same net return to all cultivators. No product is lost, and there is no idle class to support. The owners of best land must cultivate their own soil in order to live.

Thus, we have the reasons for Ricardo's conclusion that rent is not a true cost of production. Rent arises, not in payment for the services of land (for these services exist, payment or not) but to obtain the permission of the landlord to use his land. Rent is *explained* by economic analysis; it is *created and supported* by social processes and conventions.

In summation, then, rent arises in a free-market economy for three reasons: first, the continually increasing pressure of population; second, the varying fertility of different parcels of land; and third, the legal institution of private property in land.

Rent and the Law of Diminishing Returns

Rent is an aspect of the basic economic fact of scarcity. The existence of rent does not depend upon the necessity of using land parcels of varying fertility. Ricardo knew that rent will arise on land of the *same* fertility if it is farmed more intensively. As he pointed out in his *Principles of Political Economy and Taxation* (1817), if more capital and labor are applied to the same soil, the increase in total product will be accompanied by the generation of rent. This is a manifestation of the law of diminishing returns. This law is fundamental to economics, for it provides a rigorous way of treating the general fact of scarcity. Ricardo was not the first to observe the existence of diminishing returns; the physiocrat Turgot had stated the principle before. It was accepted by the classicals, although Ricardo was one of the few to give it clear expression. We have seen a hint of it in Malthus' description of the tendency of the rate of increase in the means of subsistence to lag behind the rate of increase in the population.

THE STATEMENT OF THE LAW.   The law of diminishing returns is a simple idea. It says that with technology and the resource base of the economy held constant (the "other-things-being-equal" idea), at some point in any productive process further equal additions of a variable resource will yield successively smaller *increments* of output.[4]

---

[4] The classicals stated the law somewhat differently, however, the basic idea is the same, and the simpler version given here is more widely used today.

A HYPOTHETICAL EXAMPLE. Assume a farmer works a parcel of soil of uniform quality with a certain amount of capital (seeds, barns, fertilizers, plows, and so on). We want to see how the output of the plot varies when the application of one of the variable inputs (labor, for example) is increased. When the farmer does not work the ground at all, the soil yields no useful crop. If he works the soil by himself, he obtains a yield of, say, 100 units of crop per acre per year. Now, let us suppose that he uses himself plus one hired hand in the field; that is, he uses two units of the variable input (in this case, labor). A division of labor between the farmer and the hired hand is possible; the farmer does not have to do everything himself. Let us suppose that their total product is 250 units of crop per acre. The *extra* product made possible by the addition of one extra input unit (the hired hand) is 150 units. There is no diminishing return here. Indeed, returns are increasing; output has increased in greater proportion than input—doubling the input of labor has more than doubled output. Suppose the farmer adds still another worker and the total output of the three workers is 425 units. By adding a third laborer, the farmer has increased his production by 175 units. Returns to the variable input are still increasing.

If the farmer hires a third field hand (making a total of four workers), the total product might rise to 600 units. The addition of a fourth laborer has caused output to rise by the same amount (175 units) as did the addition of the third worker. The returns to labor are now no longer increasing; they are *constant.*

Where do *diminishing* returns come in? Suppose that the hiring of a fifth worker increases the total product to 750 units. Total output still is increasing, but now it is increasing *at a decreasing rate.* The addition to output when a fifth laborer is used is 150 units—25 units *less* than the preceding addition to output (when labor was increased from three to four). With a level of employment of five laborers, we have encountered *diminishing* returns. We would expect that increasing the labor inputs to six workers would add less than 150 units to output. This is shown in Table 2, which presents the response of output to changes in input through nine units.

Diminishing returns, as we use the term here, means not that total output declines but only that its rate of increase diminishes. *Total* output increases through the addition of the eighth worker. However, beginning with the hiring of the fifth worker, the *additions* to total output from the increments in inputs are successively smaller. When

TABLE 2 *Input and Output Data for a Hypothetical Farm*

Inputs of labor	Total output	Extra (marginal) output
0	0	
		100
1	100	
		150
2	250	
		175
3	425	
		175
4	600	
		130*
5	730	
		65
6	795	
		30
7	825	
		0†
8	825	
		−30
9	795	

* Point of diminishing marginal returns.
† Point of maximum total output.

the employment level has reached seven, total product is at a maximum, and the so-called extra, or marginal, productivity of labor is zero. Expansion of the number of input units from seven to eight adds nothing to total output. (This is the region of *zero returns*). If nine laborers were used, total output would fall. Thus, the extra (marginal) product figure is negative at that level of employment; we have *negative returns* to the variable factor.

The situation marked by the dagger in Table 2 is often erroneously referred to as the point of diminishing returns, as when, in popular usage, we say, "I've reached the point of diminishing returns," as an excuse for quitting work. However, the true point of diminishing returns, that is significant here, is the point in production at which the *rate of increase* in total product falls off. Our version of the law is, strictly speaking, a law of diminishing *marginal* returns, or a law of diminishing *marginal* productivity. ("Marginal" is simply an equivalent expression for "extra.") At some point in the productive process, the *extra* product falls off as the application of variable resources is increased; at the same time, however, *total* product continues to increase.

Over some range in production, total product may increase at an *increasing* rate, as it does in Table 2 up to the point at which the level of employment is three input packages. This phenomenon does not vitiate the law, which holds merely that *at some point* total output, although continuing to increase, will do so at a decreasing rate. The reason for the initial increasing returns, in contrast to that for diminishing returns, is easy to see. As long as increasing returns prevail too few units of variable resources are being used relative to the fixed resources. The farmer, when he worked by himself, was spreading his efforts too thinly. There is no "law of increasing returns." Economic theory does not hypothesize that increasing returns must precede diminishing returns; diminishing returns may set in at the outset of production.

A real-world farmer desirous of increasing his output of wheat would, quite possibly, increase all or some of his inputs. For example, he might try to obtain a greater crop using more labor *and* more seed. There is no reason why he should increase his use of these two resources, or any resources, in the same proportion. The exact resource combination he chooses will depend upon which produces the most wheat for the least cost. If, for example, seed is relatively cheap compared with labor, the farmer may attempt to add to his output by increasing his use of seed more than he increases his use of labor; or, if he can, he might even try to decrease his labor usage by putting out more seed.

In studying the law of diminishing returns, only *one* resource is varied; the others remain constant. This is to permit us to see how output varies in response to the change in a particular input. Although resources—seed, land, labor, and fertilizer—are considerably different in nature, they may still be used, within limits, as substitutes for one another. More wheat may be raised by using either more seed, more land, more labor, or more fertilizer. But the increase in wheat output cannot go on indefinitely in response to the increase of just one resource —say, labor. Resources are substitutes for each other, but not *perfect* substitutes. Given an initial resource base, applying more labor to the soil will yield more wheat. But, obviously, labor by itself cannot do what more seeds would do or what more land would do. Eventually, *increases* in the output of wheat must fall off as successively greater amounts of labor are applied to the soil in the absence of increases in the other inputs necessary to wheat farming. In fact, at some point, total output will actually begin to decrease (see the change in output in Table 2 as a ninth worker is added). We may surmise that the reason for this negative productivity is the overcrowding of the variable resource units (labor) relative to the other resources (land, seed, fertilizer, plows, barns, and so on).

To test the law, we must have recourse to the real world, where, under the proper conditions, observations can be made of the response of output to increases in the application of a variable resource. Such tests have been made. The law always has emerged uncontradicted. But, more importantly, that the law has stood uncontradicted for several centuries attests to the perspicacity of the classicals in stating it and to its validity as a basic proposition of economics.

RENT REVISITED. How does rent arise, given, as in the situation depicted in Table 2, a single landowner and one parcel of land of uniform quality?

Suppose that the going wage rate for farm labor is 65 units of crop per year.[5] The farmer will find it worthwhile to hire *up to* six labor units. Why? Because up to the sixth unit, each resource unit contributes more to output than it costs. Each of the first five units of input yields at least 65 units of extra output (see the right-hand column of the table). Thus, if the farmer used 5.9 labor units (he can use .9 of a labor unit by hiring a part-time laborer for only 90 percent of the normal work period), an additional .1 of a labor unit would add more to the farmer's revenues than it would to his costs. When the farmer employs six men, his total costs are 390 units of crop per year (six laborers at 65 units each). The total product of his farm when he employs six laborers is 795 units of crop per year. This leaves him with an income of 405 units of crop per year (795 units of total product less 390 units of total labor cost).

Now, let us examine the disposition of this 405 units of crop per year gross income. To simplify our example, let us assume that the farmer

_____

[5] Here the return to the variable resource (labor) is expressed in real terms. To convert the return into monetary units, we need to know the price at which the crop sells on the market. If it sells for $2 per unit, the yearly resource cost would be $130 per laborer per year.

has ceased to work in the fields himself. He employs six *other* men to do the field work.

In the production of his total output of 795 units of wheat, the farmer has incurred costs for productive services other than field labor. For example, he has supplied seed and fertilizer. His tools and his barns are gradually wearing out, and someday he must replace them. Thus, for example, if a plow has a life of five years, the farmer must count one-fifth of the cost of the plow each year as depreciation expense. Barns must be treated in the same way, except that they will probably last longer than five years—say, thirty years. In this case the farmer must count one-thirtieth of the cost of the barn each year as depreciation expense. Suppose that the farmer's costs for seed, fertilizer, and depreciation charges are the equivalent of 10 units of wheat. At this point in our calculations, 395 units of wheat remain to be accounted for.

Field labor is not the only labor involved in running a farm. Someone must manage the enterprise. Let us suppose that the farmer could hire a manager, or, alternatively, could hire himself out as a farm foreman for 80 units of crop per year. Then, *his* wages are 80 units of crop per year.

Besides supplying managerial labor, the farmer has also furnished capital in the form of plows, barns, and so on. He has also advanced wages to his farmhands before the crop that they have helped to grow could be marketed. He must receive interest as a return on his investment in fixed plant and equipment and on his advances to his workers. Let us assume that the going rate of interest would yield him another 80 units of crop.

At this point in our calculations, the farmer's *earned* reward is 160 units of crop. Is all, or part, of the remaining 235 units of wheat earned or unearned income? The answer depends on the view you have of entrepreneurial activity. If you assume that entrepreneurial activity is passive, that all the so-called entrepreneur does is furnish the services of management and capital, then our farmer-enterpreneur's *normal* profit consists entirely of the wages of management plus the interest on the capital he has furnished. The remaining 235 units of crop, then, by definition, accrue to him without any productive service being supplied in exchange for them.

But now, let us assume that there is something about the role of the entrepreneur that distinguishes it from the roles of the manager and the capitalist. Suppose that the entrepreneur is the factor who must bear the burden of initiating, organizing, and supporting the enterprise. This function may be quite different from managing a going enterprise. There may be many people who would be willing to work as managers who would not, at least in the absence of compensation in excess of managerial wages, assume the burden of being the ultimately responsible agent behind an enterprise. We have assumed that our farmer could earn 80 units of crop by working as a foreman for another farmer, and we have also assumed that he could earn another 80 units of wheat furnishing the same amount of capital he uses in his own business to any enterprise. Why should he be willing to organize and support an enterprise of his own without the additional compensation called profit (the income share of the entrepreneur)?

Suppose that the operation of the free market has fixed the reward of farmer-entrepreneurs for farms of the nature and size of the farm owned by our hypothetical farmer at 100 units of crop per year. This is the *normal profit* for being a farmer-entrepreneur. That is, when the farming industry is in equilibrium—when profit is neither so high as to produce a movement of entrepreneurs into farming nor so low as to drive some enterprisers out of agriculture—the reward for such entrepreneurial activity as is involved in our example is 100 units of crop per year.[6] In other words, regardless of how much greater the return is from his farming operation, all the reward our farmer requires to serve as an entrepreneur is 100 units of crop per year (his normal profit). Therefore, any payment over and above this amount is a payment that society does not have to make in order to obtain his entrepreneurial services: It is an unnecessary payment, it is a surplus, it is rent.

Now, how much rent is our hypothetical farmer receiving? He receives 135 units of wheat per year. How do we arrive at this figure? The farmer *demands* 80 units of crop per year if he is to act as a manager. If he is to furnish capital to the economy, he must receive an additional 80 units of crop per year. Finally, if he is to offer his entrepreneurial services, he must get at least the profit he regards as normal —100 units of wheat per year. That is, he *requires* 260 units of crop per year to compensate him for the productive services that he furnishes to the economy. The 260-unit figure is the sum of his wages, interest, and normal profit. They are *incentive* payments. But, in fact, society is paying him 395 units—135 units more than he requires to offer any

[6] Remember our discussion of *normal* returns in Chapter 3, p. 66.

productive service. Take any or all of the 135 units of crop away, and he will still perform the functions the economy wants him to perform. Therefore, this 135-unit payment is a surplus over and above the necessary incentive payments. Any surplus above incentive payments is defined in economics as rent (see p. 93).

It may be argued that the 135-unit payment compensates him for the use of his land. The correct statement is that the ownership of land *enables* him to extract a rental payment from the economy, but the land itself will work for nothing. The 135 units of crop that the farmer, as a landlord, receives as rent gives him no incentive to do anything. Should something happen to reduce the rental payment—even to zero—the farmer would continue to supply the economy with the resources necessary to produce 795 units of grain per year.

To test this proposition further, consider this situation. The farmer need do nothing at all in order to receive this 135-unit rent other than allow someone else to work his soil. Any other entrepreneur who can net the 100-unit normal profit in agriculture would be willing to pay our hypothetical farmer a rent of up to, and including, 135 units of crop per year for the use of the farmer-landlord's soil. If this happens, we should drop the word "farmer" from our description of him. The possibility of receiving rental income from the ownership of a natural resource—a parcel of soil—may relieve the owner of the necessity of being a farmer at all; he may be able to convert himself from a sturdy yeoman into a country gentleman.

THE BASIS OF CLASSICAL THEORIZING. The law of diminishing returns is a hypothesis to explain how the total output of an economy changes as the population expands. It is the theoretical basis for Malthus' belief that the rate of population growth would tend to exceed the rate of expansion in the means of subsistence. This is shown graphically in Figure 3.

Population is measured along the horizontal axis. The total output of wheat is measured along the vertical axis.[7] Curve *OQ* shows the response of wheat production to increases in the population. The shape

---

[7] Those who prefer to abstract more than we have here may regard wheat as representing all food production or even all the things that constitute "the means of subsistence." If, however, the vertical axis is used to represent a mixture of heterogeneous goods, we must specify that they be combined in equal "packages" consisting of the same proportions of all the goods.

of OQ (concave with respect to the horizontal axis) is explained by the law of diminishing returns. We are assuming that diminishing returns set in at the outset of wheat production. ON_1, N_1N_2, and N_2N_3 represent equal increases in the population. With each increase, there

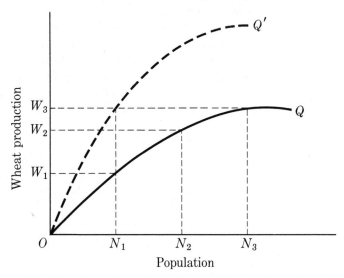

FIGURE 3 *The Operation of the Law of Diminishing Returns*

are more people to work the soil *and* more people to be fed from it. As the population increases, the total output of wheat also increases, as shown by the successive increments OW_1, W_1W_2, and W_2W_3. Note, however, that each increase in wheat production is *less* than the preceding increase as the population grows; that is, OW_1 is greater than W_1W_2, and W_1W_2 exceeds W_2W_3. Thus the classicals, epitomized by Malthus, were not optimistic about the future of the human race— they predicted that the food supply would increase less than proportionately in response to the increases in population.

Happily, however, the very nations for which the classicals predicted a gloomy future have escaped starvation. What has been the West's escape route? Technology. If inventive minds and visionary entrepreneurs are free to work, the output curve OQ can move upward. Western economic history tells us that it has. In the West, particularly in the United States, a flood of tractors, harvesting machines, fertilizers, pesticides, and new plant strains has moved OQ steadily and rapidly upward. Consider OQ'. If technology lifts the output curve, a population the size of N_1 will enjoy an output of wheat equal to W_3 instead of W_1.

Although the unforeseen rapidity of technological progress ruined the classicals' prophecy of an eventually static society hanging on the edge of subsistence, does technological progress vitiate the law of diminishing returns? No. Consider the shape of OQ'. Its *position* is determined by technology. Its *shape* is determined by the law of diminishing returns. Unless something *external* to the productive process happens (innovation), the economy faces diminishing returns on its land. Technology *offsets* the effects of this law; it does not repeal it. An external force is required to avoid diminishing returns. That force is continual technological progress and innovation; its successful application in first the West and now Japan are proof of its efficacy. Since the curve must be followed, the only hope is to raise the curve itself; such is the pervasive effect of scarcity. (Note, of course, that the response of output to increases in inputs, as we have depicted it, is characteristic of all productive processes, not simply farming.)

The Other Income Shares

Having disposed of the reward of landlords, Ricardo went on to explain the returns to the other two classes, employees and their employers. Our main purpose in looking at Ricardo's theory of income shares is to see how he created a *system* of analysis. We know now that his theories of wages and profits, in contrast to his rent theory and statement of the law of diminishing returns, are inadequate and faulty.

Before looking at the other income shares, let us note how much of Ricardo's system we already have encountered. The cornerstones of his system are his own rent theory and the Malthusian principle of population. Workers must receive their subsistence. This requirement sets a floor to wages. "Subsistence" is a sketchy term, but, in general, it is the amount of real income (food, clothing, housing) that will enable the worker to do his job and reproduce his own kind. According to Ricardo, in the long run wages tend to a subsistence minimum. Here is a major element in the so-called pessimism of the classicals. However, for reasons yet to be explained, wages may temporarily rise above the subsistence minimum. When they do, the population will expand. As long as wages stay at the subsistence level, the population remains static;

but once workers earn more than their subsistence, the Malthusian principle takes effect, and the population rises. A greater population requires more food but also furnishes more labor to help produce that food. However, as Tables 1 and 2 and Figure 3 show, the increase in food production is subject to diminishing returns, with the consequent creation of rent. This process will result, eventually, in a situation where wages are again at the subsistence level. Let us see why.

The first division of income, that between landlords and everybody else, has now been explained. What is left over must be divided between employees and employers.

Again let us abstract, by going through a time sequence. In technical language, this is the "classical dynamics." In economics, a "dynamic" analysis is one that views a process over time, while a "static" analysis presents a situation at a given moment of time. An analogy would be to a motion picture and a snapshot, respectively.

Let us assume initially that workers are receiving subsistence wages. The portion of total product remaining after the payment of wages and rent belongs to capitalist-employers. Ricardo called this difference "profits." Part of this income rewards the businessman for providing capital and is thus interest. The amount over and above the necessary interest payment, if any, may be regarded as the reward for risk-taking or perhaps, if the amount received by the businessman is more than enough to induce him to furnish his entrepreneurial services as rent.

The main route to economic expansion is the formation of capital. Ricardo, like Smith, considered the principal form of capital to be the wages fund. Employers will be *able* to augment the stock of capital— wage goods (goods consumed by workers)—if their profits exceed their own living requirements; that is, they can save only if they have enough income left after spending for their own consumption needs. They will be *willing* to employ their savings to add to the capital stock if they can earn a return on their investment. A return (profit, in the Ricardian sense) is possible if there is a difference between what must be paid to employees in wages and what landlords receive in rent.

Let us assume that this is the case initially. Employers provide more capital, leading to an increase in the wages fund. The increase in the wages fund and competition among employers for employees to operate the expanded productive capacity of the economy (we are assuming that some investment takes the form of new plant and equipment) will force the wage rate above the subsistence level. As the wage rate increases, profits will be squeezed. Yet, as long as it is possible for employers to earn a net return by hiring more laborers, they will continue to do so, all the while driving up the level of wages. Eventually, a point will be reached at which profits will be reduced to zero. Wages and rent now eat up the entire output of the economy. The reasonable conclusion is that since capitalists are receiving no income they will cease to form capital, and economic growth will come to a halt. How can it resume?

At this point in his theory of economic growth, Ricardo brought in his friend Malthus' principle of population. What is the response of the working population to a wage level in excess of their subsistence requirements? Malthus had argued that population will inexorably expand up to the subsistence level; Ricardo accepted this idea. Malthus reasoned that when wages rise above the subsistence level, human beings will more than reproduce themselves. Eventually, the increase in the working population will be large enough to drive wages back down to the subsistence level as people compete with each other for jobs. In Malthus' view, human nature causes workers to equate their wage level to the subsistence level by increasing the size of their families whenever wages rise above the level of subsistence. This is the root of the notion, fondly held in the nineteenth century (and even today in some quarters), that the poor are responsible for their own poverty.

The process we have described continues repeatedly. When wages are at the subsistence level, and there is a gap between wage and rent payments, capitalists will invest. As they employ more workers, the wage rate rises, and profits are squeezed. When profits are reduced to zero, employers cease to form capital. However, in response to the higher-than-subsistence wages, workers increase the size of their families, adding enough new laborers to the work force to drive wages back to the subsistence level. Once again, there is a gap between wage and rent payments that capitalists can garner if they will supply capital to the economy.

Rising wages during economic expansion are, of course, not the only cost squeezing profits. In fact, profits and wages are *both* being squeezed by rent. The costs of a subsistence wage rise as economic expansion continues. Remember that the Ricardian rent theory holds that rent increases as the population grows. The landlords' income becomes ever larger, while the income shares of employers and employees become smaller in relation to rent, even though the economy continues to grow.

Let us return to Figure 3. The working population is the variable resource; land (natural resources) is the fixed resource; and wheat (food) is the output. As the variable input of labor is increased, the output of grain increases. However, the expansion of total output follows the path described by OQ. There are diminishing returns to the variable resource (the working population). Each equal increment in the variable resource produces a less-than-proportional increase in output. For example, if the work force increases by 10 percent, output will increase by less than 10 percent. So employers and employees are receiving successively smaller increases in the output produced by their efforts. You can see this in Figure 3. Even though *total output* rises as the economy moves along OQ, *output per capita* is falling. If each total output (shown on the vertical axis) is divided by the number of people needed to produce it (measured on the horizontal axis), it will be found that output per member of the labor force is a smaller figure for each higher level of employment.

Meanwhile, however, the income of landlords increases. Rent is a social phenomenon. The more people there are to feed, the scarcer land (the fixed resource) becomes relative to variable resources and the higher the price its owners can charge for its use. Thus, the landlords' share of output (rent) increases, while the employer-employee share wages and profits) decreases.

Employers and employees, then, have a common cause against the landed class. Their combined share of the national income grows at a decreasing rate, and that share suffers from the increasingly large incursions of the landlords' share. This is what united two ordinarily antagonistic forces against the Corn Laws. Wages could rise, but the lot of workers would not improve for long. Increased food costs would vitiate the potentially salutary effects of a rise in wages, and higher subsistence costs would also mean greater wage outlays for employers. Thus, although employers and employees might quarrel over the apportionment of the income share remaining after the landlords had been paid, both classes could see that ever-rising food prices were inimical to their interests.

It did not require any unusual insight to deduce that rent was a substantial part of the cost of grain. In the classical era, the price of a good was thought to be determined by its cost of production. Therefore, one supposed reason for the high cost of grain was the high cost of the land on which it was grown. What Ricardo's acute insight showed was that the price of land (rent) was high because the cost of grain was high, not vice versa. As shown in Table 1, rent is price-determined, not price-determining as is the case with incentive payments to the owners of nonland resources. Ricardo's theory revealed that the landlords were becoming wealthy as the result of social and economic processes in which they played no part. And the Corn Laws compounded this inequity by import duties that kept out the foreign grain that, had it been allowed to enter England freely, would have lowered food prices and reduced the landlords' rent.

Ricardo's theory made all the hitherto poorly understood economic processes so clear that opponents of the Corn Laws were finally able to argue successfully for the repeal of one of the most outrageous examples of special-interest legislation in Western economic history.

Thus, the Ricardian theory of income distribution had important policy ramifications. In essence, it is a simple theory. Its heart is the theory of rent, which, in turn, relies heavily upon the Malthusian principle of population. The amount left over after the payment of rent is divided between employers and their employees. The way it is divided is a reflection of Malthusian population theory. Wages tend to a subsistence minimum. When competition among employers for workers is keen (in periods of prosperity), wages may rise above the subsistence level; but the workers' biological instincts act to extinguish their gains. Whether wages are at or above subsistence, the residual belongs to employers and is the share Ricardo called profits, although today we would separate it into the components of interest (a return on capital) and profit (a return on entrepreneurship).

Since OQ rises at a decreasing rate and the number of workers (population) inexorably expands in accord with Malthusian population theory, Ricardo and his classical successors surmised that at some stage in economic growth rent and the *subsistence level* of wages would consume the whole of the national output. Then, what would happen? The end of the process of economic growth is the classicals' stationary state. Progress comes to an end. The prospect for society, other than landlords, is bare subsistence. With Ricardo, therefore, the seed of classical pessimism planted by Malthus has flowered. With Marx it will become a bramble bush. Although Marx was to discard Ricardo's distinction between classes of property owners, the germ of Marxism class conflict can be found in Ricardo's analysis. Rent is the inevitable consequence of population pressure and diminishing returns. Therefore, as long as property rights are respected, society is saddled with that burden by the very nature of things. Although wages and profits are subject to adjustment, one varying at the expense of the other, attempts by employees to increase their share to the detriment of employers are futile, for both shares are doomed to fall.

In spite of the doleful predictions of the classicals, they and their contemporaries in the business world adhered to laissez faire. Why? Because they felt the whole process to be inexorable. There was no known method of intervention that could stop it. The prospect was, in fact, that intervention would probably make matters even worse. More important, of course, was the classicals' belief that the static state, like all days of retribution, was a long way off. In the meantime, the businessmen of Great Britain and the nation itself were doing very well. Why should anyone rock the splendidly appointed boat for the benefit of his great-great-grandchildren?

Ricardo and his contemporaries could not possibly have foreseen any helpful type of governmental intervention, except perhaps the expropriation of land rents (repeal of the Corn Laws could be considered an indirect form of expropriation), because the economy had not yet evolved to the state in which booms and crises began to assume damaging proportions. Their greatest failure was their inability to see that the curve OQ could move upward. Indeed, when Ricardo finally wrote an in-depth analysis of machinery as capital in the last edition of his *Principles,* he concluded that machinery was likely to be labor-displacing and that, therefore, employers would be able to enlarge their share of income at the expense of the working class. Ricardo's reasoning suffers from some internal inconsistencies and a lack of foresight. He neglected the classical postulate of full employment, which, coupled with the upward movement in OQ occasioned by increasing the number of machines, could ameliorate labor's problems. And he did not see the possibility that, even if labor's share of the income "pie" should grow smaller—and there is no convincing reason why it should if capital becomes relatively more plentiful—an increase in the size of the pie (the rise in OQ) would allow everyone to have more even if his percentage share were to drop.

The Practical Consequences of Ricardo's Work

The practical consequences of Ricardo's differential-rent theory and law of diminishing returns are eloquent testimony to the power of the tools of economic analysis. The response to Ricardo's theorizing was momentous. Businessmen and workers already were restive under rising food costs. As a result of his reasoning, Ricardo turned from theoretical abstraction to political economy, to support the demand of the urban classes, for the repeal of the Corn Laws.

What Ricardo had shown by the process of abstraction was not that the cost of bread was high because the price of grain was high, but the reverse. Grain was expensive because the price of bread was high. A major component of the price of bread is rent, but rent, unlike wages and profits, is not a true social cost of production of bread. Rather, the price of bread determines rent.

Ricardo's deductive analysis—which we have explored—convinced Parliament, and in 1846 it repealed the Corn Laws. In fairness, however, we must note that Ricardo's basic argument received adroit propagandizing at the hands of some extremely skillful pamphleteers.

The repeal of the Corn Laws was a significant event in Western economic history. It did not mean simply that a long-accepted duty on grain ceased to exist or even just the victory of the urban classes over the landed gentry. With the demise of the Corn Laws, Britain embraced free trade as an instrument of national policy, and the victory of free competitive capitalism over mercantilism was complete.

"Free trade" means that a nation does not encumber her international transactions with tariffs, duties, quotas, and other restrictions. She lets goods move across her borders as if those borders did not exist. Often, nations avoid free trade to promote what they believe to be their national interests. They may wish to become self-sufficient or to protect certain domestic industries and workers. Was Great Britain acting from altruism in allowing foreigners to send their goods into the island kingdom untaxed? The record shows that this action was one of enlightened self-interest. David Ricardo's reasoning shows how this was so.

INTERREGIONAL AND INTERNATIONAL TRADE

International trade is a political, not an economic, phenomenon. The reason for trade is not international boundaries. It would be more correct to say that trade is carried on *despite* international borders. The argument for free trade is very simple: "more." More of everything for everybody.

Regional Specialization

Specialization causes trade between geographic regions. In economics, specialization does not mean that a nation produces only one good. It means that a person, a region, or a nation produces more of some goods than the producer can use, creating a surplus that can be sold to others. Rational geographic specialization arises from the distribution of natural and other resources. Is it rational to try to produce in your home those things you can buy more cheaply from someone else? California does not attempt to produce maple sugar, and Vermont stays out of the orange business. If these two states attempted to become self-sufficient in the production of both goods, might not the main result be less palatable breakfasts for both Californians and Vermonters? The basis for trade between California and Vermont is specialization, and the basis for specialization is regional differences.

International trade is only a special case of interregional trade. Trade takes place between different regions; these regions may or may not lie in different national sovereignties. If an international boundary line does split trading regions, the opportunities for human obtuseness to prevail are increased.

Absolute and Comparative Advantage

The early classical economists, including Adam Smith, believed that the case for specialization and, therefore, trade rested on the possession of an *absolute advantage* in the production of a particular good. Climatic differences ensure that California has an absolute advantage in orange growing and that Vermont has an absolute advantage in the production of maple syrup. Therefore, there will be a flow of the two commodities between the two states, oranges, in effect, being traded for maple syrup.

What happens when, as is often the case, a region possesses an absolute advantage over another in the production of *all* goods? Is trade impossible? Would trade benefit only one of the regions?

Let us work out a completely hypothetical example of interregional trade between the states of California and Nevada to see the basis for mutually advantageous trade even when one state enjoys an absolute advantage in the production of every traded item. Essentially, we are repeating the Ricardian argument that upset the old idea that trade occurs only between regions having absolute advantages in their respective specialized commodities.

Assume that both California and Nevada can produce grapefruits and watermelons. The production of a crate of grapefruits cost one dollar in California; in Nevada production of the same quantity costs twenty dollars. Watermelons also cost one dollar per crate to grow in California, and in Nevada, the cost is five dollars per crate. Clearly, California has an absolute advantage in the production of both goods. We can assume that California's absolute superiority comes from differences in resource endowments—in the soil, the climate, the labor force, the supply of farmer-entrepreneurs, and the presence of supporting industries.

The question is: Is there any basis for trade between the two states? According to the principle of absolute advantage, there is not. However, let us look at California's absolute advantages. California is twenty times as efficient as Nevada in the production of grapefruits. She is five times as efficient in the production of watermelons. Although California is *absolutely* superior in the production of both items, she is relatively superior in the production of only one—namely, grapefruit. Since she is relatively superior in one item, she must be relatively inferior in the production of the other. And, since we are comparing California and Nevada, the latter must have a relative superiority in watermelons, although she is absolutely inferior in their production.

To simplify our discussion, let us drop money prices and use barter terms. In California, one dollar will buy either a crate of grapefruits or a crate of watermelons; therefore, one crate of grapefruits will exchange for one crate of watermelons. In Nevada, where the cost of a crate of grapefruits is twenty dollars, and the cost of a crate of watermelons is five dollars, one crate of grapefruits can be exchanged for four crates of watermelons. To raise one crate of grapefruits costs four times as much as raising a crate of watermelons.

It will be advantageous to both states for California to specialize in the production of grapefruits and for Nevada to specialize in watermelon growing. Assuming full employment in both states, if Nevada gives up the resources necessary to produce one crate of grapefruits and transfers them into the production of watermelons, she will get four crates of watermelons. If California transfers resources from the production of grapefruits into watermelon production, she gets one crate of watermelons for every crate of grapefruit that she sacrifices. Therefore, a mutually advantageous trading situation can be predicated upon the indicated specializations. It will be worthwhile to California for her to trade Nevada one crate of grapefruits for anything more than one crate of watermelons, since anything more than one crate of watermelons in exchange for one crate of grapefruits is a better exchange than Californians can get at home. And it will be advantageous to Nevada to send California anything less than four crates of watermelons in exchange for one crate of grapefruits, since Nevadans must give up four crates of watermelons to gain one crate of grapefruits in domestic production.

Now, to use the language of interregional economics, the *terms of trade* between California and Nevada are:

> One crate of grapefruits is worth one crate of watermelons,
>
> and
>
> one crate of grapefruits is worth four crates of watermelons.

The exact (barter) price lies somewhere between these two extremes.

We cannot know the final prices for grapefruits and watermelons unless we can observe the workings of the forces of supply and demand in the market, but suppose that the exact barter price settles at the ratio of one crate of grapefruits to three crates of watermelons.[8]

By sending, or giving up, one crate of grapefruits to Nevada, California receives in exchange three crates of watermelons. Internally, a self-sufficient California could gain only one crate of watermelons for its one crate of grapefruits. So there is a clear gain for California—three crates of watermelons for every crate of grapefruits foregone, instead of one for one.

Nevada also gains. For every three crates of watermelons that she sends to California, she receives in exchange one crate of grapefruits. If she attempted to be self-sufficient, she would have to give up *four* crates of watermelons to produce the one crate of grapefruits.

Therefore, the gains from trade are one crate of grapefruits for Nevada and two crates of watermelons for California. By specializing and trading on the basis of their *relative* superiorities, instead of according to their absolute superiorities, both California and Nevada are better off— if, of course, we define being "better off" as having "more."

---

[8] Supply-and-demand analysis is discussed in Chapter 6.

This is Ricardo's principle of comparative advantage. It shows that regions can trade to their mutual advantage even if one particular region has all the cost advantages on its side. If one nation were absolutely superior in the production of everything, a mutually advantageous trading situation would nevertheless exist if *differences in the ratios of the costs of production* obtained between any pair of countries producing wanted commodities.

We have used states rather than nations in our hypothetical example. To convert the general case of interregional trade into international trade, all that is necessary is to imagine that the state line between California and Nevada has become an international border. The trading situation will not be altered in any respect. The major difference in working out a hypothetical example of trade would be the currency differences between the two "nations." We would have to state the prices in our example in terms of the currency of either of the two "nations"—a complication we have avoided by using states.

Barriers to Free Trade

Free trade is a tool; it makes the best of a bad situation. We want coffee, but we do not have Brazil's climate. Other nations want steel, but they do not have our accumulation of steel-making capital. Free trade helps to overcome the inequities produced by the random endowments of natural and other resources on the earth.

As we have repeatedly emphasized, there is only one economic problem—scarcity. The more efficiently the resources of the world are redistributed, the less oppressive will be the problem of scarcity. When a country specializes in the production of the goods that it can make most efficiently and trades those goods for other goods that it cannot make as efficiently, it will have more of everything. Placing barriers in the way of free trade reduces the gains open to a nation. Obstacles to free trade intensify the problem of scarcity. Why, then, would anyone oppose free trade?

Usually, it is special-interest groups that favor the impairment of free trade. In Ricardo's time, the landed aristocracy benefited from restricting the flow of imported grain into Britain because duties kept the price of domestic grain high and allowed them to live on their land rents. This enabled the gentry to consume part of the total product of the British economy without making any contribution to that product.

It is not only the landed classes who have been selfish. Both business and labor groups in all nations have, at some time, clamored for protection. Typically, laborers demand protection from "low-paid foreign labor," and businessmen ask for insulation from the competition of "lower-priced foreign goods."

In our own time, the best known and most significant free-trade movement is the European Common Market. Though its present record of accomplishment is somewhat inconclusive, it has had as its aim the partial erasure of international boundary lines insofar as the movement of goods and resources is concerned.

Britain's Reward

It would be too much to claim that Britain embraced free trade because of Englishmen's appreciation of the logic of Ricardo's argument. Free trade became a British policy because it clearly benefited the newly powerful elements in British society. Britain adopted free trade at a most propitious time. The goods flowing into Britain duty free offered little competition to British manufacturers and their employees. They were either goods Britain was not interested in making herself or raw materials, which British ingenuity transformed into the finished products that the rest of the world badly wanted.

The United Kingdom as a whole built up a great surplus of goods—a surplus in the sense that a part of the outpouring of goods was not consumed by Englishmen. Perhaps Britain should have used her surplus to alleviate the poor living conditions of her workers. She chose not to do so, however, and her surplus was employed in making her the center of world economic development. From the productivity of her inventors, enterprisers, and laborers, Britain derived the means to finance an empire. Beyond this, she was a prime source of the development capital needed by the growing economy of the United States. In its crucial years of growth, the United States was a major beneficiary of British foreign investment. This was not foreign aid. The United States was an ideal borrower from the British point of view; not only was the rate of return high from funds invested in American industry but the Americans fully intended to, and did, repay the loans granted to them by Englishmen.

David Ricardo: An "Action Intellectual"

David Ricardo is an excellent example of how a thinker can be affected by and, in turn, affect the world of affairs. Two of his major theories—the theory of differential rent and the theory of comparative advantage—were born of the technological changes that were transforming Britain from a self-sufficient agricultural nation into an industrial power dependent upon other, less industrially developed areas for food. Conditions dictated the area of Ricardo's interests. In turn, Ricardo's analysis helped to win the argument that the Corn Laws were an offensive piece of special-interest legislation, inimical to the full economic development of the British nation. His rigorous demonstration that the price of wheat is not high because the price of land is high, but rather the reverse, enabled Englishmen to see that the Corn Laws benefited only the idle landlords.

Ricardo's principle of comparative advantage showed that a nation would improve its economic well-being if it would engage in the productive activities in which it is relatively superior to other nations. Britain was becoming demonstrably superior to other countries in the production of manufactured goods, which meant that she would be better off if she let foreign nations serve as her breadbasket.

Thus, Ricardo's analysis provided the theoretical basis for one of Britain's greatest policy changes. Repealing the Corn Laws, Britain adopted free trade (trade according to the principle of comparative advantage) at a fortunate time. By concentrating her efforts on those things she could do better than any other nation and trading internationally without erecting tariff barriers, a small island kingdom became a world power—perhaps *the* world power—for over a century. At the same time, she contributed to the economic development of the nation that was to succeed her as the leader of the free world.

THE RATIONALE FOR LAISSEZ FAIRE: SAY'S LAW

In this chapter and the one immediately preceding, we have referred repeatedly to the classicals' basic assumption that a free-market economy tends automatically to the full employment of labor and capital. If this tendency is automatic, it is a powerful argument for laissez faire, for even the best-intentioned interferences with the economy must then be at best useless and at worst disruptive. Now it is time to look at the rigorous statement of the basis for this belief. This hypothesis, *Say's law of markets,* bears the name of Jean Baptiste Say (1767–1832), who, though a Frenchman, belongs to the English School of classical economics.

Say was greatly inspired by Smith's *Wealth of Nations,* but this did not blind him to its deficiencies, among which lack of a system and internal inconsistencies were two of the most glaring. Say was the great popularizer of classical economics in at least two countries, his own and the United States. The English translation of his *Treatise on Political Economy* (1803) was for a long time the standard economics text in American colleges. But Say was far more than a rewrite man for Smith. In his *Treatise,* Say not only corrected a number of Smith's errors and created a system of economic thought but he contributed many new and valuable ideas of his own. For example, the common use of the French word "entrepreneur" instead of the English expression "enterpriser" is a tribute to Say's early recognition of this function as a unique productive factor.

How does a free-enterprise economy automatically tend to full employment, subject only to short-run aberrations? Suppose you are Smith's self-interested baker. You are a *specialist* in the sense that we used the word in international trade. You bake a few loaves for your own consumption, but the majority of your output is *surplus.* You bake bread to sell to nonspecialists in baking so that you can consume the products in which the nonbaking specialists specialize. Your very act of baking surplus bread constitutes your demand for the products of others. Similarly, the butcher and the brewer, from whose self-interests we expect our dinner, put their surplus goods on the market so that they can have the products of others. The only reason a producer furnishes a supply of goods is that he has a number of unfulfilled demands. So, if we assume that we have a three-man economy, the supply on the market of each producer's goods constitutes a demand for the products of the other producers. Thus, we have one form of Say's law, for which Say himself was not, however, responsible: *Supply creates its own demand.*

The implications of this simple statement are very important. Not only was this a basic premise of classical and neoclassical economics, but, as the theoretical economic justification for the politically motivated arguments for laissez faire, it blinded later economists to the causes underlying depressions in mature capitalistic economies.

What does it mean to say that supply creates its own demand? It means that *general* overproduction is impossible. Therefore, there is no basis for other than trivial and ephemeral unemployment, and depressions are impossible. Note very carefully that the kind of overproduction ruled out by Say's law is *general* overproduction. Say's law holds that there can never be an insufficiency of *aggregate* demand.

Say's law is most clearly seen in the context of a barter economy. Suppose, for example, the brewer decides to brew more ale. Let us assume throughout this example that additional resource supplies and new technology make it possible to move the production-possibility curve outward. The reason he decides to brew more ale is obvious: He wants more meat and bread. The increase in the supply of ale constitutes an increase in the demand for meat and bread. Assuming that the thirsts of the baker and the butcher can accommodate more ale, they will provide the brewer with more of their goods. An increase in the supply of ale, which, in essence, is an increase in the demand for bread and meat, has caused the total output of the economy to grow; for in meeting the increased demand of the brewer for more meat and bread, the butcher and the baker have had to increase their own outputs. Clearly, an increase in supply (of ale) has created its own increase in demand (for meat and bread). There is no glut; there is no unemployment; there is an increase in the gross national product.

But suppose the brewer has miscalculated. He has brewed too much ale. How do we know it is "too much"? Because it cannot be sold at the going price; the barter price of ale falls. This is the same as saying that the prices of meat and bread in terms of ale have risen. But does not the fact of "too much" ale indicate a glut? Yes, but a glut in ale *only*. Say's law does not rule out *particular* overproduction. There is no general overproduction. There still is an increased demand for meat and bread. If this were not so, the brewer would not have made more ale. In essence, the overproduction of a particular good (ale) is matched by the underproduction of other goods (meat and bread). The signal that meat and bread are underproduced is the rise in the price of each. Their prices would not have risen if there had been no shortage. With the overproduction of one good and the underproduction of everything else counterbalancing each other, there is no general glut. There is no force to lead to a general depression.

This does not mean that the economy is spared all the pains of readjustment. Since the prices of meat and bread have increased, profit-seeking businessmen will see that more of the economy's resources are applied to meat and bread production and fewer to brewing. The process followed is that of the Smithian invisible hand. Temporarily, there may be unemployment in brewing, but it is not the kind of unemployment that will precipitate a depression. Resources will simply move from brewing into baking and butchering, where new jobs will be available because of the expansion in the production of bread and meat.

Of course, there is nothing to prevent butchers from becoming over-exuberant and putting so much meat on the market that its price falls. But this new situation is exactly the same as the preceding one. There is no *general* overproduction. The overproduction of meat is offset by the necessary underproduction of other items. All that is needed is a simple readjustment of resources, and the economy will again move to a full-employment equilibrium. The importance of Say's hypothesis of the impossibiilty of a general glut (too much of everything) is that there are no forces in the economy capable of leading to a depression—that is, to the widespread and prolonged unemployment of resources.

All this is easy to see in a barter economy. After all, why would anyone brew ale over and above an amount sufficient to slake his own thirst, unless he intended to trade it for someone else's products? Even if we now admit saving (the abstension from consumption) into our analysis, the conclusion is the same. What happens to goods that, as a result of the desire of consumers to save, are not consumed? They constitute the wages fund, the stock of goods out of which workers are paid during the period of production. Since the classicals con-ceived of the wages fund as being the chief form of capital (capital necessarily being the wage goods on which the workers subsist), there could be a glut neither of goods nor of capital.

Next, admitting money into the analysis makes no difference either. The classicals, as we have noted before, were *real* theorists. They con-ducted most of their analysis, as we have, in real, or barter, terms. Re-garding money as a veil—as having no life of its own—they be-lieved that money could not affect the real variables in the system. Changes in the supply of money affect the *general* price level, but not the relative prices of particular goods. Suppose, in barter terms, one keg of ale exchanges for 100 pounds of sirloin or 500 loaves of bread. Then, with a given quantity of money in circulation, the price of each of these goods, in the units given, must be the same, say, $50. Now, sup-pose that the quantity of money is doubled. There will be a rise in the general price level. If prices double, the same quantity of ale, meat, or bread will cost $100, but one keg of ale will still exchange for 100 pounds of sirloin or 500 loaves of bread.

In the 1930's, John Maynard Keynes was to attack Say's law and the notion that money is passive as part of his explanation of the Great Depression, which the law and the then existing systems of analysis that were founded upon it held to be impossible. But long before Keynes, Thomas Malthus, in reasoning overshadowed by his population theory, rejected Say's law. Splitting with Ricardo over this matter, Malthus was convinced that there could be a general glut. Malthus' explanation is a form of the "oversaving" thesis, of which there are several.

Malthus believed that it was possible for capitalists to save too much, the result of which would be a decline in aggregate demand. Most of the classicals denied this, holding that what would be saved would be channeled into investment by the payment of interest, so what was saved by consumers would be spent by business firms. If interest rates are high, consumers will defer as much consumption as they can to lend their savings to businessmen. If interest rates are low, consumers will be less inclined to forego immediate consumption. The complete flexibility of prices and the interest rate assured the classicals that the practice of laissez faire would avoid a general glut and depressionary unemployment.

Malthus did not share this sanguine view because he thought he saw a maldistribution of income in Britain that created a wealthy class with a somewhat irrational propensity to save. Since wages tend to subsistence, the difference between wages and the total output of the economy, which is what accrues to landlords and capitalists, may be very large. Those who thus become wealthy may have some difficulty spending all their incomes. If this class now comes to think of saving as good in itself, regardless of the rate of interest, they may save more than the going rate of interest warrants, these "excess" savings then being applied to the accumulation of more capital than the economy can utilize. There will be excess capacity in the economy. The capital investment will turn out more goods than the economy can absorb. This does not mean that the problem of scarcity has been more than solved. The mass of the people still would like to have more goods, but they cannot afford them. There is a deficiency of aggregate demand. Goods go unsold; unwanted inventories accumulate; workers are discharged; and machines stand idle. Thus, said Malthus, we could have the depression ruled out by Say's law.

How can this be? The workers, whose purchases constitute the bulk of the aggregate demand, cannot buy all the goods they want because their wages tend to the subsistence level. The value of the goods placed on the market by their employers must equal the subsistence wage plus the employers' profits and the landlords' rents. Workers can only purchase, at most, a total value of goods equal to their subsistence wages. This leaves goods having a value equivalent to total profits and rents. Why do not the purchases of employers and landlords absorb the remaining goods? Because the employers and landlords do not want all those goods, they have become inordinate savers and will not spend all their incomes on the unsold goods, preferring to intensify the already grim result by adding still more productive capacity to an already troubled economy.

Did Malthus have an answer to this problem? Yes, but it was not nearly as satisfactory as that of Ricardo and the other classicals who put their faith in Say's law. Strangely, Malthus differed with Ricardo on the repeal of the Corn Laws. How could a man who predicted starvation for his fellows reasonably urge action that would keep grain scarce? Because, in the span of time before the natural checks took effect, Malthus had a useful role for the *rentiers* and other "nonproductive" persons to fill. Malthus followed the erroneous physiocratic and early classical practice of classifying certain occupations—such as those of physicians, lawyers, clergymen, and artists—as "unproductive." We know now that this is completely untenable. The test of the productivity of any occupation is whether it fills a human want. Today's economists are fully prepared to agree that man does not live by bread alone. The work of the clergyman and the artist are as fully productive as the work of the carpenter, and all productive activities add to the gross national product. These people, who Malthus believed produced nothing, added nothing to the flow of goods, could solve the glut problem by using their incomes to buy that portion of the output that would otherwise go unsold. There is an echo of Mandeville in this idea, and, later, we will see what some people thought were echoes of both Mandeville and Mathus in the work of John Maynard Keynes.

Malthus' theory of the possibility of a general glut did not become a part of the great body of classical and neoclassical economic thought. Rather, the mainstream of economic thought was guided by Say's law, following a course that, for a time, was probably wise enough. Before large-scale industrial capitalism became dominant, the economics of David Ricardo, with subsequent modifications and corrections, was highly useful. It was not until the 1920's and '30's that this closely reasoned system was to run into real trouble. Then, Say's law, the fundamental premise of the classical system, was called into question. How could a useful economics be deduced from a faulty postulate? Among the tasks to face the economists of the '30's was the necessity of investigating the validity of Say's law and the need to construct a new economics if, in whole or in part, it could no longer be regarded as tenable.

KARL MARX:
A TRADITIONALIST
WHO BROKE
WITH TRADITION

5

"A specter is haunting Europe—the specter of communism." So Karl Marx and Friedrich Engels ominously announced in 1848 in the *Manifesto of the Communist Party*,[1] and today that specter haunts not only Europe but the world. The word "specter" is well chosen, for Marxian communism, like all phantoms, does not exist. Communists are indeed real, but communism is not. Marx himself (1818–83) had great reservations about the chances for the creation of a communist society. Why then are he and his progeny so hated and feared by so many? This is a question we shall explore in the present chapter by considering the two main parts of Marxism: the Marxian *economics* that has occasioned fear and contempt in anti-Marxians and the less understood, more nebulous, Marxian *vision*. It will be well to keep this distinction in mind.

The end of the *Manifesto* is a good springboard into the study of Marxism. These are the lines that have awakened hope in some and loathing in others: "Let the ruling classes tremble at a communist revolution. The proletarians have nothing to lose but their chains. They have a world to win. WORKINGMEN OF ALL COUNTRIES, UNITE!" What thoughts and events stand behind this dramatic call to arm for class warfare?

[1] The English edition appeared in 1888.

INDUSTRIALISM AND CAPITALISM

History reveals that industrialization is a trying experience for human beings, and, the more rapidly industrialization proceeds, the more are people tried. Ironically, the postrevolutionary history of the Soviet Union is the best example of this historical lesson. The wearisome experiences of past industrialization have led some peoples in underdeveloped areas to shun it. On the other hand, with aggravating but understandable inconsistency, many underdeveloped nations now demand the fruits of industrialization while refusing to pay the price. The educated among them have read the record of what happened to the ordinary man in England during the Industrial Revolution, and many are aware of the hardships of Russia's agonizing industrialization. Whatever the case, the underdeveloped nations in general are sure that there must be a better way to national wealth.

In the search for this better way, many people have tended to confuse industrialism with capitalism. The two are not identical. *Industrialization* is the social and technological process of moving from a principally agricultural economy based on manual labor and small economic units to an economy that uses machines, mass-production techniques, and large-scale economic organization. *Capitalism* is one *way* of effectuating the process; socialism is another. Both ways have been tried, and, as we know, both have been difficult experiences.

Industrialization *is* unpleasant because it is severely dislocating. It makes obsolete old and respected skills. It forces people to move from the country to cities that are ill-prepared to receive them. This is still happening; witness the continual migration of displaced Negroes from the rural South to the urban North in the United States. Although England can be forgiven for much of the hardship that occurred there, since she had no previous encounters with industrialization upon which to draw, many practices of the early industrial era do seem inexcusable to us. There is no denying that hours were long, that women and children were ill-used, that workers were forced to live under conditions that might have been tolerable in the country but meant filth, decay, disease, and death in the city.

It would seem that the process of industrialization ought not to be as painful for underdeveloped areas today as it was for England, for now men know what it is like to live with an industrial system and have developed a greater social awareness of the needs of the individual worker. The mistakes of the past need not be repeated, but the dislocating effects of the transition from a rural, agricultural, handicraft-based society to an urban, industrial economy will be present even if attenuated.

MARX ON CAPITALISM AND SOCIALISM

Karl Marx was convinced that the road to national wealth is rocky. A political refugee from his native Germany, Marx lived in England during the period of tremendous industrial expansion and was deeply impressed with the misery and degradation of the English working class. A confirmed radical, he blamed the ills of industrial society upon the *economic system* of capitalism, rather than on the process of industrialization. Private ownership of the means of production, said Marx, inescapably causes man's inhumanity to his own kind. He argued that capitalism is so faulty that not only must it lead to the destruction of the lives of workers but it is inexorably suicidal; in the end it must, by its very nature, destroy itself.

Marx did not despise industrialism; he glorified it. He felt that the techniques of mass production offered the only basis for a better life for the vast majority of individuals. As a self-professed materialist, he, unlike many social reformers, did not advocate retreating to the simpler life of the preindustrial era. The *basic* fault of the industrial system, Marx believed, was not in forced urbanization, in the cultural lags that accompany an advancing technology, or in factory life but solely in the private ownership of things—plant and equipment—that make other things. He preached that under socialism (that is, the ownership of the means of production by the workers themselves) the imperfections of capitalism would not exist to impair the functioning of the industrial order.

But Marx did not think that *any* socialist system is viable; he insisted that the only true and workable socialism was his own. There have been many socialists before and after Marx, and for those who did not accept him as master Marx had only scathing denunciation. He called them utopian dreamers and asserted that because their work was "unscientific," they proposed plans that were, if anything, more faulty than capitalism itself. The difference between Marx and all other socialists is that Marx (according to Marx) had discovered the *true* principles of economic development. He alone was scientific, and non-Marxian socialist thinkers were at best muddleheaded social reformers and at worst charlatans. Nothing but more disappointment and despair for the working class could come of their pathetic schemes.

Marx had a versatile intellect, and he pursued with varying degrees of success the occupations of economist, historian, philosopher, sociologist, journalist, prophet, and revolutionary. Although none of his activities is completely separable from the others, we shall, in the first part of this chapter, focus on the work of Marx the economist.

THE MARXIAN ECONOMICS OF CAPITALISM

It may come as a surprise to some students that Marxian *economics* is not concerned with socialism at all; it is about capitalism. Marx was not only an economist of capitalism but a faithful classical economist. His economics is in the analytical tradition of three stalwart defenders of the capitalist order—Adam Smith, Thomas Malthus, and, particularly, David Ricardo. How can we legitimately call Marx a classical economist, even though the "orthodox" classicals would have had only distaste for his theories? Because Marx was a thorough student of the classicals. Because, in expounding his theory in *Capital* ("Das Kapital"), he used the tools, the concepts, and the theoretical constructs of classical economics.

Because he was a good classical economist, Marx knew better than to write a theory of something that did not exist—that is, an economics of socialism. Although he did produce a *vision* of ideally functioning "socialist" and "communist" economies[2] (which leaves him open to the charge of being as wildly visionary as the well-meaning dreamers on whom he poured forth his opprobrium), in his economic theorizing Marx confined himself to the subject of capitalist economic development. His theory does have a twist—in contradistinction to the work of his companion classical economists, Marx produced a theory of how capitalism does *not* work. But it is a theory of capitalism nonetheless.

Marx's strict classicalism left him open to attack in two areas. First, he was so steeped in classical economic literature that his mind could not accommodate subsequent changes in economic analysis. When Marx was writing *Capital,* a number of other economists, with the

[2] These two terms are not interchangeable in strict Marxian usage, as we will see later.

notable exception of John Stuart Mill, were already discarding much of strict classical analysis for more fruitful methods of studying the economy. Marx remained, almost alone, a prisoner of unregenerate Ricardian economics. Second, Marx was such a devoted disciple of the classicals that he was eventually forced to contradict himself. Some of his theorizing is inconsistent with classical analysis, and he himself knew that it was. When it came to a showdown, as it did in the last volume of *Capital*, Marx repudiated his own thesis rather than abandon the faith of Smith, Ricardo, and Mill.

Capital

Marx expounded his theory of capitalism in his tersely and appropriately entitled work, *Capital*. Marx began writing this earth-shaking three-volume book in 1851. Volume I did not appear until 1867, and the author did not live to see the remaining volumes published. After his death, his collaborator and old friend, Friedrich Engels, edited Marx's massive notes. By doing a considerable amount of fresh writing himself, for which he took little credit, he brought Volumes II and III to completion, the former in 1885 and the latter in 1894.

The Marxian theory expounded in *Capital* consists of three main elements: (1) a theory of capitalist economic development, (2) a materialistic economic interpretation of historical causation, and (3) a thesis of social revolution.

THE MARXIAN LABOR THEORY OF VALUE

Marx's chief intellectual debt to the classicals was for their labor theory of value. The labor theory of value is the basis of Marx's economic analysis of capitalism, for it is essential to his explanation of how capitalists exploit the working class.

Although the labor theory of value troubled Marx (and some economists have contended that Marxian economics is improved by eliminating it), he clung to it. Despite all the trouble it caused him, it was essential to the conclusion he wanted to reach—namely, that only laborers have a right to share in the income of society and that when they are prevented from having all the social product, they are the victims of expropriation. This conclusion had embarrassed Ricardo and the other classicals, but it was the core of Marx's thesis.

Under capitalism, said Marx, there are two classes of people: those who have property and those who do not. ("Property" should be interpreted as capital. The workers' ownership of personal property has no significant economic consequence here.) The propertied are the capitalists, and the propertyless are the workers. But labor creates all wealth. Capitalists add nothing to the total wealth of an economy. They are worse than useless; they are parasites living off the efforts of others.

Utility

Marx knew that the old, bald labor theory of value was hopeless, so he reworked it. Let us look at some of the problems he faced to see how he attempted to solve them. Suppose you set up a firm to produce hats for cats, but no single cat owner ever bought one. Would Marx insist that you be allowed to trade a cat hat for any other good embodying an equal quantity of labor? This question is not an empty one; some utopian socialists have been this foolish. In a few actual experiments in utopian socialism (often financed by wealthy but reform-conscious individuals), a worker could produce whatever he wanted. For example, he could sit at home and spend ten hours making a cat hat, and when he had finished it he could bring it to a central warehouse, where he would be given a labor certificate for ten hours of labor. He could exchange this certificate for anything else containing up to ten hours of labor, and that something else could well be more worthwhile than a cat hat. Obviously, such experiments in socialism failed, and Marx was probably more derisive of these experimenters and their efforts than many capitalists would be.

To prevent occurrences as foolish as the cat-hat example, Marx modified the labor theory of value to say that goods must be wanted—that is, they must possess *utility*. In this, he did no more than Ricardo and some other classicals, who knew that a good must have utility for it to be valuable. Marx's treatment of utility is consistent with classical theorizing and, like the classicals', his explanation is wholly inadequate. No sooner did the classicals show some insight into the idea of utility than they backed away from it. The varying amounts of utility that different goods might possess did not matter. Once they were satisfied that a good had utility (no critical level was specified), its value was determined by its cost of production. So with Marx. What they all missed is that goods can obviously possess different amounts of utility and that the value of those goods will vary accordingly. More importantly, they did not consider that units of the same good consumed in succession will not add to a consumer's satisfaction at an unvarying rate. If the classicals had thought about this, they could have solved Smith's "Diamond-Water Paradox." [3]

Homogeneous Labor Units

Another problem in using amounts of labor time as a standard of value involves the varying *quality* of labor. Not all workers are alike. Suppose we have two firms making an identical product. One firm employs vigorous young college students, while the other hires the inhabitants of a senior-citizens center. The firm employing the residents of Retirement Village takes, say, three times as long to produce a given quantity of output as does the firm using college students because the senior citizens are slower, get sicker oftener, and cannot work as long at a time. Under the labor theory of value, is not the firm using the oldsters smarter than the one employing the college students? The amount of labor time in a unit of output produced by the oldsters' firm is triple the amount in the same quantity of output produced by the collegians. Therefore, is not the output of the "senior" company three times as valuable as the same output of the "junior" firm?

Marx avoided an absurd answer to this question by reducing labor to homogeneous units of labor time. He made the elemental unit the amount of work done by a worker of average, or representative, skill in a certain amount of time. Therefore, the more highly skilled, stronger, or faster laborer possesses more labor units (and the inefficient laborer fewer) than the average worker. Thus, each unit of output is of the same value, whether it is produced by the elderly people or by the college students, for its worth is determined by the labor time that a worker of average skill would spend making it.

Machinery and Technology

The problem posed by the use of capital is answered in a similar way. If two plants are producing identical automobiles but one uses hand labor and the other uses today's methods, it is evident that

---

[3] We take up the resolution of this vexing problem in Chapter 6.

there will be more labor time embodied in the hand-built cars than in the mass-produced ones. Unless the labor theory of value is amended, the hand-built car, although identical in every way to the mass-produced model, should be more valuable. Marx avoided this untenable result by stating that for products to exchange at the value of the labor time embodied in them, the generally prevailing level of technology must be used. The value of a firm's product will not be enhanced if it uses hand labor in processes for which machine labor could be substituted.

The "Socially Necessary" Labor Theory of Value

We now have the three important elements in Marx's revision of the labor theory of value: First, the goods produced must be wanted (although Marx did not consider the variation in the intensity of a want as additional units of a good are consumed). Second, the unit of labor time used in measuring the value of goods is an abstract, homogeneous unit based on the work of a representative laborer of ordinary skill. And third, the latest available technology must be used in production. Marx called his refined labor theory of value the *socially necessary* labor theory of value.

THE THEORY OF SURPLUS VALUE

Given the conditions of the socially necessary labor theory of value, all goods exchange at the value of the labor time embodied in them. If that is so, how can there be any surplus left over for the capitalists to exploit? In order to see how the capitalists can live upon—prey upon—the earnings of labor, we must consider the Marxian formula for the value of goods.

The Value Equation

Marx contended that the value of a given good depends on three separate elements: variable capital, constant capital, and surplus value. We may write this as an equation:

$$V = v + c + s$$

(V is the value of a good; v is the amount of variable capital embodied in it; c is the value of constant capital transferred to it; and s is surplus value.)

VARIABLE CAPITAL. "Variable capital" is Marx's expression for labor time, so the lower-case *v* stands for the value of the labor time used in producing a good. At this point, it may appear that the equation contradicts Marx's argument that the value of a good is determined solely by the amount of socially necessary labor time in it, for in the formula two other components enter into the value of a good. Let us look at them.

CONSTANT CAPITAL. "Constant capital" is the name Marx gave to what we call capital. As plant and equipment are employed to produce an output, they are used up. This idea is not peculiar to Marxian economics; it is a truism recognized in accounting procedures and evidenced in the accounting records of firms under the item "depreciation." The value of the equipment used up in the production of other items must be part of the value of the finished goods. For example, suppose that a firm buys a printing press for $10,000 and that the press will have a useful life of ten years; then, on the average, the machine is used up—depreciates—at the rate of $1,000 per year. In order to recover the cost of the machine, its owner must add its value (or cost) to the value (or price) of the output produced during the working life of the press. Therefore, Marx's usage conforms to our usage.

But does not the act of providing the machine entitle its owner—a capitalist—to a reward? According to the orthodox theories of capitalism it does, but not according to Marxian analysis. To grasp Marx's position, recall the original labor-theory-of-value argument. How did the machine get *its* value in the first place? Just like everything else— from the amount of socially necessary labor embodied in it. It is labor that gave the machine its value; and, therefore, it is laborers, not capitalists, who should have the reward for supplying the press. When the laborers built the press, they were not simply making a piece of printing equipment; they were helping to make a final future output—the printed material that would be run off at some later date. The workers who made the press were *storing up* the value of their labors to be released whenever printed material came off the press. Consequently, according to Marx, the printing press, or any item of capital, is "stored up," "congealed," or "crystallized" labor.

Up to this point in our discussion, labor is still the only item contributing value to production: the *present* labor of the variable capital (in our example, the printers) and the *past* labor of constant capital (the workers who made the press).

SURPLUS VALUE. We are now left with the final element in the Marxian equation, surplus value. The expression "surplus value," considering the classical use of the term "surplus," suggests that there is something spurious about this element. It is "surplus"; hence it is not needed. Surplus value is that part of the total value of a good that, under capitalism, is taken by the capitalists. Capitalists live on part of the surplus value, using what they do not spend on consumer goods to buy the plant and equipment required for the productive process. Did Marx stumble into an inconsistency here? He admitted that capitalists save part of their incomes to buy the goods used in production. Should not this fact, recognized by Marxians and non-Marxians alike, entitle capitalists to a reward? No, said Marx, the mere act of buying the plant and equipment of the economy does not entitle capitalists to anything. After all, plant and equipment are congealed labor; therefore, the recompense for their use should go to laborers. The status of ownership does not entitle capitalists to a reward, for the way capitalists come into the possession of plant and equipment is by theft. They expropriate it from its "true" creators and owners, the members of the laboring class.

Capitalist Expropriation

The real task of Marxian economics is now clear: to explain how capitalists exploit laborers. This is equivalent to showing how surplus value is created. Since the basic premise of Marx's argument is that labor is the source of all value, labor must create surplus value. To explain how laborers create surplus value and how capitalists take it away from them, we must look to Marx the historian.

According to Marx, in a primitive, precapitalist society, goods exchange at their respective values, and expropriation cannot be a problem. Expropriation becomes possible only when the economy uses money. However, in a more advanced but still noncapitalist economy (for example, feudalism), money may be used without the possibility of expropriation. Goods are exchanged for money, and then the money is exchanged for some more goods. In this instance, goods still exchange on the basis of their true, or labor, values.

In capitalism, the mode of production, to use the Marxian expression, is vastly different from that of all earlier forms of economic organization. The productive process is so complicated that individual craftsmen and workers cannot finance it. The period of production is lengthened. The methods used are "roundabout," that is, in contrast to the individual craftsman who undertakes the making of a specific good from start to finish, many seemingly unrelated workers, plants, managers, and firms are combined to produce a final good. In a capitalist economy it may be a long time before the ultimate good is sold, and in the meantime all these apparently unrelated workers must subsist. Capitalists, as we saw in the preceding chapter, make subsistence advances (from the wages fund) to laborers in the interval between the time the workers render their services and the time the final good is sold to the ultimate consumer. Therefore, Marx reasoned, in a capitalist economy, the money-goods cycle is rearranged. First, capitalists advance money to laborers to tide the latter over the period of production; the workers produce the goods to be sold for money; the capitalists collect the money; and so the process repeats itself.

Let us sum up the cycles associated with the three fundamentally different historical periods:

1. Primitive barter economy: $G_1 \rightleftarrows G_2$, where G_1 and G_2 are two different goods. Goods exchange directly for goods. Obviously, $G_1 = G_2$ in value. If G_1 embodied twice as much socially necessary labor time as does G_2, then our representation would be: $G_1 \rightleftarrows 2\ G_2$.

2. Precapitalist, money-using economy: $G_1 \rightarrow M \rightarrow G_2$. Goods are exchanged for money, which is exchanged in turn for other goods. Again, the value of $G_1 = G_2$. We know that each good embodies equal amounts of socially necessary labor time.

3. Capitalist economy: $M_1 \rightarrow G \rightarrow M_2$. Capitalists advance a sum of money, M_1, to the workers who produce G goods. The goods are then sold by the capitalists for the sum M_2. Out of M_2, the capitalists make the next round of advances to the workers. The process repeats itself continuously.

No sensible person would advance another a sum of money to receive back only the same sum. The original sum might as well have been kept in the first place. Thus, a self-interested capitalist will not advance workers wages to produce goods that he can sell at a total revenue that just equals the workers' wages. There is no

profit, or surplus value, in that; and profit is the mainspring of capitalist enterprise. Capitalists want back an amount larger than that
with which they began the process. Therefore, M_2, the amount for
which a capitalist sells the goods produced by his workers, is larger
than M_1, the sum of money that he advanced to them. The difference
between the initial amount he advanced to the workers and the amount
he receives from his customers is surplus value. We may express this
as

$$s = M_2 - M_1$$

The Marxian value equation may now be rewritten:

$$V = v + c + (M_2 - M_1)$$

The Iron Law of Wages and the Cost of Production Theory

We now understand the process by which surplus value is created,
but what is important is why it happens. What makes this process
possible? How can capitalists force workers to produce goods having a
certain total value (the total value being the value of the labor
power embodied in them) and then withhold part of that value from
the laborers? This withheld portion is the income (surplus value) of
the capitalists.

The creation of surplus value is explained, in part, by the so-called
iron law of wages. This law is simply a name for the theory that
wages tend to a subsistence minimum. Malthus held that this tendency
would occur because of the increasing pressure of population. Marx
accepted Malthus' conclusion but not his biological premise, rejecting
the latter as a slur upon the common sense of the working class.

Marx's argument is completely economic. The only thing of value
that the laboring class has to sell is its labor power. What determines
the value of labor power? The value of the labor time necessary to
produce (or reproduce) the labor power itself. In other words, the
value of labor power is the value of the means of subsistence of the
laboring class.[4] What a man's labor power is worth on the market
is the value of the things he and his family must have to live at the
subsistence level. This is the *market value* of the labor power of a

[4] "Subsistence," as we have noted before, is an imprecise concept; it varies from
place to place, time to time, and culture to culture. It is the amount of goods
and services necessary to maintain and reproduce the labor force required by a
viable economy.

laborer—the market, or exchange, value of the one thing a laborer has to sell.

And the laborer does receive exactly what his labor power is worth in terms of its cost of production. Marx did not accuse capitalists of trying to gouge workers by paying them less than the going market rate. Marx, in common with the other classical economists, assumed a highly competitive capitalistic economy.

Since, according to classical theory, competition forces the prices of all commodities down until the price equals the cost of production and forces buyers to pay the same prices for the same goods, employers *must* pay workers the market (subsistence) rate. Suppose that the subsistence requirements of a laborer and his family amount to $8 per day. Then that is what his labor power is worth on the labor market, and that is what he *will be* paid. (Marx never claimed that under capitalism the worker is a slave. He is free; but he is free, Marx wryly noted, to sell his labor power at the going wage to whomever he wishes or to starve.)

If, as Marx and the classicals insisted, all commodities, including labor, exchange at their values, and *if* the employed worker receives the full value of his labor power from his employer, how, then, can he be a victim of capitalist expropriation? Perhaps he is not. Perhaps, instead of paying the worker less than his value, the seller charges the *consumer* more for the good than it is worth. But Marx did not allege that capitalists expropriate their profits from their customers. Obviously, this, too, would violate the precept that goods exchange at their true values. We must, therefore, search elsewhere for the source of surplus value.

Marx found that source, in part, by preserving the classicals' invalid distinction between value in use and value in exchange. The worker, as a propertyless human being, has only his own labor power to sell. He sells it to the capitalist for its *exchange* value—its cost of production. But is that all the capitalist gets in return for paying the going wage rate? No, contended Marx. The employer pays for the *exchange* value of labor power, but he gets the *use* value for his outlay. And the exchange value of the goods he sells is determined by the *use* value of the labor embodied in them. Moreover, the use value of labor power is necessarily greater than its exchange value (that is, labor can always produce more than what it needs for its subsistence).

How does the employer extract this greater use value from the labor power he has bought at its exchange value? He forces the laborer to produce more value than the value of his own subsistence. We assumed earlier that the going wage rate—the cost of the worker's subsistence—is $8 per day. It will take the worker a certain length of time each day to turn out a product equal in value to his wage. Suppose that time is six hours. But there is no necessity for the working day to be six hours. Why shouldn't it be twelve hours? The working day would be six hours if the worker could determine its length, but he cannot. He is in no position to dictate the terms of his employment.

Capitalists operate in a buyers' market because they have a unique monopoly; they own the economy's productive equipment. Private ownership of the means of production is, according to Marx, the root of capitalistic expropriation. Denied access to capital, the workers can produce nothing. So they must work on the capitalists' terms or join the pitiful "reserve army of the unemployed." And what are the capitalists' terms? That the workers put in more than a "necessary" working day; that they remain at their benches for a "surplus" working day. In this lengthened day, they produce *surplus value* for their capitalist-employers.

Suppose the working day is twelve hours. In the first six hours, the worker produces goods having an exchange value of $8. He has earned his wage. In the remaining six hours, he produces goods also having an exchange value of $8. At the end of the twelve-hour working day, his efforts have created goods having a total exchange value of $16.[5] But the worker does not receive $16 in exchange for the equivalent value that he has created. The capitalist withholds $8 from the sale of the goods and expropriates it. This $8 taken by the capitalist is *surplus value*. The worker has been expropriated although he has been paid the full market (exchange) value of his services. In other words, surplus value is the difference between the use value of labor power and its exchange value. Therefore, Marx's basic classical premise that all goods exchange at their values is maintained intact even though there is a discrepancy between the exchange value of a worker's labor power and the exchange value of the goods the worker's labor power has created.

[5] Remember that the exchange value of the goods a worker produces is determined by the *use* value, not the exchange value, of his labor.

Marx attributed the existence of this discrepancy to the capitalist mode of production. In a capitalist economy, there are two classes: those who have property in the form of the means of production and those who do not. By definition, the former are capitalists and the latter are workers. Production requires the use of both capital and labor; neither is of any value without the other. Without capital, the worker is helpless. He and his family must eat, and so he must work. Capitalists also need workers; but there is a shortage of capital relative to the number of people who would like to combine their labor power with it, and capitalists have a monopoly of the capital. Therefore, the capitalists have the upper hand. The worker can command his exchange value in the market, but the difference between what he is paid and the exchangeable value he creates will be taken by his employer.

If capitalists can withhold the means of production from workers, could workers not withhold their labor services from the capitalists? Marx dismissed this possibility so long as the capitalist mode of production exists. The state is the instrument of the capitalists, Marx held, and the state will not permit the workers to organize. Unorganized workers have no power. They have nothing to tide them over should they refuse to work on the capitalists' terms. On the other hand, the capitalists can afford to wait. A work stoppage, or the threat of one, would be only a minor inconvenience. In the unlikely event that a strike brings work to a complete halt, the capitalists have the resources to sit it out. The workers do not. Their daily wages just cover subsistence. And the capitalists have an unintentional but powerful ally, the reserve army of the unemployed. The presence of this grim brigade helps to keep employed workers docile. Outside the factory gates are numerous people willing to take the place of any worker who feels inclined not to pay the capitalists' price for a place at the workbench.

This is why Marx demanded *social* ownership of the means of production. Labor is the source of all value. The institution of private property permits capitalists to dichotomize the exchange and use values of labor power to their advantage. If the expropriators could be expropriated, the workers would own the means of production themselves, and the exchange and use values of their services would be equal. In short, the surplus value now appropriated by capitalists would go to the workers themselves.

Marx never attributed any evil intents to capitalists. Capitalists are just as much prisoners of the system as are workers; they may not wish to exploit workers at all, but they are driven to it. Capitalism, as Marx and many non-Marxians agree, is a fiercely competitive system. Any capitalist who tries to avoid exploiting his workers will be bankrupted, since classical economic theory holds that the costs of production are driven down to the lowest point consistent with production. Anything that raises the costs of production, such as paying wages higher than the going rate, will cause a firm to suffer losses, and these losses eventually will destroy the firm.

These are the basics of Marx's economic analysis of capitalism. We shall now turn to Marxian dynamics, that part of Marx's work in which he predicted the *inevitable* downfall of capitalism.

DIALECTICAL MATERIALISM

Philosophy and History

The future Marx predicted for the capitalist system involves Marxian economics, Marx's theory of history, and Marxian philosophy.

When Marx was a university student in Germany, he studied under the great philosopher G. W. F. Hegel. Hegel is renowned for his dialectical method, roughly summed up as "thesis, antithesis, and synthesis." Although Marx was Hegelian in method, his approach to understanding reality is an inversion of Hegel's, for Hegel said that the most fundamental things in the universe are ideas—hence the expression "dialectical idealism." Not so, said Marx; the most fundamental thing in life is economic reality, specifically the mode of production. Therefore, the philosophical basis of Marx's interpretation of history is dialectical *materialism*. In this process, the thesis (for example, a primitive economy) develops within it a number of contradictory elements (perhaps the evolution of money and the development of trade). The contradictions grow in number and intensity producing an "anti-thesis" or antithesis. The thesis and the antithesis cannot coexist. Eventually, the two yield a synthesis—a new stage in history (for example, feudalism). The synthesis then becomes a thesis, since the synthesis itself (in our example, feudalism) contains contradictions, and the process will repeat itself. Repetition of the process is assured until a synthesis is reached that possesses no internal contradictions.

Elements of Marxian Historiography

There are four major elements in the Marxian theory of historical development: (1) the economic structure of a society; (2) its noneconomic superstructure; (3) the dialectical interrelationships between the structure and the superstructure, which impel society forward; and (4) the philosophical analysis that attempts to explain the dialectical process of historical change or progress.

STRUCTURE.   The structure of a society is the base on which a society is founded. Marx's most important contention is that the structure is purely economic—hence, his theory that history is economically determined. The structure has two components: the forces of production and the social relations of production. The forces of production are somewhat similar to the factors of production of orthodox economics; they are all the elements directly affecting the production of goods—essentially, the technology and resources (both natural and human). The social relations of production are the institutional arrangements by which a particular society organizes itself for production. For example, in capitalism the social relations of production are private property, the monetary system, the market process, and so forth.

THE SUPERSTRUCTURE.   The superstructure is a catchall; it comprises everything not specifically assigned to the structure. On the economic base, or structure, a society erects its religions, family life, arts, customs, laws, sciences, philosophies—indeed, all its ideas, economic and noneconomic. Thus, the ideas of Karl Marx are themselves part of the superstructure of capitalist society and are therefore founded upon its economic structure.

The structure of a society, Marx held, is more flexible than its superstructure. His evidence is that history shows a number of changes in the mode of production. Since primitive times, several different modes of production have developed: the self-sufficient family unit or clan of the cavemen, the slave-master, serf-lord, and now, in our own time, proletarian-capitalist modes of production. When the mode of production changes, forces are released that alter the nature and organization of a society.

THE DIALECTICAL PROCESS.   Social institutions, conventions, and ideas change slowly, and when they do the changes cause dislocation and pain. Generally, Marx held, the flow of historical causation is from the structure to the superstructure; however, he did not rule out the possibility of some reverse current. In most instances, the superstructure must adapt itself to changes occurring in the structure. Changes in the mode of production cause inconsistencies, or *contradictions,* to develop in the superstructure. These contradictions develop into stresses that are cumulative and eventually become unendurable. The old superstructure crumbles, and a new one is built. Changes in the structure cause the indefinable historical process known as "progress." [6] The contradictions combine to form the antithesis, which faces the thesis (the old economic system); and, when these contradictions have become so powerful that they force the superstructure to change, a new synthesis has appeared in the historical process.

The Marxian theory of historical causation holds that all social arrangements are transitory. Just as feudalism gave way to capitalism, so, argued Marx, capitalism must give way to something else. For example, feudalism came to an end as the emergence of modern industrial technology, the opening of trade routes, the institution of private property, and the mobilization of financial resources combined to produce a change in the structure. While these changes occurred in the structure, the superstructure remained relatively rigid. The old feudalistic social institutions, customs, and beliefs acted as fetters on the mode of production. But the burgeoning forces in the structure became too powerful for the moribund superstructure, and a social revolution ensued, culminating in the economic system Marx called capitalism. Similarly, Marx prophesied, capitalism will pass as contradictions develop within it. Let us look at the contradictions Marx saw in the capitalist order.

Classical economics depicts capitalism as an extremely competitive and progressive system in which the capitalist-entrepreneur is motivated by his hope of profits. Marx agreed with this picture. In fact, in the expansionary, premonopolistic phase of capitalism, Marx's conception of the system at its worst is more competitive than our present economic system. According to both classical and Marxian economics, capitalists must use the latest equipment and techniques in production or their lower-cost competitors will force them out of business. But Marxian

---

[6] For Marxian historians, defining progress is easy. Progress means simply moving from one mode of production to the next in a sequence leading from the primitive economy through capitalism to ideal communism.

economics holds in addition that capitalists can realize nothing upon their investment in plant and equipment, because such constant capital adds only its own value to final output. The capitalist rendered full value for the machine when he bought it, so it is impossible for him to extract more value out of it than it is worth. Capitalists can get income in only one way: by exploiting workers.

THE INEVITABLE END OF CAPITALISM

As capitalists sell more and more goods—as the capitalist economy grows —they must have more labor with which to produce these goods. But, as their demand for labor increases, they may reduce, perhaps eliminate, the reserve army of the unemployed. Without the presence of a sizable reserve army to hold down wages, wages will rise. They may rise well above subsistence levels, and the workers will enjoy a measure of affluence. All this is transitory, however. The increase in wages squeezes the capitalists' profits, and capitalists look for a way out.[7] They seek relief in mechanization. They buy more constant capital in hopes of replacing high-cost labor with lower-cost machinery.

Marx readily admitted that the capitalist system does have a built-in mechanism to assure that the latest industrial technology will be used. However, replacing workers with machines solves one problem only to create others. First, as the workers are sent out of the plants to rejoin the reserve army of the unemployed, wages will fall back toward the subsistence level. The capitalists have succeeded in cutting their wage costs, but this blessing has an accompanying curse. Who buys the bulk of the capitalists' products? The triumph of capitalism is mass production; and it produces goods for the masses. But unemployed, impoverished workers cannot contribute much purchasing power to the economy.[8] Second, the labor theory of value and the theory of surplus value show that capitalists gain their incomes by exploiting laborers. They cannot expropriate the product of machines. Constant capital adds only its own value to a capitalist's output, and he paid the full value for it when he bought it. Another contradiction, named by

---

[7] Marx dismissed the possibility of both profits and wages rising together—the situation in which the *proportionate* share going to each class remains constant but the *absolute* amounts both increase. That is, he did not foresee that a rise in productivity *per capita* might result in more for everybody.

[8] See Chapter 4, p. 109.

Marx "the law of the falling tendency of the rate of profit," is forming. This "law" holds that as capitalists replace workers with machines to reduce their costs and retain their competitive positions, they are concurrently reducing the base from which they derive their incomes.

Capitalists face another dilemma. If they do not maintain a sizable reserve army of unemployed workers, their profits will be squeezed. To remain competitive, and in business, they must substitute capital for labor. But, in substituting machines for workers, they diminish their own possibilities for exploitation. How do capitalists attempt to meet this dilemma (a Marxian "contradiction")? They force the remaining workers to produce more surplus value. A given amount of workers can produce more surplus value if they are compelled to work longer, if the work flow is speeded up, or if cheaper workers—workers who have less value in exchange, such as women and children—are used.

The Cyclical End

In Marx's system, these events lead to the demise of capitalism. Capitalism does not fall in domino fashion, with the first business failure leading to the successive collapse of other firms until the entire system lies in ruins. Death comes in spasms; capitalism approaches its end in a cyclical pattern. The membership of the reserve army rises and falls. When capitalism begins to decay, there will still be upward turns in the cycle. Workers will be put to work; wages will rise; the economy will exhibit all the outward signs of prosperity. Inwardly, however, the contradictory death forces continue to work. The cycle must turn downward, for capitalists, caught by higher wage costs, look to new capital innovations to replace workers. The resulting unemployment causes total purchasing power to fall. Eventually, when purchases must be made to sustain life, and when wages have fallen so low that it becomes worthwhile for capitalists to put the unemployed back on the payroll, the cycle will start upward once more.

The cycles are not even. As capitalism rocks toward its doom, their amplitude increases. The peaks become higher and are marked by irresponsible optimism; the troughs become deeper and are characterized by greater despair. Capitalism, Marx believed, is inherently unstable, and its instability is progressive.

A glance at economic history shows some basis for Marx's prophecy. Most economists agree that economic fluctuations *are* a capitalistic phenomenon. For a long time, many believed that cycles were an inescapable accompaniment of capitalism. In addition, in advanced capitalist nations cycles did increase observably in amplitude. The economic history of the United States exhibits this pattern. Nearly every thirty years, up to 1940, the United States experienced a major depression, bringing economic ruin to many persons and firms. In between there were booms, and it seemed that the higher the boom, the worse the depression that *inevitably* followed. The process culminated in 1929, when, after an unprecedented spiraling boom, the economy broke down almost totally, and the United States experienced a depression that lasted until its commitment to the Allied side in the Second World War. During this intensely troubled period, there were in this country many conversions to Marxism as well as to non-Marxist socialist schemes, and a good many people in every status of life sincerely doubted the ability of the capitalist economy to recover.

As we know now, however, the Great Crash was not the death knell of capitalism. Since the end of the Second World War, we have had some minor downturns; but there have been no economic experiences remotely approaching the Crash of 1929 or the regularly spaced panics that were once a regrettably familiar part of American life. On the contrary, not only the United States but all the nations of the West—capitalistic nations—have experienced continued economic growth and affluence. The historical record that once supported Karl Marx seems to have been severely shaken, if not destroyed. Have economic cycles been tamed or perhaps even eliminated? The possible reasons for the post-war record of the West will be discussed in Chapter 7. For now, let it suffice to say that we know more economics than did Marx and his contemporaries.

Decadent Capitalism

Whatever we now know and are willing to do to prevent economic fluctuations from destroying us, Marx appears to have been on fairly firm ground in his time when he predicted that cyclical fluctuations would continually worsen. As the cycles became worse, he foresaw, not only would workers become more miserable, but the lot of businessmen would deteriorate; businesses would fail and disappear permanently. Capitalism is an intensely competitive system; capitalists who could not survive the increasing instability of the economy would be pushed down into the ranks of the proletariat. Their places would be taken by larger business units.

With this prophecy, Marx leaves behind the competitive capitalism of the classicals and portrays capitalism entering a monopolistic phase. In its initial phase, capitalists meet competition in the usual ways: by increasing efficiency, by mechanizing, by introducing new goods, by stepping up sales pressure. But, as capitalism sours from growing contradictions, ordinary competitive behavior becomes inadequate in the struggle for survival. Business firms become cannibalistic; they grasp for life by *eliminating* competition, by swallowing up subviable firms. In doing this, the surviving firms increase the concentration of ownership. As the process continues, capitalism becomes an economy of ever fewer capitalists—capitalists of increasing avariciousness and power—and ever more workers—workers suffering deeper degradation and longer periods of unemployment. The contradictions become increasingly unbearable. The workers cannot find work and therefore cannot buy the vast output of the capitalistic economy. Further, their employment is necessary to the capitalists, for workers alone are the source of surplus value.

Out of this context, capitalist imperialism and a propensity for war develop. Having eliminated the source of surplus value at home and having dried up the purchasing power of the workers, the few remaining capitalists now turn to desperate measures to enhance their power. They colonize homelands of backward peoples, hoping to exploit new sources of hitherto untapped surplus value. They foment wars so that their governments will be forced to employ the capitalists' excess productive capacity to make war materiel. Useless expenditures are necessary to feed the monster the capitalistic economy has become. But the monster, in aggrandizing its power, has commenced its final, suicidal act. As Marx's account of the days of capitalism comes to a close, the system is proceeding to an inevitable and untenable form: one gigantic monopoly. With millions of miserable proletarians as its penniless would-be customers and enemies, the doom of capitalism is at hand.

The time will come, wrote Marx, when the contradictions of capitalism will destroy it. It will have lost its reason for being. Capitalism is a necessary, and inescapable, part of economic development, according to the Marxian conception of history. It prepares the industrial base and trains workers for the next economic system. Capitalism is a dynamic system—a system of change and growth. When it loses its dynamism, when it ceases to grow because its ability to provide an ever-greater flow of goods of ever-increasing diversity is weakened and when it attempts to survive by turning inward and feeding upon itself, it will be finished.

Prologue to Revolution

While capitalism sickens, said Marx, the workers will have reached unendurable depths of misery and degradation. When the human spirit will bear it no longer, the workers must revolt to end the domination of their capitalist masters. This time the revolution will not fail as have all workers' revolts in the past, for the very system of capitalism that has brought the workers to ruin has also brought with it their salvation. By making workers conscious of the two-class nature of society, by educating, training, and disciplining them, it has provided them with the will and power to overthrow the decadent system and to set up and maintain a new order. Marx put it this way:

> Along with the constantly diminishing number of magnates of capital who usurp and monopolise all advantages of this process of transformation, grows the mass of misery, oppression, slavery, degradation, exploitation; but with this too grows the revolt of the working-class, a class always increasing in number, and disciplined, united, organised by the very mechanism of the process of capitalist production itself. The monopoly of capital becomes a fetter upon the mode of production, which has sprung up and flourished along with it and under it. Centralisation of the means of production and socialisation of labor at last reach the point where they become incompatible with their capitalist integument. This integument is burst asunder. The knell of capitalist private property sounds. The expropriators are expropriated.

THE VISION

Thus capitalism comes to an end. But now what happens? What is the new synthesis? At this point, Marx ceases to be an economist and becomes a prophet. To his credit, he left his speculations on the future course of events out of *Capital,* so that work remains, whatever men today may think of it, primarily a theory of economics. The Marxian vision of the future lies elsewhere.[9]

[9] The Marxian vision of a utopian future is largely the work of post-Marxian writers. Marx himself had little to say about an ideal society or how to achieve one. His main contribution to the operation of a socialist economy is his essay *Critique of the Gotha Program,* written in 1875 and published by Engels in 1891. The Gotha program was the result of an 1875 meeting in Gotha, Ger-

Communists and Communism

Those states that today are the inheritors of the Marxian tradition are usually called "communist," yet in none of them does communism exist. Members of the Communist party of the Soviet Union are supposedly working diligently to bring about the communist millenium. In doing this, they have had little guidance from either Marx or Engels. Marx the prophet did produce a vision of what *could* come after the inevitable death of capitalism; but he was hazy about the nature of the future society, and his writings say nothing about how that society should be run. The principles of economic planning, coordination, and supervision that are utilized in the Soviet Union were learned not from Karl Marx but from men more pragmatic in outlook than the scribbler of the British Museum.

Marx was sure that capitalism must fail. He was less certain about what type of economic system would follow it. This may seem strange, since he was not reticent about announcing his discovery of the universal principle of historical causation. Obviously, if the dialectical process explains history, capitalism will be followed by a new synthesis. So long as any contradictions exist in a synthesis, society must change. Only when no contradictions are present will the Marxist dream be realized. The end, then, of Marxist dogma is the ideal state. If this sounds quasi-religious, it should, for *personal conversion* is necessary to the attainment of Marxist perfection.

Industrialization and Alienation

Some people feel that there was a strange ambivalence—a love-hate relationship—in Marx's attitude toward the industrial order. Actually, we do not need to engage in posthumous psychoanalysis to understand

---

many, of the German Social Democratic Workers Party. The delegates to the Gotha convention attempted to set up a program for running a socialist state. Marx's *Critique* is his none-too-favorable evaluation of that program. Probably the two most famous post-Marxian guides to the operation of a postcapitalist economy are Lenin's *State and Revolution,* the first edition of which was written in 1917, and Joseph Stalin's *Foundations of Leninism,* a collected series of lectures that Stalin delivered in 1924 at Sverdlov University, Moscow. There are many other works by Lenin and Stalin on the postcapitalist economy and a great many more works by lesser-known but major figures in the Bolshevik movement. Strictly speaking, these works are in the field of *political* economy rather than economic theory.

this dualism. The explanation is simple. Although Marx admired *industrialization,* he detested the then existing form of *industrialism.* Industrialization—the employment of mass-production methods—is the means to the good life for the masses. Plainly, there is no other route to material affluence for everybody. Marx admired the industrial development wrought by the capitalists. But he rejected the way the capitalists distributed the fruits of their creation, and he hated even more fiercely what he thought capitalist industrialism was doing to the workers.

The worst fault of capitalism, in Marx's eyes, was not that workers were expropriated—that was bad enough—but that they were alienated from their work and from each other.

Marx the psychologist felt that an individual could realize his potential as a truly *human* being only through the creative process. Capitalist industrialism prevents the worker from attaining the joy that can be his through work. Here is an important insight into Marx's personal values. Many people believe that Marxism, with its slogan "to each according to his need," is a system designed to benefit dawdlers and ne'er-do-wells. Not so far as Marx was concerned. He was *pro*-work and somewhat of an ascetic (he certainly lived that way himself). Marx believed that joy comes not from acquiring things or manipulating people but from work. Work is good, and good is work. This may sound a little Calvinistic, for there is something in common between communists and Puritans.

Capitalist work is work perverted. Capitalistic institutions (such as private property, competition, the market exchange process, the maximizing principle) preclude the worker's dominion over his own work, and he is thereby alienated from it and from the whole fabric of the economy.

What are the forms of the workers' alienation under capitalism? First, their *product* is alienated because the capitalists take it from them. Marx thought that this was about as unnatural as separating a mother from her child at birth.

Even worse, the worker becomes alienated from *himself* in that his work is not of or for himself. Capitalism can bring the worker ephemeral happiness in goods as items only of *consumption,* not of production or creation. Here Marx differs fundamentally from Adam Smith, for their models of man are entirely different. Smith, the moral philosopher, reassuringly tells us that the whole end of production is consumption. Marx, the materialist, says that the end of human action is production.

Since capitalism prevents the worker from realizing his deepest nature, he is *dehumanized*.

Finally, men become alienated from *one another*. Obviously, workers are alienated from capitalists, but they are alien to one another as well because they are competitors for, and in, their work. Marx saw the worker under capitalism as nothing more than "an appendage of a machine." But this does not mean that Marx believed machines would inherit the earth. Alienation is the product of capital*ism,* not of capital. Indeed, in the postcapitalist society, Marx foresaw the use of capital in greater quantity than under capitalism, but unaccompanied by worker alienation.

Welfarism Denounced

Marx predicted that the capitalists would not allow capitalism to die without trying to save it by enacting welfare measures to relieve the misery of the reserve army of the unemployed. This did not trouble him. At best, all it could do would be to prolong capitalism's death agony.

A surprising aspect of Marx's personal philosophy is that he did not believe in share-the-wealth programs or look with favor on pushing all people down to the level of the least capable member of the race. He believed in people *earning* their livings, as we shall see shortly. As he had no use for non-Marxian socialists and welfarists, so he had only contempt for *crude* systems of communal ownership of incomes and wealth. He would have regarded an Israeli *kibbutz* as pure hokum. He was quite sure that workers would be more miserable under crude communistic schemes than they were under capitalism, for social reformers, he thought, lacked the rationality of the capitalists.

The Revolution

As we have said before, Marx was certain that capitalism must fall. That certainly is part of his inexorable law of historical development. But when it collapsed, he felt, the workers must act to assure that the power of the state fell into the hands of their representatives. The representatives, of course, are the members of the Communist party. Their mission is to organize and execute the revolution and then to prepare the way for the ultimate noncontradictory economic system. The first item, therefore, is revolution.

Marx believed he knew when, where, and how the workers' revolt would take place. But like the early Christians, who believed that the kingdom of God was at hand and then revised their predictions as time went on, Marx finally took refuge in the safe prediction that the revolution would occur when the time was right. When would the time be right? When capitalism was fully developed.

The answer to when the revolution would occur also gives us the answer to where. It could come only in fully developed capitalist countries, of which, according to Marx, there were only two, the United Kingdom and Germany. The reason Marx answered the "when" and "where" questions in this way was that he felt that the next economic order had to build on the fully developed industrial base of capitalism. Without a large industrial base, a socialist economy could not survive.

History, of course, has since forced all Marxists to abandon this prerequisite. Obviously, Marx did not write the script for the twentieth-century communist revolutions. Bolshevik revolutions, as we know, have come in agricultural, underdeveloped countries, forcing protagonists of Marxian prophecy, such as Lenin and Stalin, to revise Marx's predictions. Current Marxist dogma asserts that a capitalist industrial base is not a necessary prelude to revolution.

Ideal Socialism

How does the transition to a finally noncontradictory state come about? This is the vaguest part of Marx's vision. Marx may be partly excused for his blurry foresight here because he had relatively little interest in this question. After all, he had developed a clear theory of history; why should he be criticized for not also providing a detailed plan for the future?

The first phase in the *ideal* postcapitalist economy Marx called "ideal socialism." Despite the implications of Marx's stirring passage about disciplined workers taking over from the capitalists, Marx himself and later Marxists, particularly Lenin, did not believe that the workers could move immediately to ideal socialism. Actually, Marxist dogma holds that the workers are not ready for self-government. In the beginning, an élite must govern in the name of the workers. This is "the dictatorship of the proletariat." The élite is, of course, synonymous with the thoroughly indoctrinated, toughly disciplined, intensely loyal, completely dedicated inner cadres of the membership of the Communist party. Without the dictatorship of the proletariat, chaos would probably follow the workers' uprising. The task of the élite group is to prepare the way for the ideal state. Its dual responsibility is to keep the productive capacity of the capitalist economy intact, augmenting it if possible, and to purge the postcapitalist society of all possible elements of bourgeois thought. As it has turned out, this has usually meant the physical annihilation of the bourgeoisie. But it means even more than this horrible necessity. The workers themselves, as full of hatred as they are supposed to be for their former, now defunct, masters, are still possessed of a "bourgeois mentality." These thought patterns have to be erased, and proper Bolshevik thought patterns must be infused. While the workers are on their way to right thinking, the Communist party can get on with its work of building an ideal socialist state. If all goes well in this phase, there is a possibility of building the final, noncontradictory economy of ideal communism.

Marxists have definite ideas about the nature of an ideal socialist state. Examining these ideas is helpful in understanding some of the actions taken by the Soviet Union and the People's Republic of China.

In keeping with Marx's predilection for the massive use of industrial techniques, ideal socialism will be highly industrialized and will employ capitalistic methods of production. This is not a paradoxical statement. Although great amounts of capital will be used (hence, the capitalistic methods of production) to achieve an economy of affluence, all capital will be owned by the state in the name of the workers. Since the workers are not yet ready to manage all aspects of the economy themselves and since they still harbor the regrettable bourgeois tendency to want to be paid for their work, they will be paid differential rates. The differences in wage rates will reflect differences in productivity, as they are supposed to do in a capitalist economy. The most wanted workers will receive the highest pay. Socialism's crucial difference from capitalism in determining who is the most productive is that the central planners, rather than consumers, decide what output is wanted. Moreover, capitalist expropriation of wages will be impossible, for there will be no capitalists. Finally, during this period the workers will be losing their old bourgeois mentality and, it is hoped, replacing it with the new communist mentality.

In this state, even though it is not perfect, one great thing has been accomplished. The workers are no longer alienated. Alienation, the product of the two-class system, is an impossibility because now there is only one class.

In Russia, which is presumably in this period today, production is directed by the central planners of the Communist party. Marx himself was exceedingly hazy on the details of the economy in this government by the representatives of the proletariat, but his disciples in the Soviet Union have built up, with trial, error, pain, failures, and successes, an enormously complicated, highly sophisticated planning and coordinating system.

Ideal Communism

Obviously, Marx's well-known, and poorly understood, prophecy that under ideal socialism the state will wither away has not been fulfilled. The complex Soviet bureaucracy attests to that. Ideal socialism, say the Marxists, is not a perfect society; ideal communism is.

Now, the Marxian trumpet becomes uncertain. The Marxist prediction of an ideal communist society is a *contingent* possibility. Whether ideal communism can become reality depends on two things. First, ideal socialism must have generated such an enormous expansion of production and productive capacity that the economy has become *truly* abundant in all material goods. Second, "a new man" must appear. Human beings as they are are not good enough for the new society, they must undergo a complete alteration of their individual and social psychologies. Not only must all elements of bourgeois mentality be eradicated, particularly the Smithian-endorsed propensity to consume goods, but, instead of receiving his primary satisfaction from the consumption of goods, the new communist man must rejoice in his work—in producing for others (with the others feeling exactly the same way). Only with such a mentality can human beings find complete self-fulfillment, and only with such human beings is real communism possible. Apparently, filled as we are with our bourgeois mentality, we could not recognize "the new man" in ourselves or others, for such a practical Bolshevik as Lenin has said, "Communism presupposes both a productivity of labor unlike the present and a person not like the present man on the street."

Marxians have pictured the ideal communist economy as a truly affluent society—not in the Galbraithian sense, in which there are too many private goods relative to the supply of public goods, but in the sense of a virtual elimination of scarcity. It is in this final phase of history that the famous Marxian prediction about the withering away of the state is to occur. Most people, of course, wonder how a society could survive without some kind of governmental apparatus. No Marxist thinks that it could. Marx predicted, not that all state machinery would disappear, but only that the state would *wither away as an instrument of oppression.*

What is the key difference between the Marxist conceptions of ideal socialism and ideal communism? If the words are strictly construed, not just used as euphemisms for whatever it is we find reprehensible, the question answers itself. *Socialism* implies the social ownership of the means of production. *Communism* comprehends the communal ownership of the totality of national wealth. There is no private ownership of anything. There need not be. Allocation and distribution problems in the communist economy will be of little consequence because of the virtual elimination of scarcity. Within the framework of what governmental organization survives, the workers collectively decide what to make and how to distribute it. Only at this stage, in the Marxist scheme, is the distribution of income based on need instead of productive contribution. This seemingly impractical distributive criterion will work because scarcity no longer plagues man and, more importantly, because the bourgeois incentives to work that existed under both capitalism and socialism are not needed. The communist man is a new creature; and his fulfillment comes from work itself, not from consumption.

CONCLUSION

We have distilled, from the thousands of pages of Marxist literature, some essence of Marxian economics, philosophy, history, and prophecy. Can we redistill this essence still further to state simply what Marx was about? Marx himself tells us that he discovered neither the existence of classes nor the class struggle. What he claims as original is the ideas that the existence of classes is the motivating force behind historical causation and that the course of history has been, and is, inevitably fixed in the path he describes. The key word in Marx's theory of economic determinism is "inexorability"; history *must* move according to his thesis.

Many people believe that Marx betrayed a lack of belief in his own system by working so relentlessly for the cause of revolution and for the building of the Communist party. If he believed that all he said was inevitable, why did he not content himself with writing

Capital and apply himself to more remunerative pursuits than his endless outpouring of essays, critiques, and letters? Marx's thesis of inexorable historical progress ends with the suicidal death of capitalism. But Marx knew where his theory ended and his wishful thinking began. He believed that the workers would revolt; but he was vitally concerned that the revolt, when it occurred, be purposefully directed, that power be seized by the Bolsheviks in the name of the workers, and that, under the dictatorship of the proletariat, a viable economic system be set up. As an atheist, he believed that the only chance for human joy is in one's own mortal lifetime. Marx was not sure that man could, or would, make his heaven for himself on this planet, but he was sure that if power were not seized by the élite of the Communist party upon the demise of capitalism, chaos could result. Marx was horrified by the thought of postrevolutionary anarchy, in which all that he hoped for could be lost at the moment of its birth. He devoted his life to the cause of the proletariat, but he had no faith in the ability of its lower orders to rule the new world until the élite had made the world safe for them and them safe for the ideal society.

Marx, as we said early in the chapter, was, among many things, an economist, a revolutionary, and a prophet. He had the good sense to know, even if his readers do not, which hat he was wearing at any particular time.

THE RECONSTRUCTION
OF ECONOMICS:
NEOCLASSICISM

6

By the mid-1800's, the noble structure that Smith, Malthus, Ricardo, and their followers had erected was getting shaky. Some patchwork had been done by John Stuart Mill, Nassau Senior, and others, but there could be no doubt that classical economics was in trouble. Karl Marx was not the troublemaker. His economics was essentially classical, and in fact shared many of the increasingly apparent difficulties of the classical system. Besides, Marx was at the time obscure and disreputable and so far removed from "the establishment" of the economics profession that, no matter how telling his arguments may have been, he lacked the status to make any orthodox economist feel insecure.

The turmoil in economics came from two respectable sources: one external and the other internal. The external challenge, the more serious of the two, was simply this: *Classical economics seemed unable to explain some patently obvious phenomena.* Its theories were breaking down, and, what is worse, no really new and tenable theories were being offered to take their place. The internal source of trouble, emanating from economists themselves, was a conflict over *methodology* —how economics should be studied. In the mid-1800's, economics was being pulled in three directions—by English classical economics, by Austrian marginalism, and by German historicism. Classicalism and marginalism would eventually unite to save economics; historicism was too unwieldy to survive; it would fall of its sheer bulk.

THE APEX AND FALL OF THE CLASSICAL SYSTEM

The developers of classical economics had brought to it an elegance of method not found in any other social science. (In fact, one reason economists could battle over method was that economics was one social discipline that was sufficiently rigorous to be able to utilize methodical analysis.) The last two classical economists we shall consider are Nassau Senior and John Stuart Mill. Although neither of these men are of the stature of Smith, Malthus, and Ricardo, they are the economists who, with J. B. Say, brought the classical system to its analytical and influential peak.

Nassau Senior (1790–1864)

Nassau Senior's earnest concern was to make economics scientific. He wanted no part of *political* economics. What he desired was a pure science, in the manner of astronomy or physics, into which morals, conventions, philosophies, and politics could not intrude, simply because they would be of no consequence. Senior attempted to base the whole structure of economics on four *a priori* principles, and from them he proposed to deduce the explanations of economic phenomena. (Whether Senior's objective is worthwhile is still debated among economists, some economists proudly claiming the title "*political* economist," and others disdaining anything but the most pristine *a priori* discipline.)

Senior's greatest contribution was not, however, his delineation of the proper sphere of economics but his interest-rate theory. Although it is by no means a perfect explanation, it is of particular interest to us here, for in the preceding chapter we dealt with a man who denounced interest as unearned income. Senior was not nearly as colorful as Marx, but in his sober way he raised serious questions in the minds of thoughtful readers about Marx's hostility to the payment of interest.

In the first place, Senior shared Smith's optimism that labor and capital could work together to the mutual advantage of both. Senior did not doubt that population growth would continue, apparently accepting, as who did not (save Karl Marx), the acuity of Malthus' postulate about the strength of the passion between the sexes. But, said Senior, and this is an all-important "but," capital will so enormously increase the productivity of labor that the welfare of laborers must necessarily improve with an increase in capital accumulation. Senior may have been too optimistic in asserting that the power of labor to produce wealth could be expanded indefinitely by devoting some of the products of labor to the production of goods rather than all of production to consumption. But he was on much firmer ground than either Malthus or Marx, for he saw that despite the law of diminishing returns, curve OQ (in Figure 3, Chapter 4, p. 108) could be raised by increases in capital and that everybody—all "classes" —could be better off. Since capital has the power to aid in the creation of wealth, it *can* generate an income for its owners.[1]

Now, the question is: Why *must* the owners of capital be paid? Because *all* people have a demand for capital. Why? The answer is in one of the two fundamental postulates of economics: Everybody wants "more." Given a certain quantity of labor and natural resources, the economy can produce "more" only as its stock of capital grows. The more capital is used, however, the more complex, or roundabout, the productive process becomes, and the longer is the wait for finished goods to be sold to generate income for the vast anonymous army of workers who contributed to their production. Not everyone can afford to wait. The draftsman drawing the plans for a coking plant cannot wait for his dinner until the suit that was sewn with a steel needle tracing its ancestry back to the coking plant is sold in some men's shop. But somebody somewhere has to wait, and waiting is disagreeable. If someone is to perform a scarce service, he can command a price. That someone is the capitalist. Moreover, it seems reasonable to conclude that the longer the period of waiting, the greater the recompense must be to the one who waits.

Waiting, however, is not the most important reason capitalists are rewarded, Senior reasoned. If a man buys a piece of capital to make goods for others, he is doing without; he is *abstaining* from consumption. Senior was so impressed with this argument that he declared that "abstinence," not capital, is a factor of production. Again, for most people, abstinence (saving) is unpleasant. Why do without anything until tomorrow when you can have it today? Besides, you may not have a tomorrow. Thus, argued Senior by implication, does anyone seriously believe that someone will abstain for the benefit of

[1] Recall our analysis of the net productivity of capital in Chapter 3, p. 76.

others when going without goods and facing an uncertain future are unpleasant? Society must either pay the capitalists or forego the obvious benefits of capital.

The cost of abstinence (capital), then, is a true cost of production. Although Senior remained in the classical camp as a cost-of-production theorist, he destroyed the notion that labor is the sole true cost of production. He argued that if workers receive all the product (as Marx urged) and consume it all, their lot will soon be far more piteous than even Marx predicted. If they or anyone else is to abstain from immediate consumption to bring about a better tomorrow, as even Marx knew is necessary, the abstainers must be paid for their sacrifices. Of course, one could argue, and many have, that people with low incomes cannot abstain because they must use all that they receive just to keep alive. The abstainers must be persons who find it easy to do without (because at worst they do without some luxuries, not without necessities). Therefore, why should they be paid? One side of this question is ethical, and we must recall that economics does not deal with questions of ethics. But another side of the question is nonethical, and if Senior did not have a convincing answer to the nonethical side, it simply means that he did not have a perfect theory of interest. Nevertheless, he did have more insight into the nature of capital, interest, and the costs of production than any other classical. Later in this chapter we shall find that the trouble with Senior's analysis is endemic to classical economics—it stems from the failure to produce a viable theory of value. The general answer to why interest is paid, however, is simple: So long as capital is scarce and wanted, it can only be had at a cost.

John Stuart Mill (1806–73)

John Stuart Mill made some original contributions to economics, but had he done nothing more than complete his task of making Ricardo readable he would deserve to be revered in the annals of economic thought. Ricardo's brilliance was masked by an unbelievably turbid writing style; and if Mill, whose enthusiasm for Ricardo was unbounded, had not rearranged and rewritten the master's work, modern economics would no doubt be even more obscure than it is. Mill's treatise on the classical system, *Principles of Political Economy* (1848), suceeded Say's *Treatise on Political Economy* as the favorite text on the subject in English-speaking countries for several generations.

Mill tried to keep economics from becoming a tool of special interests by separating what he thought were immutable laws from those that are susceptible to change by human action. To this end, he classified all economic hypotheses under one of two headings: the laws of production and the laws of distribution. The *laws of production* are derived from the law of diminishing returns and are therefore expressions of the natural order. Obviously, these are beyond the power of man to change. The *laws of distribution* are, however, in part man's doing, so he can effect changes in them. Mill was wrong here; for just as the classicals' distinction between productive and unproductive labor is invalid, so is Mill's artificial dichotomy between the "laws" of production and distribution. Production and distribution cannot be divorced.

Mill's error was a fruitful one, however, for it led him to denounce, in work subsequent to his *Principles,* the classicals' completely unsupportable doctrine of the wages fund. The idea of a wages fund of predetermined size, out of which workers are paid, was an excellent antilabor device. If the upper limit of wages is rigidly fixed by the fund, any labor action to obtain higher wages is fruitless, inasmuch as beyond the wages fund there is nothing. At the same time, the wages fund is an anticapitalist tool, too. If the workers accept the wages fund as an inherent part of capitalism, preventing them from bettering themselves, it will surely occur to them to abandon capitalism in favor of a more advantageous system. Thus, Mill's denunciation of the wages-fund idea helped to eradicate the seeds of class conflict loosely sown by the classical analysis and to restore to economics a measure of optimism lacking since the days of Adam Smith.

Obviously, there is no set stock of "wage goods" stored up somewhere in the economy waiting to be disbursed to workers. Wages are prices, and, like all prices, they vary with supply and demand (a matter we shall discuss shortly). If capitalists decide to produce more capital and give more employment, wages and interest can both grow.

"METHODENSTREIT"

In the last quarter of the nineteenth century, as we have said, professional economists engaged in a battle interesting only to themselves —but a battle whose results benefited everyone. While many persons were concerned with the increasing inapplicability of economics to observed phenomena, what worried economists was how to study economics. The battle over methods was appropriately named, by the German-speaking antagonists, the *Methodenstreit*.

At the time, there were three distinct ways of studying economics: English classicalism, Austrian marginalism, and German historicism. The first two had some things in common, as we shall see, but German historicism was unique, and the *Methodenstreit* was essentially between the English and Austrian approaches on the one hand and the German method on the other.

In building the classical system, English economists had relied heavily on deductive reasoning. Deduction was also the mainstay of the Austrians. Not so with the German historicals; they fervently believed in inductive reasoning.[2]

The members of the German historical school were loudly hostile to the method of the English classicals because they repudiated the results so fervently sought by the classicals—the formulation of general laws of economic behavior. The historicals were not interested in producing "laws"; in fact, they were contemptuous of the concept of "law" in economics. What they wanted to do was to accumulate a mass of painstakingly detailed historical data. In this quest, they were eminently successful. Our heritage from them is a set of voluminous studies of the economic aspects of their own and earlier times and a set of techniques of economic historiography.

History, to which the German school was so passionately attached, has settled who won the *Methodenstreit*. The Germans produced no lasting body of economics. Largely owing to their influence, continental European economics was stultified, with the result that, until recently, it lagged far behind the work done in the United States and the United Kingdom. Although we may say, then, that the English classicals and the Austrian marginalists won, we cannot say that the end of the *Methodenstreit* was a victory for the deductive method. The quarrel itself was absurd. Scholars use whatever methods or combinations of methods will bring them closer to their desired ends. Moreover, neither English classical economics nor Austrian marginalism was the final victor. Both were soon to yield, to use the Hegelian expression, to a new synthesis.

[2] Deduction is the process of reasoning from general information to a particular conclusion. Induction involves reasoning from particular instances to a generalized conclusion.

AUSTRIAN MARGINALISM

On the Continent during the late 1800's, a group of economists centering around the University of Vienna began to develop an economics to counterbalance English classicalism. Although they are called *Austrian* marginalists, they had, as did the English classicals, adherents in other countries. Indeed, a few outstanding early marginalists were Englishmen. And the Austrians were just as impressed with the deductive method as were the classicals. What, then, were their differences?

The English classicals were *objective* theorists, and the Austrians were *subjective*. The English were objective in that they were cost-of-production theorists. Cost is an objective fact. The classicals desperately tried to show that the cost of production of a given good explains its value. The Austrians, seeing the obvious pitfalls of this method, tried to attack the problem of value by taking a subjective, or psychological, approach. Goods have value because they are wanted. Utility is the power of a good to satisfy a want, so the marginalists worked on the concept of utility.

The classicals, including Marx, believed that a good must have utility in order to be valuable. But that was the end of the matter. "Possessing utility," went the typical classical explanation of value, "goods will tend to exchange on the basis of their costs of production." And, with that as their basic proposition to explain value, the classicals continued to be confounded by Smith's "Diamond-Water Paradox" and other related problems of valuation. When they used "utility" in their discussions, the classicals did not know what a powerful concept they had in their hands. If they had been better mathematicians, the development of economic analysis would have proceeded much faster.

The marginalists, on the other hand, were unwilling to stop with the weak "possessing utility" preamble to classical value theories. They inquired deeply into the matter of utility and, using some mathematical concepts, were able to solve Smith's "Diamond-Water Paradox," although they too, like the classicals, failed to produce a generally satisfactory theory of value.

The marginalists are aptly named. They were concerned with magnitudes at the margin—that is, with "extra bits" of some relevant total rather than with the total itself. And this is where Smith went astray. He fell into the "Diamond-Water Paradox" because he was concerned with *total* utility. If he had comprehended the idea of *marginal* utility he would have found no paradox in comparing the values of life-sustaining water and envy-inspiring diamonds.

The central idea of marginal utility is very simple: The more the consumer has of a given good, the less his satisfaction will *increase* with additional purchases of the good, although his *total* satisfaction continues to rise. Now let us see how this concept solves the "Diamond-Water Paradox." How can it be that water is less valuable than diamonds when water is a vital necessity?

Suppose a desert dweller can obtain only one quart of water per day; it will mean very much to him, for his life may depend on it. Thus, he may jealously guard his quart against all comers. The water is so precious that perhaps he would take no price for it. If, however, he can obtain two quarts of water, what will his situation be? His total utility will be greater than if he had but one quart. Yet the subjective value (utility) to him of *either one* of his two quarts is less than the subjective value of one quart was when he possessed only one. When he had but one quart of water, that single quart determined whether he would live for the rest of the day; with two quarts he can assign some of the water to less urgent uses, since he does not need it all to keep him alive. In other words, the additional amount of water is of less value to him than the original amount.

And this is how he will continue to regard his situation with respect to water the more quarts of it he has. As he gets more and more water, he can assign it to less and less important uses, and each new increment of water will be worth less to him than the preceding increment. In other words, the *total* utility he derives from water increases with each additional quart (he can devote it to more and more uses), but the *marginal* utility of water is falling (each new quart is put to uses less important than the uses of the preceding quarts).

By now it should be easy to see that the more water a man has, the less will be the marginal utility of water to him, even though the total utility is greater. And this analysis applies to any good. We are saying simply that the more one has of a given good, the greater will be his total satisfaction; but the larger his collection is of the good in question, the less important the addition or subtraction of one unit of the good will be to him. As a person's access to a supply of water is increased, he will cease to confine his usage of it solely to the maintenance of his internal chemistry and will begin first to wash himself with it, then to wash his clothes, his dishes, and his car, and, finally, with enough water at his disposal, to fill his swimming pool with it. If a consumer has enough water to fill his swimming pool, giving to him or taking from him one quart of water will be a matter of almost no consequence.

If, then, a consumer has several hundred thousand quarts of water and only two diamonds, a quart change in his water supply will not be noticed, but a positive or negative change of one diamond will matter very much to him. The scarcity of diamonds alongside the relative abundance of water means that our hypothetical subject will assign diamonds to their most urgent uses—for example, in ornamental display—whereas he may use water for trivial purposes, not caring whether the garden hose runs an extra hour or so.

Thus, in comparing the subjective values of water and diamonds to him, he is interested not in the total utility that each good provides but in their utility to him *at the margin*. (Remember, "marginal" means "extra.") He compares an *extra* (marginal) unit of water with an *extra* unit of diamonds, and, since an *extra* quart of water has virtually no significance to him while an *extra* diamond would have a great deal, he would be willing to forego many quarts of water in order to gain one more diamond.

The principle of diminishing *marginal* utility—the hypothesis that the utility of a good can decline at the margin, while the total utility it furnishes its consumer rises as he buys more of the good—is the great contribution of the marginalists. This commonsense observation eluded the classicals, and thus they could not solve Smith's "Diamond-Water Paradox."

THE ROCK OF VALUE

The theory of value is a rock upon which economic analysis is built. It is also a rock upon which the classical and marginalist ships crashed and came to ruin. The classicals were chided by the marginalists for the inability of their cost-of-production theory to explain value unambiguously. But it soon became apparent that the marginalists had no explanation either.

Was the work of the Austrians entirely futile? No. They corrected the deficiencies of the classicals' cost-of-production theory by showing that the intensity of desire for a good, though not itself enough to determine value, must be taken into account in any theory of value. Somehow the two components of value must be brought together. The classicals sailed the route of cost of production; the marginalists took the lane of subjective utility. Each school got into stormier seas as the deficiencies of both analyses became more embarrassingly evident, and both of them finally crashed on the rock of value. Economics was wrecked with them. Was there anyone who could rebuild it?

ALFRED MARSHALL (1842-1924)

The wretched state of economics was ended virtually single-handedly by the Cambridge University economics professor Alfred Marshall. Marshall brought life to a decadent science. The revivified discipline is known as *neoclassical* economics—the new classical economics. It is, in part, a fusion of the objective economics of the English classicals and the subjective economics of the Austrian, and it is the foundation and core of modern economics. The approximately one-half of a first-year textbook that deals with so-called price theory or value and distribution theory is heavily based on the work of Marshall and his neoclassical successors.

Marshall, like so many other major contributors to economics, came to the field from philosophy and mathematics. As a deeply socially conscious individual, he combined his interests in utilitarian ethics, mathematics, and social reform in the pursuit of a more useful economics. To Marshall, being "useful" meant bringing the good life to the English workingman.

Marshall made a tremendous impact on economics and was the developer of a valuable "tool box" for economists. Among the concepts he pioneered are demand-and-supply analysis, the refinement of the partial-equilibrium method, the use of time periods, the concept of the representative firm, and the idea of an elasticity coefficient. None of these items may mean anything to you now, but if you study first-year economics they will become your property in common with all other students of economics. We shall consider one of these concepts, demand-and-supply analysis, in this chapter.

Marshall made this impact through his great book, simply titled *Principles of Economics*. This book and *The Wealth of Nations* are two of the most important works in economics. Marshall's *Principles* appeared in 1890, having required ten years to write. In it, Marshall virtually rebuilt the discipline. What had become an unscientific, ineffectual, divided, and demoralized field gained a new life from this one book. Marshall drew together the diverse strands of economic theory, discarded the erroneous and trivial, gave rigor to the salvageable parts, and added numerous new contributions. Once again, this time with Marshall as its protagonist, economics reacted to the real world; and once more, as with Smith, Malthus, and Ricardo, the message of economics was understood, and the *Principles* became an immense and lasting success.

"Lasting" is a precise word to use in describing Marshall's *Principles,* for not only has the book gone through nine editions since it first appeared in 1890 but it is still in print today. It may still be read with profit, and, since much of it is incorporated into present texts on economics, a good part of it is read by readers unaware of their author's debt to Alfred Marshall.

The whole spirit of the *Principles* is mathematical, yet all actual mathematical formulations are confined to footnotes and an appendix. The most difficult aspect of Marshall's work is the necessity for the reader to assure himself from time to time that he has grasped what the author has said, for Marshall's style of writing is deceptively simple. It is easy to pass through his well-fashioned and commonsensical sentences and paragraphs without ever realizing the depth and complexity of his statements.

Marshall had great influence also as a teacher. As a professor at Cambridge, he taught some of the greatest of all neoclassical economists. Among his more noteworthy students were Francis Y. Edgeworth, Arthur Cecil Pigou, and John Maynard Keynes—an economist to whom the last chapter of this book is devoted. These students, and those they influenced, have continued, enlarged, corrected, and modified economics into what it is today.

DEMAND AND SUPPLY

Marshall's demand-and-supply analysis put an end to foolishness about "value in use" and "value in exchange" and to questions about whether the value of a good is determined by objective supply conditions or subjective demand criteria.

But, if the old value theories were foolish, there is also much foolish-ness in the popular conceptions of demand-and-supply analysis it-self. Some people think that the expression "demand and supply" summarizes economics. Others feel that it is an empty phrase, that anyone who can say "demand and supply" fancies himself an econo-mist. Still others, overly impressed by the expression, demonstrate their belief in its profundity by saying something such as, "You can't repeal the law of demand and supply."

The truth is that demand-and-supply analysis is a useful tool of economists; it is an especially useful tool with which to *begin* the study either of economics or of a specific economic problem. But, in any case, it is only a beginning. The immediate purpose of demand-and-supply analysis is to find which of an infinite number of possible prices for a particular good will actually be the price at which that good will exchange in the market. But economists' observations of the effects of demand and supply are not the end of their investigations of an economic event. Of more interest to economists, and of greater importance, are the forces lying behind demand and supply. What causes consumers to act the way they do? What causes business firms to decide how much of a given good they will place on the market? What will be the effects of a change in the investment plans of business firms? How will consumers react to an increase or decrease in income-tax rates? The greater part of a standard economics text is devoted to examining the forces underlying demand and supply. In this section, we shall introduce the analytical apparatus of demand and supply and then use the remainder of the chapter to consider how the nature of business firms affects the process of economizing.

Consumer Demand

Adam Smith gave us a timeless maxim when he declared that the end of all economic activity is consumption. The world economizes because consumers have demands. What are these demands? Obviously, demands arise from wants. But wants exist only in contemplation. A demand, on the other hand, is a want that a consumer can effectuate. Demands are felt in the market. The market is oblivious to wants.

To consider the demands for all the countless things that con-sumers buy is sure to induce acute frustration. Instead, let us for the moment focus on the demand of *one consumer for one particular good.* We can work out some hypothetical examples of consumer demand for, say, the abstract good "gizmos." [3]

Can you analyze your demand for a particular good into its components? Among the most important determinants of a consumer's demand for a good are his tastes, his income, the price of the good, and the prices of all other goods.

The various determinants of demand mean that we have several variables with which to contend. Where shall we start? Suppose that if the price of a gizmo were $7 a consumer would buy three per week. Suppose, alternatively, that if the price of a gizmo were $6 he would buy five. This seems to be about what we would expect. We do not know how many gizmos he would actually buy, but it seems reasonable that the lower the price, the more gizmos he would purchase.

However, suppose that one week, when the price of gizmos was $7 each, the consumer did, in fact, buy three, but the next week, when the price of gizmos fell to $6 he did not buy more gizmos—in fact, he bought none. A fall in price did not induce the consumer to buy more gizmos. Why not? Because the price of gizmos is only one of the determinants of the amount of gizmos demanded. One or more of the other determinants obviously has changed. The consumer may have lost his taste for gizmos completely; or his income may have fallen so he feels that he can no longer afford gizmos, even at a lower price; or the prices of the other goods he buys may have risen so there is nothing left for gizmos. All these things may have changed together, or some may have moved in opposing directions. In the latter case, if the forces operating to weaken his demand for gizmos preponderate, then the consumer will demand fewer gizmos despite the fall in price.

Obviously, we have a very complicated situation if we are going to be concerned at once with all the components of consumer demand. With such an unwieldy group of variables to contend with, it is doubtful whether we could make any sense of consumer behavior at all.

What we want to do is to form a hypothesis about consumer behavior.

---

[3] We shall use an abstract good so that we will not have to be concerned about the actual prices of real goods and also to make a point, later on, about what kinds of goods may properly be treated by demand-and-supply analysis. As we move through this discussion, think about what kind of a good a gizmo must be and what kinds of firms must produce gizmos if we can determine their market price from demand-and-supply analysis.

The real world is extremely complex—too complex to be studied directly; thus, in order to understand reality better, we must abstract from it. We must simplify our problem.

The procedure we shall use is already familiar to you. It is the partial-equilibrium (or "other-things-being-equal") technique described in our discussion of Ricardo's differential rent theory. We shall select one variable from our determinants of demand and hold all the others constant. For their purposes, economists commonly choose the price of the good under consideration as the variable. This does not mean that economists believe that the price of the good itself is the most important determinant of the quantity of gizmos demanded, but, as the end of demand-and-supply analysis is the determination of the market price of the good, price is used as the variable magnitude.

In the study of consumer demand, we are interested in finding out what amount of a particular good a consumer will buy in a specified time period at different prices, when, for the sake of analysis, all other determinants of demand are held constant. We want to observe the influence of our chosen relevant variable—the price of the good in question—on consumer behavior. To do this, we shall draw up a hypothetical demand schedule of a consumer for gizmos covering a period of one week.

TABLE 3   *The Demand Schedule of an Individual Consumer for Gizmos*

Price	Quantity demanded per week
$5.00	0
4.50	1
4.00	3
3.00	6
2.00	12
1.00	16
0	22

Table 3 shows precisely what economists mean by demand. The demand of a consumer for a good is a *schedule* showing how many units of a good a consumer will buy at a given price within a set of prices. To make any sense of such information, we must understand how to use the schedule. First, as was stated before, all the determinants that cause a consumer to buy a certain quantity of gizmos are held constant, with the exception of the price of gizmos. Second, the demand schedule covers a definite time period. Our schedule is for a week; it could just as well have covered an hour, a year, or the consumer's lifetime.

The most important thing to note in using the schedule is that it shows the amount of gizmos the consumer would buy *if* the price were at a particular level for the week. In other words, the schedule conveys "if-then" information. Specifically, starting at the top, the schedule says that *if* the price of gizmos were $5 each, the consumer would buy no gizmos at all for the week. Given his tastes, income, and the prices of other goods, he is not interested in purchasing gizmos if he must pay $5 or more apiece for them. But what if the price were somewhat lower, say $4.50? Our schedule shows that the consumer would buy one gizmo. From this point on, our consumer's demand schedule for gizmos proceeds in even-dollar "jumps." If the price were $4, he would buy three gizmos. Looking down the schedule, we see that if the price were $1, the consumer would buy sixteen gizmos per week. In the unlikely event that gizmos were a free good, the consumer would demand twenty-two of them per week. To use the schedule properly, *we pick a specific price* to see the amount of gizmos a consumer would buy at that price.

Usually, we are not interested in the demand of a single consumer for a particular good. One consumer ordinarily plays a negligible role in the determination of the market price of a good. For our problem, we are interested in the *market* demand for gizmos—that is, the sum of all the individual demands of gizmo buyers. If we had the demand schedules of all gizmo buyers, we could simply add the quantities bought at each price together, and we would then have the market-demand schedule for gizmos. Doubtless, each individual will have a demand schedule somewhat different from that of any other individual. For simplicity, however, let us assume that the demand schedules of all the individual buyers of gizmos are sufficiently alike to permit us to multiply the quantity demanded at each price by ten thousand hypothetical gizmo buyers. Thus, we have added a component to the determinants of market demand not included in our list of factors determining individual demand—namely, the number of consumers in the market. Our market demand schedule is shown in Table 4.

TABLE 4   *The Market-Demand Schedule for Gizmos*

Price	Quantity demanded per week
$5.00	0
4.50	10,000
4.00	30,000
3.00	60,000
2.00	120,000
1.00	160,000
0	220,000

Economists usually find tabular lists difficult to work with; they prefer graphs, so the material shown in Table 4 is presented graphically in Figure 4.

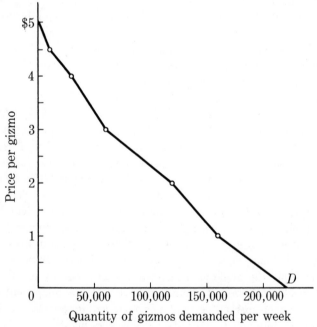

FIGURE 4   *The Market Demand for Gizmos*

The graph has the advantage of a picture. It brings out certain economic principles more quickly and even more fully than an array of figures. For instance, we can read from the graph the quantities of gizmos that would be bought at other than round dollar prices. For example, at a price of $1.50, consumers would demand 140,000 gizmos.

Note the slope of the demand curve; it portrays the law of demand. The demand curve slopes downward from left to right. Mathematically, this is called a negative slope—negative in that a change in price results in a change in the opposite direction in the quantity demanded. Thus, as we "ride down" the demand curve, price *decreases,* while the amount of gizmos that consumers are willing to buy *increases.* This is the law of demand. It says that, given a demand schedule, a fall in the price of a good will induce consumers to purchase greater quantities of the good. The law may be stated more succinctly by saying that there is an *inverse* relationship between price and quantity demanded.

The law is tested like any other scientific proposition—by making observations of relevant phenomena. Therefore, economists have simply watched what happens in the market, and, as a result, they have been satisfied that the law of demand holds true except for the miniscule and problematical case of a very odd class of goods under extremely unusual conditions. Actually, we are entitled to say that the law of demand is a universally noncontradicted hypothesis.

You may believe that you know of some exception to the law of demand. For example, suppose the owner of a drive-in thinks, "Hamburgers are not selling at all well, so I must stimulate demand. But I will not cut the price; I'll advertise." The statement may appear to contravene the law of demand. Here is a seller proposing to sell more, although he wants to keep the price at the same level (or, alternatively, he may wish to sell the same quantity as before and raise the price).

The problem is not a fallacy in the law of demand; the problem is loose terminology. When we work with a particular demand curve, the only variable determinant of the amount demanded is the price of the good itself. That is, within a *given* demand schedule, the only way to sell more is to lower the price. This does not mean, however, that other actions cannot change the demand schedule itself. Let us examine this idea.

Economists say that a change in the *price* of a good causes a *change in the quantity demanded* of the particular good, not a change in demand. A *change in demand* occurs whenever there is a change in any one or any combination of the *other* demand determinants (other, that is, than the price of the good). Since it is·these *other* demand determinants that fix the shape and position of the demand curve, a change in them must *shift the entire demand curve.* This is the same as saying that a new demand schedule has been established. If there has been a change in demand, all the figures in Table 5 under the heading "Quantity demanded per week" will now be different.

To increase his sales of hamburgers, then, the drive-in operator can do one of two things: He can lower the price of his hamburgers to increase the quantity demanded, or he can advertise in an attempt to shift the entire demand curve—that is, to cause an increase in demand. The difference between these courses of action is shown graphically in Figure 5. The first possibility is shown in panel A. Here the restaurant owner has caused a *change in the amount demanded* of hamburgers. He has moved down a given demand curve from point *A* to point *B*, lowering price from $.75 to $.50 and thereby increasing the quantity of hamburgers sold from 400 to 500 per week. The increase in sales is attributable solely to a fall in price. (Remember,

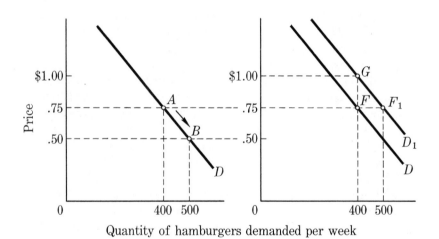

Quantity of hamburgers demanded per week

A. B.

FIGURE 5 *A Change in Quantity Demanded Contrasted with a Change in Demand*

a movement along a *given* demand curve is produced only by changes in the price of the good itself.)

The restauranteur's second alternative is illustrated in panel B of Figure 5. Here, in the movement from F to F_1, the enterpriser has caused the same end result as in panel A (he has sold 100 more hamburgers per week), but he has not had to lower the price to do so. Price remains at $.75. He has, however, by advertising, altered a determinant of demand, namely consumer taste, so as to shift the entire demand schedule from D to D_1. He has achieved what economists call a *change in demand*—that is, a change in the demand schedule or curve. *An increase in demand* is shown by the *rightward* shift in the demand curve. This means that consumers will buy more of the good at each particular price. A look at panel B of Figure 5 will show you that this is true. Similarly, *a decrease in demand* would be shown by a shift in the demand curve to the *left* of its initial position. With the demand curve moved to the left, consumers will buy less of the good at each particular price.

The rightward shift of the demand curve from D to D_1 in Figure 5, panel B, shows that, as a result of advertising and the consequent stimulation of consumer demand for his product, the restauranteur can sell the same amount of hamburgers (400) at a price 25 cents higher than before, or $1 each. This is not a violation of the law of demand because it is accomplished by a shift in the demand curve and does not involve a movement along the original demand curve, D.

Supply

We now turn to the supply side of the market, the side based upon objective cost information. What induces business firms to put a certain amount of a desired good on the market? Upon reflection, you would probably say (1) the price at which the good sells, (2) the cost of producing the good, which means the prices of all the things a firm must buy to produce its goods, and (3) businessmen's expectations about the prospect for sales or the future state of the economy in general. Doubtless, there are other things that induce a firm to market a certain quantity of goods, but these are probably the most important. Just as in the case of demand, since there are several variables with which we must work and since our ultimate goal is the determination of market price, we shall use the price of the good itself as the variable and hold all the other supply determinants constant.

We shall skip the depiction of the supply curve of an individual producer and turn immediately to the market-supply schedule—the schedule that shows the amounts of a good that all producers together will put on the market at each of a range of possible prices. The market-supply schedule for gizmos is presented in Table 5.

TABLE 5 *The Market-Supply Schedule for Gizmos*

Price	Quantity supplied per week
$0	0
0.50	0
1.00	10,000
2.00	50,000
3.00	130,000
4.00	160,000
5.00	180,000

The schedule shows that producers are unwilling to supply gizmos as a free good. Even at a price of $.50 per gizmo, they remain uninterested in satisfying any potential demand. But a price of $1 is sufficiently attractive to induce some manufacturer, or manufacturers, to put 10,000 gizmos on the market. A price of $5 would cause the gizmo industry to offer 180,000 gizmos for sale.

The same information is portrayed graphically in Figure 6. The most striking aspect of the supply curve, S, is that it slopes upward from left to right. Its *positive* slope shows the *direct* relationship between price and quantity supplied: As the price rises, the quantity supplied also increases; as the price falls the quantity supplied declines.

The reasons for the direct correlation between price and quantity are simple. The promise of higher prices for their goods is an incentive for businessmen to expand output. First, a rise in prices holds out a hope for greater profits. The promise of higher profits then acts to expand output in two ways: (1) Firms already in the gizmo industry will expand production to gain more profits. This will

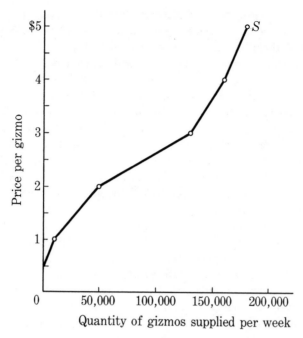

FIGURE 6 *The Market Supply of Gizmos*

cause a movement along a given supply curve; in other words, the expansion of production by firms in the gizmo industry causes *an increase in the amount of gizmos supplied.* (2) Enterprisers not currently in the gizmo industry will be led to enter it to get some of the lucrative gizmo business for themselves. The higher the price rises, the more will businessmen be induced to provide buyers with gizmos. Higher prices mean that higher-cost producers (less efficient producers) can enter the gizmo business, for the expanding differential between the selling price and the costs of production reduces the chances of business failure. The entrance of new firms into the gizmo industry causes the supply curve to move rightward; in other words, the entry of firms causes an *increase in supply.*

The Determination of Market Price

So far, we have said nothing about the actual price at which gizmos exchange. We have said such things as "*Assuming* that the price of a gizmo is $2, consumers will demand 220,000 of them per week," or, "If the price of a gizmo is $3, entrepreneurs would be willing to put 140,000 of them on the market each week." What we want to know now is what the *actual* market price will be with our given demand and supply schedules.

To find out what price will in fact "clear the market" (that is, will leave no buyer without gizmos and no seller with unsold ones), all we need do is juxtapose our demand and supply curves, as we have done in Figure 7. As Marshall put it, the forces of supply and demand act like a "scissors" to determine the market price. Neither the supply side nor the demand side alone establishes the price, as the English classicals and the Austrians, respectively, thought; both "blades" are necessary for price determination.

Our demand and supply curves intersect at point *E*, at which the price is $2.50 and the quantity is 90,000 gizmos. This price ($2.50) is called the equilibrium price because once it is established there will be no tendency for any other price to obtain—assuming, of course, the absence of forces acting to change the demand and supply curves themselves. Given our present demand and supply curves, the price at which gizmos must exchange is $2.50; it cannot be higher or lower. If any other price does momentarily exist, the market price must tend to the $2.50 level. Do you see why?

Take a price above $2.50—say, $4. Figure 7 shows that at that price consumers demand only 30,000 gizmos, but producers put 160,000 of them on the market, leaving a 130,000-unit *surplus* of gizmos. This surplus is shown by the distance *AB* between the demand and supply curves at $4. But manufacturers of gizmos do not want surplus stock. What can they do about the unwanted inventory accumulation? They can cut price in order to stimulate sales, and this is what they will do. As they lower the price, two things happen. First, sellers will be less interested in offering gizmos at the lower prices. The quantity of gizmos supplied will drop. Second, buyers will be willing to buy more gizmos as price falls. Thus, the quantities supplied and demanded move closer together. The process will continue until the two quantities are equal and the price is $2.50, for, so long as price is above $2.50 per unit, there will be a surplus quantity on the market, and sellers will have an incentive to cut price. And each cut in price will bring closer together the quantities demanded and offered for sale. At a price of $2.50 per unit, the quantity demanded equals the quantity supplied.

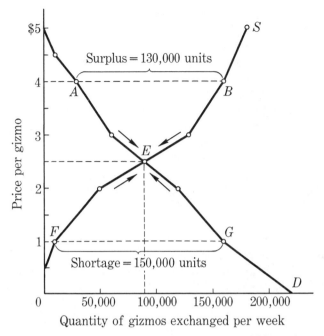

FIGURE 7   *The Determination of the Market (Equilibrium)*
Price for Gizmos

The surplus has been wiped out, and there is no force to drive price
any lower.

What about upward pressure on price? Suppose the price is temporarily at $1. At this price, the quantity demanded exceeds the quan-
tity supplied: Only 10,000 gizmos are offered for sale, but consumers
would like to buy 160,000 of them. At a price of $1, there is a *shortage*
of gizmos equal to 150,000 units, shown by the distance *FG* between
the two curves. The shortage will also be eliminated by the free action
of buyers and sellers in the market. The demand schedule shows that
10,000 gizmos can be sold for much more than $1. Actually, at as much
as $4.50 all 10,000 gizmos would be bought (demanded). Therefore,
so long as the amount supplied is 10,000 and the price is below $4.50,
buyers will bid against each other and cause price to rise. But the supply
will not stay at 10,000, for the rising price induces sellers to put more
gizmos up for sale. At the same time, the rising price will make gizmos

less attractive to buyers, causing them to demand fewer gizmos. Once
again, two forces are working to bring the quantities supplied and demanded into equilibrium. Price will continue to rise so long as there
is a shortage of gizmos; and there will be a shortage at any price less
than $2.50, for at all lower prices, the quantity demanded exceeds the
quantity supplied. Only at $2.50 does the quantity demanded equal
the quantity supplied, eliminating both the shortage and any further
upward pressure on price.

Thus, as we have shown, at a price of $2.50, there is neither down-
ward nor upward pressure on price. The market is in equilibrium, and,
unless the supply and demand curves themselves are changed by external forces, there will be no change in price. Equilibrium price is
often referred to as a "market-clearing price" because it does just that.
When quantity demanded equals quantity supplied, there is neither
surplus nor shortage, and the market is therefore cleared.

Will the $2.50 price persist forever? It will unless, as we said, there
are changes in demand or supply or both. Any change in the forces
that affect the positions of the two curves will act to change market
price. Thus, if there were an increase in gizmo consumers' incomes, we
would expect an increase in demand, shifting the demand curve to the
right. The price of gizmos would then rise.[4] The process described in
the preceding paragraphs would cause the price to rise from $2.50 to
the new equilibrium price. Similarly, if there were to be a fall in the
price of one of the productive factors used in making gizmos, the cost
of their production would fall. Profits would tend to rise, and we would
expect the supply curve to shift to the right, reflecting the entry of
new firms. A new and lower equilibrium price for gizmos would then
be established. Again, the process we described would occur and the
price would fall.

Applications of Demand-and-Supply Analysis

Demand-and-supply analysis has many useful applications. We cannot exhaust the possibilities here. One thing should be clear, however,
and that is that "surplus" and "shortage" have no real meaning apart
from considerations of market price. A free-market price ensures that

[4] To prove this to yourself, try drawing a new demand curve in Figure 7 to the
right of the one shown there; then find the new equilibrium price where your
new curve intersects the supply curve.

neither surplus nor shortage can persist. If there is a persistent shortage of a particular good, we know that some force outside of the market is keeping price below the equilibrium level. Similarly, if there is a stubborn surplus of a good, some force is maintaining price above the equilibrium level. In short, either a lingering surplus or a continuing shortage is clear evidence of interference with the free-market mechanism.

Why should anyone interfere with the operation of the free market? Because someone regards the equilibrium price as an *unsatisfactory* price. There is nothing sacrosanct about an equilibrium price; some people may find it quite objectionable.

For example, some farmers have found the equilibrium prices for their crops to be too low to allow them what they believe to be a "proper" or "fair" standard of living. Determining what a "proper," "fair," or "just" price is, of course, involves a value judgment. For many years now, Congress has agreed with a great number of farmers that the market, or equilibrium, price for many of their crops is not likely to be a just price; so, at a cost of billions of dollars, the federal government has seen to it that these prices are maintained above the equilibrium level. The result has been persistent surpluses of supported crops.

As an illustration of the opposite case, that of deliberately induced shortages, consider the imposition of ceiling prices during the Second World War. The lack of civilian production during wartime meant that the intense bidding among consumers would have driven the equilibrium prices of numerous goods far beyond the reach of many consumers. Congress, which did not believe that this result of the price system was an equitable way of distributing civilian production, imposed legal ceilings on the prices of many goods. These prices were below the equilibrium levels, so the civilian economy was faced with shortages of many goods. Since the price system is the normal determinant of how goods will be distributed, Congress now had to devise some other means of distributing the regulated goods to civilians. And, since the ceiling prices were invoked in the name of equity, the means they devised had to be what they considered equitable. The procedure adopted was a system of point rationing. In actuality, the country then had a two-price economy. One price was the conventional, but below-equilibrium, money price, and the other required the use of ration points. A "point price" was placed on certain consumer goods by the

Office of Price Administration (the federal agency charged with price regulation), and coupon books and tokens with which to pay the point price were issued to civilians.

The money-price system alone *could* have rationed the goods. There would have been no shortages.[5] Of course, goods would have gone to the highest bidder, and many people would have been priced out of the market; but quantity demanded would have equaled quantity supplied. The American people were unwilling to allow the money price mechanism to perform its usual rationing function. It was deemed to be unjust in wartime to allow goods to flow to those persons with the highest incomes. But, by establishing ceiling prices, the American people inescapably created shortages of price-controlled goods in the sense that, at those prices, there was a greater demand for goods than could be satisfied.

Agricultural price supports and ceiling prices show that the concept of an equilibrium price reflects a real economic situation. Unless prevented, the operation of the free market does tend to an equilibrium price. Avoiding an equilibrium price involves high costs and much effort. The agricultural price-support program of the federal government, begun in the thirties, has cost billions of dollars. It has resulted in the production of countless bushels of crops that no consumers demanded at the supported price, and these surpluses have had to be removed from the market and stored to prevent them from depressing the selling price below the support level. Similarly, the price ceilings imposed during the Second World War required the creation of a large federal bureaucracy to establish, administer, and police the rationing system. Since there were both buyers who were willing to pay more than the ceiling price for controlled products and sellers who were willing to sell the goods at higher prices, constant surveillance and a readiness and ability to institute criminal prosecutions against violators was necessary to limit the formation of black markets.

Marshall's Contribution

The graph of the intersecting supply and demand curves is important for two reasons. First, it summarizes the market actions of buyers

---

[5] That is, there would be no shortages in the sense that the demand for goods *at the market price* would not have exceeded the supply. This does not mean that people would have had as much as they wanted (or usually had) of all goods; there would still have been scarcities.

and sellers. We see at a glance the array of potential deals that demand-
ers and suppliers are prepared to offer each other, and, at the price and
quantity combination determined by the point of intersection of the
two curves, we see the one deal that clears the market. Out of all the
possible deals that might be consummated, this is the *one* deal to which
the market irresistibly gravitates.

Second, in the supply-and-demand diagram we have a constant reminder of Alfred Marshall's work in uniting the classical cost-of-production economics with marginalist economics, each of which, alone,
had theoretical deficiencies, to form what is now called neoclassical
economics.

Behind the supply curve is classical economics, with its emphasis on
the objective costs of production. Businessmen incur costs in producing
goods. Some of these costs, such as the investment in plant and equipment, are fixed over a period of time. There are "sunk" costs and exist
whether the firm produces anything or not. Other costs, such as payments for labor and materials, change with output. The more the
businessman produces, the higher will be these variable costs. Of course,
his total costs rise too, since to the costs that remain fixed at any level
of output, he must add the costs that rise as output increases. But, as
the businessman's costs rise with increases in output, so do his revenues
because he has more goods to sell. In the face of the increasing costs
and increasing revenues that the businessman incurs as he expands
production, how many goods will he want to put on the market?

Certainly, so long as the increase in his total receipts exceeds the
increase in his total costs for each unit that he adds to his output, the
businessman will find it worthwhile to expand his output because his
profit will rise. If a gizmo producer is able to sell all the gizmos he
produces at any given price, then any increase in price will induce him
to expand his output, for the rise in price is a signal that it is possible
for him to increase his profits if he will put more gizmos on the market.
This is what the upward slope of the supply curve shows. The supply
curve also, then, reflects the production costs that businessmen must
take into consideration in deciding how many gizmos to produce.

The negative slope of the demand curve, on the other hand, summarizes the attitude of consumers toward gizmos. Consumers do not
care about the costs of production. They only know that they want a
certain number of gizmos enough to be willing to give up a certain
amount of money (which they could have used to buy other things)

to have them. The lower the price, the more gizmos consumers will buy. Why does the demand curve slope downward to the right? Behind its slope is the law of diminishing marginal utility. As we saw in the discussion of the marginalists' work, the more one has of a good, the less difference the addition or subtraction of one unit of the good makes. If the consumer has to give up dollars for gizmos, the more gizmos he has, the fewer dollars he will part with to get another one. Other things being equal (for example, if the tastes of consumers for gizmos are not stimulated and there is no increase in the incomes of gizmo buyers), gizmo purchasers can be induced to buy more gizmos only if the price is lowered. Thus, the *subjective* valuation of gizmos on the part of consumers is made *objective* through the prices that they are willing to pay for the goods.

There are an infinite number of price-quantity combinations on each supply and demand curve. Clearly, neither the producers' costs of making gizmos nor the consumers' subjective valuation of them, by itself, determines the selling price of the good. Of the infinitude of possible prices, only one will clear the market—the one at which the quantity of gizmos supplied equals the quantity of gizmos demanded. To say that this price is the result of the forces of supply and demand is only to summarize the many combinations of forces present. Behind the supply curve is the objective fact of scarcity, which is reflected in the costs of production. Behind the demand curve lie the subjective valuations of consumers, which reflect the law of diminishing marginal utility. In bringing together both sides of the market, Alfred Marshall bridged the gap between subjective and objective valuations and between the theories of the classicals and the marginalists. In so doing, he produced a determinate theory of market price. The expression "supply and demand," which has become almost synonymous with economics in the popular mind, is a reminder of the work of the great scholar who, to a very great extent, recharted the course of economics.

COMPETITION OR NOT?

Competition and Its Benefits

Have you thought about what kind of a good a gizmo must be and what type of firm would produce gizmos? The name "gizmo" was given to our hypothetical good to avoid coloring your thinking by using an actual good while we explored demand-and-supply analysis. Now, let us ask what kind of good a gizmo must be to have its price impersonally determined in the market. Does this kind of pricing make sense to you? Are you not able to think of firms that do not passively accept a market-determined price but have an active price policy? A firm producing a good such as a gizmo, for which the price is established in the market, cannot have a price policy. It takes from the market the price at which the good sells, and it must live with this price. What qualities must such a good and its producing firm have for this to be so?

If a firm produces goods that are in some way unique, that firm can exercise some measure of control over the price at which its goods sell. The uniqueness may be real or imagined—that is, any differences may be implanted in consumers' minds by public-relations procedures. If, however, consumers do not care from whom they buy because the goods from all sellers are exactly alike, it will be extremely difficult for a firm to set a price on its goods unequal to the prices of identical goods sold by others. (How could such a firm induce buyers to pay a premium for its product?)

Homogeneity of goods, then, is one of our requirements. There is another. A firm must be so small in relation to the market that its entry or exit does not move the market supply curve appreciably. If it cannot, alone, affect the supply curve, then it cannot, alone, change the equilibrium price. This inability, coupled with the requirement of a homogeneous product, means that the firm must be a "price-taker." It simply takes the price obtaining in the market and does the best it can with that price. The firm cannot charge any premium for its goods without pricing itself out of the market, for buyers can get from other producers all the (identical) gizmos they demand at the (lower) equilibrium price. And it makes no sense for the firm to charge *less* than the market price, for it is such a small part of the industry that it can sell all it can produce at the going price. It cannot, therefore, increase its sales by selling gizmos for less than the market price.

What actual kinds of goods and firms fit these specifications? Any good that is homogeneous—such as corn, wheat, potatoes, or coal—would be similar to gizmos in that a buyer would not have the slightest interest in making a distinction between the firms that produced the goods. It is increasingly more difficult these days to find firms that both produce nondifferentiable goods and are small enough so that their presence or absence in the market has no effect upon price. However, a major example of such firms would be farming enterprises. (Of course, if agricultural price supports are involved, we recognize that this constitutes an interference with the free market, but the prices of all crops are not supported.)

You will recognize that the requirements for a firm to be a price-taker are in large measure the same as the conditions required for Adam Smith's "invisible hand" to function. In Chapter 3, we noted that the invisible hand is an eighteenth-century expression for perfect competition. The price-taker operates in a perfectly competitive market. Now is a good time to recall all of the benefits, enumerated in Chapter 3, that we are supposed to receive from the invisible hand, for we are about to call them into question.

The price-taker, like all other enterprisers, is a profit maximizer. But, since he can do nothing about the price at which he sells his goods, the only way open to him to maximize his profits is to sell that quantity of goods which gives him a maximum profit. Since an individual price-taker cannot affect the market price of a good no matter what quantity he, individually, puts on the market, it might seem that it would be profitable for him to put an unlimited quantity of goods on the market. This would be true were it not for the fact that a business firm has positive costs of production. As any business firm expands output, not only do its revenues increase,[6] but its costs also increase. And, because of the law of diminishing returns (see Chapter 4, pp. 100–04), costs and revenues do not often increase at the same rate. The price-taker tries to operate so as to produce that quantity which will yield the greatest *difference* of revenues over costs; in other words, by adjusting the quantity he sells, he attempts to operate at the maximum-profit output.

Since the price-taker is given the price at which he must operate, the sole set of variables over which he has any control in deciding what quantity of goods he will put on the market are his costs of production. Even here, many costs are given, such as the prices he pays for his factors of production. The lower his costs, however, the greater will be his profit at every level of output. Thus, the price-taker has a real incentive to keep his costs down. Moreover, the lower his costs, the greater also will be the output at which his profit is maximized (the

---

[6] The total revenue of a business firm is equal to the price of a particular good multiplied by the quantity sold. Profit is the difference between revenues and costs.

point of the greatest difference of revenue over cost). It might be concluded, therefore, that a price-taker is the most efficient producer—he gives consumers the most goods for the least cost—and that the existence of such firms should be encouraged.

Departures from Competition

MONOPOLY. At the opposite extreme from the type of competition underlying the operation of the invisible hand is monopoly. "Monopoly" literally means "single seller." A monopolist is the single seller of a good for which there is no substitute. Obviously, a true monopolist is difficult, if not impossible, to find in the real world. If there are any, such as the telephone company, they are regulated by public agencies that try, with debatable success, to make the firms behave competitively. When the Aluminum Company of America (Alcoa) was the sole producer of virgin aluminum, it was sometimes cited as an example of a monopolist, but was this really the case? There are many substitutes for aluminum.

A monopolist, by virtue of his market position, is able to exercise a measure of control over price. Such a firm *can* have a price policy, in contrast to the price-taker, who can have none. However, although today there are probably no instances of complete monopoly, we know of many firms that do have deliberate price policies—steel companies, automobile manufacturers, tobacco concerns, grocers, and physicians, for example. Since a monopolist has some control over price, and a price-taker has none, the firms we have just listed, and similar firms, must be *in some sense* monopolistic. However, since we doubt that there are any true monopolies, these firms must also be in some sense competitive. These two conclusions are correct. The characteristic American business firm is a blend of monopolistic and competitive elements. In general, American firms may be said to be "monopolistically competitive."

MONOPOLISTIC COMPETITION AND OLIGOPOLY. About forty years after Alfred Marshall had rebuilt economics, the discipline needed reconstruction once more. The world had changed; new theories were needed to explain it. Marshall had provided economists with two theoretical extremes: a rigorous statement of the principles of an economy made up of price-taker firms and a theory of monopoly. Although both these basic theories were immensely useful (and are still frequently used for the valuable insights they convey), the growing importance of firms that were neither pure competitors nor pure monopolists was increasingly evident.

In the early 1930's two economists, Edward H. Chamberlin in the United States and Joan Robinson in England, produced theories purporting to explain the functioning of what had then become the most important type of firm in the economies of the West. Both of these theories built upon Marshall's work without contradicting it, so they may be said to be additions to neoclassical theorizing.

Chamberlin combined the theories of competition and monopoly to produce a theory of monopolistic competition. The hallmark of a monopolistic competitor is that he produces a good somewhat distinguishable from other goods in the same general product line. The producer is able to try to attract customer loyalty by pointing out real or imagined superiorities in his product. These differences may range from tangible quality differentials to the smile he gives customers when they enter his store. In the case of monopolistic competitors, customers *do* care from whom they buy.

Most American business firms blend monopolistic and competitive elements. They are not full monopolies, since they have many competitors producing substitute goods. But these goods are, to some degree, *imperfect* substitutes for each other, so the firms are not fully competitive either. *Within limits,* each firm can have a price policy. There are various degrees of monopolistic competition: The stronger are the monopolistic elements of a firm relative to its competitive attributes, the more control the firm has over price—and vice versa. Be sure to note, however, that even a pure monopolist does not have complete control over the prices he charges. In the absence of extra-market coercion, he cannot force consumers to buy from him. As he increases his price, more and more consumers will probably choose to do without his product.

The composition of monopolistically competitive industries varies from those in which there are two or three firms to those with many hundreds. When an industry comprises very few firms—say, for illustrative purposes, from two to ten—the firms composing it are said to be *oligopolies.* "Oligopoly" means "few sellers." Oligopoly is highly characteristic of the American economy. Most of our giant firms are oligopolies. Whenever you hear the expression "Big Three" or "Big Five" in regard to business firms, you are safe in assuming that the firms referred to are oligopolies. Examples of oligopolistic industries are not hard to find; they include the automobile, steel, copper, radio and television, tobacco, mail-order retail sales, chemical, fountain-pen, typewriter, computer, motion-picture, electric-light-bulb, and soap industries. There are so many other examples that when we say "American capitalism," we are usually thinking about oligopolies.

Problems of Noncompetitive Market Structures

In contrast to competitive firms, monopolistic firms restrict output and raise price. In our discussion of a perfectly competitive market, where the seller cannot affect the price, we showed that the competitive enterpriser can maximize his profits only by being efficient (by keeping his costs as low as possible) and by increasing his output to the point where an additional unit would raise his total costs more than it would increase his total revenue. Monopolistic firms, however, do not have to accept a market price; they can, within limits, set their own price. They find [7] that they can increase their profits by raising the price, even though that means they will sell less output (since the higher price will cause consumers to demand fewer units of the good). It seems, therefore, that the interests of consumers are defeated when extremely competitive conditions do not prevail. The public gets less of the good and pays a higher price for it. Economic analysis shows this may well be the case whenever a competitive industry becomes monopolistic.

Suppose that 500,000 gizmo firms, constituting a competitive market, were succeeded by five firms, each firm having bought up 100,000 of the smaller competitive businesses. We have assumed a severe case of monopolistic predominance by reducing the number of firms from 500,000 to five, a clear case of "fewness" or oligopoly. Fewness brings with it special problems. Our five oligopolists, like any monopolistic firms, will raise prices and restrict output in comparison with the preceding competitive context. But how high will each firm raise its prices? Who will be the first to do so? If firm A decides to chance being the leader, can it be certain that firms B, C, D, and E will follow it to the new price level? If the 500,000 original firms had been reduced only to 1,000 or 500, probably no one firm would be too concerned with what other firms might be doing. Since the competitive elements would be stronger with a larger number of firms, each firm would feel that its

[7] For reasons shown by more advanced economic analysis than we can explain here.

market policies would not be particularly noticed by its competitors. This can hardly be true in an industry of five firms of more or less equal size, so each firm must be vitally concerned with what its rivals are doing. A characteristic that belongs uniquely to oligopoly, then, is interdependence.

What are the likely results of interdependence? Interdependence breeds uncertainty, and no one really likes uncertainty very much, especially as a steady diet. If, for example, oligopolist A decides to raise the price of gizmos to a higher level, firms B, C, D, and E may let him go it alone, watching the misguided A price himself out of the market. On the other hand, if A decides to cut price below some mutually agreeable level, in the hope that he will take business away from the other four firms, the other four may follow right along, with the result that no one takes any customers away from anyone else, and all suffer from lower profits owing to the injudicious price cut.

Thus, oligopolistic prices are believed to be "sticky." That is, oligopolists may not respond well to market stimuli. Should costs of production fall, they may not pass the benefits along to consumers in the form of a price reduction because they do not want to start a series of competitive price decreases that might even take the extreme form of a price war.

Since uncertainty is so uncomfortable, oligopolists may try to rid themselves of it through any of several common practices. One of the simplest of these is price leadership, in which one firm sets a price and the others follow. The agreement as to which firm exercises price leadership may be express or tacit. Another way of circumventing uncertainty, much used in Europe before the Second World War, is the cartel. The members of a cartel agree, in writing, on how the market is to be divided geographically, what proportion of the market each firm may have, and, possibly, what prices are to be charged.

As a result of these oligopolistic responses to uncertainty, consumers are the losers, for they are denied the benefits of competition. Actions in restraint of trade are prohibited in the United States by the Sherman Antitrust Act and the Clayton Act. To the credit of American businessmen, undercover noncompetitive agreements have never fared well in the United States; American enterprisers, like the American public generally, are much more favorably disposed toward competition than are their European counterparts, by whom agreements to reduce competition, and consequently uncertainty, are often regarded as a standard business practice.

It seems, in sum, that we have a doleful picture of monopolistically competitive markets, especially in cases of extreme oligopoly. Output is restricted; prices are elevated; and, in the case of oligopoly, there is a predisposition to collusion. At the same time, oligopoly is the most important form of market structure in the United States. Should we worry?

A Dynamic View of Monopolistic Firms

We have been looking at monopolistic firms in a static, or timeless, sense. The analysis itself, properly understood, is not incorrect; but unless we examine an alternative viewpoint we are likely to be led to a questionable conclusion.

Let us look at monopolistically competitive firms, particularly oligopolies, from a dynamic viewpoint—that is, let us look at their activities over time. Simply consider your own knowledge of the American economy. Which firms come to mind as being the most progressive? Which firms contribute the most to our rising standard of living? Your list probably includes International Business Machines Corporation, the General Electric Company, General Motors Corporation, the Ford Motor Company, the Du Pont Company, Radio Corporation of America, and similar corporations. It would not be surprising if your whole list were made up of oligopolies. Do you have a single pure competitor on your list? Perhaps you have listed farmers, feeling that since an ever-fewer number of farmers has succeeded in supplying an ever-increasing urban population with an ever-larger quantity of food, some wheat farmer in North Dakota is undoubtedly very progressive. But is it the farmer who is progressive? Or is it the firms that supply him with his implements, pesticides, and fertilizers and the agricultural colleges and experiment stations that develop new farming techniques and plant strains? A farmer may be efficient, but is he, by himself, progressive?

What makes a business firm progressive? Research and development. What motivates a business firm to undertake research and development? The hope of profits. What enables a business firm to utilize the profits obtained from research and development? A protected market position.

A firm must have large resources to undertake product research and innovation. A small enterpriser simply cannot generate the funds necessary to support a meaningful research program. In addition, there is little point for a firm to put a new or a better product on the market unless the firm can enjoy the benefits of its investment in product development for at least a while. Despite the problems of oligopolistic uncertainty, oligopolies do enjoy a protected market position because they are so few in number. Indeed, precisely because of their uncertainty, oligopolies may undertake product and service innovation. Why? Because oligopolistic uncertainty, as we have described it, is most closely related to price competition; but price competition is only one form of competitive behavior. Oligopolists would rather compete with one another by providing new and improved products and services than by cutting prices. The results of such competition are far less disruptive to them. In fact, there are indications that oligopolistic firms are inherently progressive. They can exploit the fruits of innovation and use the extra profits thus generated to engage in further research. And the process may well be cumulative—progress becomes habitual. Many economists have concluded that oligopolies, viewed from a dynamic standpoint, are the most progressive firms in the American economy.

And the consumer? Consumers in a highly advanced economy do not want simply the greatest quantity of goods at the lowest possible cost. Life is made more bearable by having a wide variety of goods from which to choose and by enjoying improvements in goods over time. Suppose we do pay more for a gizmo when five firms produce the good than when 500,000 firms are engaged in its production. In the latter case, do you think that you would ever get a better gizmo? Could you possibly have a gizmo that was in any way different from anyone else's gizmo? The higher price may well be the cost of product improvement and of a measure of distinction. You may still get what you pay for. Of course, it may also be that, to some degree, you are paying a "private tax" to some oligopolist that a more competitive market structure would reduce or eliminate.

In any case, oligopolists do compete. That is the motivation behind their research and development programs. Although corporations, as a rule, are longer-lived than single proprietorships and partnerships, they have no inherent immortality. They must progress in order to survive. To fall behind in this kind of competitive struggle is to be lost. This was the opinion of the great economist Joseph A. Schumpeter, who, viewing capitalism dynamically, called it "the process of creative destruction." [8] Schumpeter argued that the important form of competition is the battle between firms for survival. Firms may prosper and remain powerful for a while; but, unless a firm can adapt, its power will be weakened, and it will lose its viability. Capitalism grows by destroying old economic structures and erecting new ones. Recall that there were once well over a score of automobile companies in the United States; today the important producers number less than the fingers of one hand. Once the motion-picture industry ruled the mass entertainment media; today the remaining studios devote much of their capacity to serving television. The process of one business fighting another for supremacy, with the battle one of life or death, is the harshest sort of competition, making price competition pale in comparison. Whether we agree with Schumpeter's rather sanguine view of oligopolies or not, surely he was right when he said that we must judge the performance of our form of capitalism over time; and the time needed for an adjudication may be very long, perhaps centuries. Schumpeter doubted that most of us would be around long enough to form a favorable opinion.

THE GENERAL EQUILIBRIUM OF LEON WALRAS

Many people, upon their introduction to the method of partial-equilibrium analysis, ask, "Isn't there any way to study how the economy actually operates?" They are affronted by the apparent artificiality of having to hold other things equal. Soon, however, either they come to agree that the method offers meaningful insights into an enormously complicated mechanism or their complaint is stifled by the sufficient complexities of the partial-equilibrium method itself. They may not be satisfied, but they are glad to leave well enough alone.

Yet many thoughtful students do wonder if there is not some way to put the bits and pieces of the neoclassical method together so that the economy can be seen functioning as a system. It is intellectually satisfying to see how scarcity leads to opportunity costs, how rent is price determined rather than the other way around, how marginal utility is the relevant variable in the want patterns of consumers, how the demand for and the supply of gizmos together determine their equilibrium price, and how the demand for and supply of the people who make

[8] Joseph A. Schumpeter, *Capitalism, Socialism, and Democracy*, 3rd ed. (New York: Harper, 1950), pp. 81–86.

gizmos determine their equilibrium wage. But all these processes are seen in isolation. From the time of the physiocrats, and especially in the work of Adam Smith, have we not seen that the economy is a system? How does the system work?

We know that the economy is not only a system; it is a circular flow, and its elements are highly interdependent. So we can begin to put the pieces together. We know that the price of a gizmo is not determined solely by the wages of the men who make gizmos or by the utility that gizmo consumers attach to the goods. Marshall showed that the subjective (demand) and objective (cost of production) concepts must be united to produce a determinate equilibrium price. Yet, in synthesizing the utility side and the cost-of-production side of a market confrontation, we run the danger of preserving the cleft between the classicals and the marginalists that Marshall tried to bridge.

We (except Marxians) have now learned the lesson that a good is not valuable because the labor that made it is valuable; rather, the labor that made it is valuable because it makes a valuable good. Where does this statement leave us? We *do* have the costs of production (which include labor) entering into the determination of value on the supply side. Obviously, the value of the factors of production is determined like the value of anything else. The demand for factors interacts with the supply of factors to produce an equilibrium price, which, in turn, becomes part of the cost of production of the good in question and is reflected in the supply schedule of the final good. Therefore, we seem to have arrived at a state in which we must make the pathetic statement that the prices of productive factors depend upon the supply of and demand for the final goods that the factors produce and that the prices of those goods depend, in part, on the supply of and demand for the factors involved in their production.

By now, you have probably concluded that traversing the circular flow involves circular reasoning. That this is not so was shown conclusively by Leon Walras (1834–1910) of the University of Lausanne. In his *Elements of Pure Economics,* Walras developed the system of *general*-equilibrium analysis. In a colorless but mathematically exact way, he showed by equations the equilibrium solution of a case much like that of the "brewer-baker" example in our chapter on Adam Smith.

Walras inseparably fused the utility and cost-of-production sides of the market, instead of merely creating a synthesis of the two. By doing this, he irrevocably exorcised any ghosts of the defunct classical cost-of-production thesis—spirits that sometimes seemed to haunt even the great Alfred Marshall. At times, the neoclassicals appeared to be driven by an urge to reenter the house of Ricardo to conjure phantoms of the labor theory of value. Any vestiges of the cost-of-production theories could not stand the light of Walras' analysis, and, thanks to his work, economists have been able to proceed untroubled by any recurring doubts about the neoclassical theory of value.

Finally, Walras "closed" the neoclassical system. He showed that there was one equation for every unknown in the system. This means that there is a determinate solution to the economizing process of the free-market economy. The system is self-contained. Rather than involving circular reasoning, the economy can be represented by a system of simultaneous equations. Walras rigorously proved what Smith had intuitively contended about the free-market economy: It is an interdependent system whose form is mutually determined by its various elements.

In the Walrasian general equilibrium, which occurs only in the context of a perfectly competitive economy, no one can increase his utility without decreasing the utility of someone else, and, as provided by Say's law, all goods are sold. This is often referred to as an "optimal" solution to the economic problem.

For accomplishing this Herculean task, some economists of undisputed repute have dubbed Walras "the greatest of all economists." Others reserve their praise for Smith or Marshall.

The mathematics of Walras' analysis are much too difficult to be even hinted at here. The mathematically adept may wish to consult an intermediate-price-theory text to see the formidable array of equations and notations of the Walrasian system. Despite his disdain for nonmathematical economists, Walras' mathematics are relatively inelegant and his prose is more convoluted and tortured than that of Ricardo. (Interestingly, Walras failed several mathematics examinations in his youth; and when, after spending a year as an indifferent engineering student, he tried his hand at writing, the result was a monstrously bad novel.) But Walras' economic insight was brilliant. Despite his inept symbolic and verbal explanations, his general-equilibrium method rounded out, closed, and polished the neoclassical system.

JOHN MAYNARD KEYNES:
ECONOMIST OF FULL
EMPLOYMENT AND GROWTH

7

Until our entry into the Second World War, living in the American economy was like riding a roller coaster—but it was not fun. The American economy (and the major European economies) up to that time was highly unstable. Americans were resigned to repeated peaks and troughs in economic activity, which culminated in the roaring boom of the 1920's and the devastating depression of the 1930's. Life was neither comfortable nor predictable. One could get caught up in an expansionary phase of the cycle, borrow, buy land, and invest, only to be caught in a downturn. For a great number of our people, this meant bankruptcy, loss of jobs, bank failures and, for the economy as a whole, the victory of "less" over "more." In short, our aggregate economic behavior was not solving the economic problem.

In previous chapters, we have noted that economic fluctuations seemed to be inherent in the economic life of capitalistic nations. The price of material abundance appeared to be periodic booms followed by inevitable downturns. Occasionally, economic prophets would herald the attainment of an irrepressible level of prosperity, but the downturn always came. The question we now consider is whether capitalism must be shackled inescapably to economic instability.

DEPRESSIONS: THEIR CAUSE AND SUPPOSED CURE

Scarcity is the essence of economics, yet people can become satiated with some of the things they buy with their limited incomes. For example, the automobile industry has bad years now and then, when it appears that consumers have fairly well satisfied their desire for cars. Suppose one day it seemed that consumers were not buying things as they had been the day before. The circular flow of income would be affected. If the trend continued, goods would go unsold, and eventually some workers would lose their jobs. As less and less is spent with each revolution of the circular flow,[1] the economy would plunge into a downward spiral having its end in a depression, or trough, in the pattern of economic fluctuations. A depression would happen *if* the trend continued. The classical economists argued that the trend would not continue, that the economy would right itself.

How could the situation remedy itself before it got serious? With competitive firms and competitive laborers, this is no problem, said the classicals. The process is as simple as the demand-and-supply analysis in Chapter 6. Sellers will begin to cut the prices of their goods so that inventories will not pile up. It will always be worthwhile to hire laborers at *some* wage rate, and the wage rate, in consequence of the temporary spate of unemployment, will begin to fall. It will continue to fall until all the workers willing to work at the new, lower wage have been put back to work. From the workers' point of view, it is better to work than to starve. The workers are not likely to suffer from the lower wage because the prices of the things they buy will have fallen too, and they will be deprived of little, if any, of the goods and services they normally consume. Thus, unemployment is only a short-run phenomenon.

Is this convincing? What was happening in the 1930's? A "short run" that was a decade or more in length? Americans standing in the bread lines or selling apples on street corners would have found little comfort in the notion that one of the glories of our economic system is that it is self-correcting and that the miseries they were enduring were manifestations of a short-run phenomenon.

The depression of the 1930's was worldwide. Europe, especially Britain, was involved in it no less than was the United States. The

[1] See Chapter 2, pp. 39–43.

British and American governments tried to remedy the situation, but their initial efforts not only achieved nothing but probably made matters worse, as we shall see.

The economics we are studying in this chapter, often called "the new economics," is rooted in Britain's experience following the First World War. Obviously, the war years were unusual. In the first normal year, 1919, the British government felt that the proper course for the nation to take was to resume as quickly as possible the serene life that had been interrupted in 1914. A little boom appeared during the year of demobilization, which seemed to prove the wisdom of the nostalgic course taken by the government. One year later, however, the boom collapsed; Britain entered a period of economic distress that would eventually engulf the world.

The United States experienced postwar prosperity and depression, too, but the boom was longer-lived. In the mid-twenties, Americans were still convinced that their country would have perpetual prosperity. Downturns in economic activity were held to be obsolete, even though in Europe, especially in the United Kingdom, unemployment ominously persisted from 1919 to 1929. The West was too closely interrelated for the economic malaise not to spread. In 1929, the United States caught it.

The world was entirely unprepared. What Britain thought was a full-fledged depression was only the prelude to her difficulties. Unemployment, which at the outset of the contraction had been at the improbably high figure of one million persons, became an unthinkable three million before the distress was over.

What does a responsible individual do when he finds himself in financial difficulty? He cuts his spending and attempts to increase his income. Therefore, was it not entirely reasonable for the British government to have attempted to keep the beleaguered island kingdom afloat by cutting expenditures and increasing taxes? In the 1930's, the United States, never too quick to learn from anyone else's mistakes, repeated Britain's. Following the decline in the aggregate demand of Americans for goods and services, President Hoover obtained the authority to reduce public spending and increase taxes. In spite of these actions, or more accurately, as we shall see, in response to them, the British and American economies continued their downward plunges. Something was wrong.

Governments and political leaders of the time should not be criticized too severely, for economists, blinded by Say's law,[2] had no answers to give them. At least the 1930's demonstrated, albeit negatively, the importance of theory to the world of affairs. Once again, economics was out of touch with the times; there was need for a new theory. The theory that emerged—one that has virtually remade the capitalist world, to say nothing of economics—was the work of John Maynard Keynes.

JOHN MAYNARD KEYNES (1883–1946)

John Maynard Keynes was a student of Alfred Marshall at Cambridge University, where he later taught. One of the most famous and influential economists of all time, he was even raised to the peerage, becoming Baron of Tilton. Keynes was not only an academician but an adviser to the British treasury and a skilled investor who won two fortunes during his lifetime.

Human beings have a proclivity for erecting monuments to great men, but most are lifeless and of relatively small value compared with the services they commemorate. The monuments the world has erected to John Maynard Keynes are more pervasive, more vital, and certainly more costly than any erected in honor of Washington, Lincoln, Nelson, or Wellington. To find Keynes's memorials, take the advice given to those who seek the monument to Sir Christopher Wren, architect of St. Paul's Cathedral: "Reader, if you seek his monument, look about you." If we look around us, we will see the living monuments that capitalistic nations have begun to erect to Keynes: the *intentional* budget deficits that are now a key part of the fiscal policies of the American and British governments.

The word "intentional" is important, for budget deficits have been a familiar, if unwanted, part of our fiscal scene since the 1930's. Now, many years since Keynes's great work, *The General Theory of Employment, Interest, and Money* (1936), was published, our national administrations have advocated intentional budget deficits to help to stimulate the economy.

Thus, you can see why Keynes has been controversial. To spend intentionally more than one earns is held, in some circles, to be grossly immoral. Earlier American administrations that incurred unintentional

[2] Say's law, as you will remember, states that the act of production creates sufficient income to purchase the total output of the economy. Therefore, insufficiency of *aggregate* demand cannot be a cause of economic slumps.

deficits were embarrassed (although some were more embarrassed than others), but now we have national administrations that actively seek to create deficits by spending more than the government receives in tax receipts. Have our standards fallen?

The embarrassment Americans of an earlier day felt at deficit spending was shared by the governments of Keynes's homeland. Not too many years ago, when Britain was a major world power, many finance ministers from underdeveloped nations left the halls of the British treasury in anguish. They had been sent by their respective governments to secure what then passed for foreign aid, and they were told by the chancellors of the exchequer that they could expect no assistance from Whitehall unless they mended their profligate ways and embraced a policy of "fiscal responsibility," meaning, simply, "Don't spend more than you earn."

THE SIGNIFICANCE OF EFFECTIVE AGGREGATE DEMAND

Lord Keynes taught that a mature capitalistic economy is likely to come to grief because people will not make the demands on it that they theoretically should. They will save part of their incomes, and the saved dollars will not reenter the income stream. Thus, consumers and business firms will not buy all the products that the economy is capable of producing, and the economy must of necessity suffer unemployment.

But Keynes also taught that resources need not be left idle and, by implication, that if the survival of capitalism is desired, resources had better not be left idle—effective demand for them must be created.

Now, what is effective aggregate demand, and how can it be created? Effective aggregate demand is Keynesian talk for spending. It is the total spending of all the members of the economy—consumers, business firms, and government—for the goods and services the economy produces. Why is spending, or effective demand, important? Because, as we have seen in the circular-flow model of the economy, spending and income are the same thing. If one individual has an income, someone else must have spent. No spending, no income. Keep in mind the important idea that the economy is a circular flow, and ask yourself what will happen if people decide to save more money at every level of income? Saving is a leak from the circular flow of income and affects the level of income the same way a water leak affects a circulating hydraulic system. In a swimming pool, the water continually recirculates. If the pool is in good working order, the rate of outflow equals the rate of inflow, and the water level remains constant. But suppose there is a leak. Some of the water is escaping from the system, and the water level of the pool will fall. Similarly, if the economy has been in equilibrium (that is, if the gross national product has remained constant) and households decide to increase their rate of saving, the level of GNP must fall unless an increased inflow of spending matches the now higher rate of saving. Without spending injections to compensate for the saving withdrawals, the economy will plummet downward.

This returns us to a question we have considered before: Is saving good or bad? Once again it seems that saving—which is the same thing as not spending—may be bad. Most of us have been taught that thrift is a virtue, but here it appears that saving leads the economy into downturns that may deprive people of their jobs. Must we argue that saving is a private virtue and a public vice? Not necessarily. It depends on what is done with the money people save. If savings are channeled back into the economy by financial institutions (banks, stock markets, insurance companies, savings and loan associations) and spent by business firms for plant and equipment, the economy will experience no leakage from the circular flow.

This, said the classicals, is just what *will* happen. Moreover, two good ends will be served simultaneously—the saving of part of their incomes by individuals and the growth of the economy made possible by additions to plant and equipment. This is Say's law. Let us review it. Not only do wages and prices fall to restore full employment; if people decide to save more of their incomes, the interest rate (the price of borrowing money) falls, and this encourages business firms to borrow more money to spend on plant and equipment. The interest rate continues to fall until the amount saved by households is equal to the amount borrowed and spent by business firms. Thus, the classicals saw the capitalist economy as a fully self-correcting mechanism. Depressions were just minor imperfections or the result of tampering— usually by government—with the self-regulating system and should be left to work themselves out.

Keynes disagreed. He felt that the classicals had underestimated the seriousness of the "imperfections," overestimated the speed with which the system would correct itself, and failed to understand the real causes of depression. In order to follow his argument, it will be helpful for us to learn a little more about aggregate demand.

THE ANALYSIS OF AGGREGATE DEMAND

To begin, we must define the term "gross national product" more precisely than we have heretofore. The gross national product of a nation is the total value of all the *final* [3] goods and services produced within its boundaries during a one-year period. The quantity of each final good is multiplied by its price, and the resulting arithmetic products are added to obtain the GNP.

Why do we use only final goods and services? Let us take a simple example. A considerable part of an automobile is sheet steel. The steel itself is the end product of a process combining coke, limestone, and iron ore. The coke was once coal. If we start with the value of the coal, add to that the value of the coke, then add the value of the steel, and, finally, add the value of the finished automobile, we shall have added in the value of the coal four times, to say nothing of the coke three times and the steel twice! We do want the values of everything we have produced during a year to be included in our GNP, but we want the value of each good to be counted no more than once. By including only the value of the finished automobile in the GNP, we avoid "double counting." For example, suppose one dollar's worth of coal is used to produce the coke used in making automobile sheet steel and it costs twenty-five cents to change that amount of coal into coke. The coal was worth $1, and the coke is worth $1.25. It would be incorrect to add these two figures together and say that the value of the fuel used to make the steel necessary for one automobile is $2.25. That way, the value of the coal would be counted twice. By simply taking the value of the coke, $1.25, we count the $1 value of the coal and the twenty-five cents' worth of *value added* to it by the coking process. Thus, by including only the values of finished automobiles in the GNP, we avoid counting the value of the goods and services used in producing automobiles more than once.

Many people understand pictures better than they do words, so let us try to work out a pictorial analysis of Keynes's main ideas.

In Figure 8, we measure the dollar amount of the gross national product on the horizontal axis. The gross national product is also necessarily the gross national income of an economy, since the economy

[3] See p. 4.

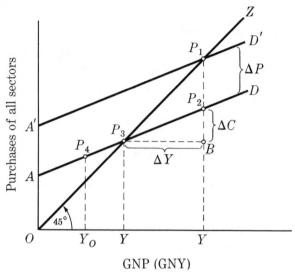

GNP (GNY)

FIGURE 8   *The Determination of the Equilibrium Level of the Gross National Product*

is a circular flow and what is output to one person must be income to another. Following the Keynesian convention, we let Y stand for income.

On the vertical axis, we measure the dollar volume of purchases for goods and services (spending) of the three sectors of the economy (households, business firms, and government). Thus, we have dollar amounts on both axes. If at any given level of GNP the three sectors were to purchase all the output of the economy, it is clear that the dollar amount of purchases would equal the dollar amount of GNP, and a graph of such behavior would be the straight line OZ, which makes a 45° angle with either axis at the origin. For example, at P_1 and P_3 all the GNP is purchased, since the amounts on both axes are equal, and these points lie on OZ. Points P_1 and P_3 are only two of an infinite number of points lying on OZ at which all the GNP is purchased.

In the short run, however, there is no reason for purchasers to wish to buy exactly the amount of the GNP. At certain levels, the GNP may not be large enough to satisfy them; they may demand an output beyond the fulfillment capacity of the economy. At other possible levels of GNP, they may not demand all the output of the economy; they may *save*.

Let us assume that AD is the current short-run aggregate-demand schedule for the three buying sectors. You should regard AD much as the individual- and market-demand schedules of Chapter 6, for AD shows what amount buyers are actually willing to purchase. There are two major differences, however, between an aggregate-demand curve and the demand curve for a particular good. The first difference is self-explanatory; AD is an *aggregate*-demand curve; it shows the demand of purchasers for *all* things (the GNP) the economy produces. The second difference has probably occurred to you already; AD has a positive slope. This does not violate the law of demand. The graphs of the Chapter 6 correlated *price* with *quantity* and showed that the relationship is inverse. Here, we are relating *purchasing* to *output,* and the relationship is direct; hence, the positive slope. Why is the relationship between purchases and GNP direct? The circular-flow concept answers this question. Output is income; that is why we have put GNY in parentheses. As the aggregate income (output) of the economy rises, purchasers will demand more output; therefore, an aggregate-demand curve has a positive slope.

What we want to know is how the actual level of GNP is determined. (For the time being, continue to assume that AD is the aggregate-demand curve, and pay no attention to $A'D'$.) Suppose that the level of GNP is OY_F. If purchasers are to buy it all, their expenditures must equal $Y_F P_1$. Since P_1 lies on OZ, we know that $OY_F = Y_F P_1$. But, in fact, purchasers' expenditures equal only $Y_F P_2$. We know this from the aggregate-demand curve AD, which tells us how much purchasers will actually buy at any given level of GNP.

Now, under these circumstances, can the GNP stay at level OY_F? No. There is a deficiency of aggregate demand equal to $P_1 P_2$. Purchasers are *saving* an amount equal to $P_1 P_2$. Although the economy is producing a dollar volume of goods and services equal to OY_F, purchasers will not buy them. A dollar amount of output equal to $P_1 P_2$ goes unsold. Here, then, is a general glut! But the glut will disappear. How? By much the same mechanism as a surplus of a particular good is eliminated in conventional demand-and-supply analysis. Producers attempting to rid themselves of unintended and unwanted inventories will cut back production until everything produced is sold. Given AD, this can happen only at a level of GNP equal to OY, for at that output (income), as demand curve AD shows, purchasers spend YP_3 for goods and services, and YP_3 is equal to OY. The glut is gone! Obviously OY is the only maintainable level of GNP, for, given AD, at no other level of output will purchasers buy all the output. OY is therefore called the equilibrium level of GNP. Once it attains that level, the economy will have no tendency to move in either direction; and, at any point on AD to the left or right of P_3, the economy *must* tend to OY. Suppose the level of output is less than OY—say OY_0. At this level, purchasers buy an amount of goods and services equal to $Y_0 P_4$. Can you reverse our analysis to see how the economy must expand until GNP equals OY?

Two things should be noted about the equilibrium level of income, OY, before we go on. First, we have said that everything produced is sold. This does not mean that inventories are nonexistent and that no one is saving. It does mean that there are no *unintended* inventories. At any equilibrium level of GNP, goods remaining unsold were intended to be in that state by their sellers. For analytical convenience, it may help to regard *intended* inventories as being sold to their producers. After all, inventories are part of the capital of a business firm. Second, although there is no net saving in the economy, one of the sectors may be saving. For example, consumers may be saving part of their incomes at OY, with all the proceeds being loaned to firms who use them to buy capital (including intended inventory). The government sector may have a balanced budget with taxes equaling expenditures.

At OY, the economy is in equilibrium. Everything produced is sold. Is Say's law fulfilled? What does Keynes have to add to the classical hypothesis? The first change Keynesian analysis makes in the classical hypothesis is to say that at OY Say's law may or may not be operative. The classicals would say that an equilibrium level of income must be a full-employment level of income. This is precisely the point Keynes challenged. He pointed out that, although the economy tends to equilibrium, it does not, in the short run, automatically tend to a *full-employment* equilibrium. In the short run, owing to the forces discussed in the next section, expenditures equal to YP_3 may be insufficient to keep all men and machines employed. To achieve full employment, expenditures may have to be equal to $Y_F P_1$. In that case, the full-employment level of GNP is OY_F, while the equilibrium level remains at OY. So long as GNP is OY, men and equipment must be unemployed. (You may regard OY as the level of GNP in the mid-thirties and OY_F as the level of GNP during the Second World War.)

There is nothing good or bad about an equilibrium level of income. It just is. Why should a free-market economy tend to an equilibrium having any kind of normative significance? If we decide that full employment is desirable, we must consciously try to make the economy produce a level of GNP equal to OY_F. But how do we do this? We have just shown that, given AD, the economy cannot maintain an output of OY_F. What must be done is to change AD—to get purchasers to buy more of the GNP at every possible level of output (income). This will cause the entire aggregate-demand curve to shift upward.

Notice that it can make no difference which sector spends more at every level of GNP, just so long as the necessary spending is done. Keynes believed, for reasons given elsewhere in this chapter, that the national government is the most logical source of the necessary increased expenditures.

Suppose we continue to use the experience of the United States in the Second World War as an example. As a result of the pressing necessity to buy war materials and supplies, the federal government was forced to engage in an unprecedentedly large volume of deficit spending. A government "deficit spends" when its expenditures exceed its tax receipts. The difference between receipts and expenditures is accounted for by borrowing. The federal government, in consequence of its monetary and taxing authority, has virtually limitless borrowing power. From the sale of its obligations (treasury bonds) to the banking system and to private firms and individuals, it acquires the money to provide new infusions of purchasing power. At the same time that the federal government was expanding its purchases through deficit spending, the business sector, in anticipation of an expected avalanche of government orders, greatly increased its investment spending to provide the additional productive capacity. The result was a rise in the aggregate-demand schedule.

Let us assume that the aggregate-demand schedule rose by an amount equal to $\Delta P = P_2P_1$, so that it was then $A'D'$. The increase in spending for goods and services caused output to expand until OY_F was reached—an equilibrium level by definition and also a full-employment level. Only by intervention with the market mechanism were the equilibrium and full-employment levels of the GNP rendered equivalent. Note, however, that this "intervention" was merely an increase in spending by two of the three sectors. (There were, of course, other peculiarly wartime interventions with the economy on the part of the federal government, but these are not part of the Keynesian prescription.)

It is unfortunate that it took a war to teach us this lesson, for experience is a hard teacher and not a good one; her lesson is always late. Keynes was a much gentler teacher, but apparently more difficult for men to comprehend.

There is an interesting phenomenon in connection with the increase in aggregate demand. The increase in purchasing—the vertical distance between AD and $A'D'$, that is, $P_2P_1 = \Delta P$—is *less* than the distance $YY_F = \Delta Y$.[4] An increase in purchases has generated an increase in the GNP larger than itself. This phenomenon has a name: the *multiplier effect*. The multiplier effect means that an increase (decrease) in aggregate demand will cause an increase (decrease) in GNP larger than itself.

Is this making something out of nothing? Many people, when they encounter the multiplier for the first time, think so. But remember the circular-flow idea. Suppose that the current equilibrium level of the GNP is \$300 billion. The level of purchasing that is, of course, also \$300 billion is insufficient to fully employ all the resources of the economy. Now suppose that business firms or the government, or both, raise their spending on goods and services by \$1 billion above the current level. One billion dollars' more purchasing power is injected into the circular flow of economic activity. Does this mean that the new equilibrium level of the GNP will be \$301 billion? Does the GNP increase only by the amount of new spending injected into the economy? If you think so, go back to Chapter 1; look at the diagram of the circular flow of income.

Business firms or government simply cannot thrust \$1 billion worth of new purchasing into the circular flow only to have it stay there. For every expenditure, there must be an income. Households, as the ultimate owners of the productive resources employed by the firms, must be the final recipients of the business sector's \$1 billion increase in spending. What will households do with the \$1 billion addition to their incomes? There are only two things they *can* do with it. Households may either spend their incomes on consumption goods and services or not spend it. (Not spending is, of course, *saving*.) Al-

---

[4] The upper-case Greek letter Δ (delta) is read "change in."

though we have defined what households *can* do, we must know what they *will* do with an increase in income in order to predict the new equilibrium level of the GNP. Suppose that investigation shows that households spend nine-tenths of any addition to their incomes. Obviously, then, they must save one-tenth of any income increment. (In other words, they have what is called a *marginal propensity to consume* (*MPC*) of 9/10 and a *marginal propensity to save* (*MPS*) of 1/10.) Thus, when the households receive the additional $1 billion from business firms in payment for the productive services that they have sold to the firms, they will spend $900 million on consumption goods and services and save the remaining $100 million. The receivers of this new $900 million worth of consumption spending are, of course, the business firms, who will then add $900 million of goods and services to their former level of output to satisfy the newly augmented consumer demand.

Let us look at what is happening in the circular flow. As a result of the initial injection of an additional $1 billion into the circular flow, consumption expenditures have increased by $900 million and saving has increased by $100 million. To the initial $1 billion of new investment spending has been added the household sector's $900 million of consumption spending *induced* by the business sector's initial expenditure. Business firms and households together wish to purchase $1.9 billion more output. Owing to the time necessary to expand output to meet the increased volume of intended purchasing, there will be a lag between the dollar amount of purchasing orders and the dollar volume of actual goods and services. But our expectation is, assuming the economy has the capacity to fulfill the new orders, that, eventually the total output of goods and services should reach $301.9 billion.

But this is not an equilibrium level of the GNP (for reasons that will become clear as we continue). *If nothing else is done*—that is, if business firms allow their spending to return to its former rate—the GNP will return to its old equilibrium level of $300 billion. The expansion of the GNP will be only a temporary surge.

For the GNP to expand to a continuing higher level, the increased *rate* of investment spending must be maintained. A one-shot injection of investment or government spending into the circular flow will not cause the GNP to rise to a higher equilibrium level.

The behavior of the economy is similar to the reaction of your car when you depress the accelerator pedal a little more to increase your speed. Say you are traveling at 50 miles per hour; if you depress the pedal a little, let us suppose your speed moves up to 60 miles per hour. Assuming that you are on a level stretch of highway, your new rate of travel can be maintained only if you keep the accelerator depressed to its new level. If you let up on it so that it returns to its original position, your automobile will begin to fall back to the old "equilibrium" speed of 50 miles an hour. Similarly, if the GNP is to reach a new equilibrium at a higher level, the new *rate* of spending must be maintained over a given time period. (For accounting purposes, the time period is customarily one year.)

Let us suppose that business firms do raise the *rate* of their investment spending by $1 billion per year—say, from $50 billion annually to $51 billion. This means that in any twelve-month period, the *rate* of investment spending is maintained at an additional $1 billion above the initial rate. Such an increase in the rate of investment expenditures can be represented graphically, as in Figure 8. Assume that the shift of the aggregate-demand curve from AD to $A'D'$ was caused by a $1 billion increase in the rate of investment expenditures. In this case, the vertical distance between AD and $A'D'$ ($\Delta = P_1P_2$) is $1 billion. As you can see in Figure 8, the distance YY_F is greater than the vertical distance ($\Delta P = P_1P_2$) between the two aggregate-demand curves AD and $A'D'$. A rise in the rate of investment spending ($1 billion in our hypothetical example) has caused an *increase* in the annual rate of output of final goods and services greater than itself. In other words, a $1 billion increase in the rate of flow of investment injections into the economy causes the increase in the annual rate of flow of total final output to exceed $1 billion! How does this come about?

Out of the first injection, households spent $900 million and saved $100 million; therefore, nine-tenths of the additional amount that the business firms had injected into the circular flow was returned to them. Business firms now use this "extra" $900 million (received from consumption expenditures) to buy the resources necessary for making the additional $900 million of output demanded by households. The resource owners receiving this additional $900 million payment are, of course, themselves members of households, and, in the aggregate, they treat a $900 million increment in their incomes exactly the same way that the first-round income recipients treated the initial $1 billion increase in income. These second-round income recipients (resource owners) spend nine-tenths or $810 million, on consumption goods and services and save one-tenth, or $90 million.

Remember, now, that the *rate* of investment spending has been increased by $1 billion. Not only, then, does the business sector disburse $900 million on the second round, but it also continues to make investment expenditures at an annual rate of $51 billion—that is, at a rate of $1 billion more than the previous equilibrium rate of $50 billion per year. Therefore, on the second round, a total of $1.9 billion in additional spending leaves the business sector to be spent by the consumer-resource owner sector. We have already noted that consumers will spend nine-tenths or $810 million, of the $900 million increase in their incomes. And, of course, they will also treat this round's additional $1 billion injection as they did the initial injection—they will spend $900 million of it and save $100 million.

Now let's take stock of where we are. In the first round, in response to the business sector's injection of $1 billion, consumers increased their consumption expenditures by $900 million and their savings by $100 million. The business sector then spent that $900 million in addition to their second-round injection of $1 billion. Consumers thus received $1.9 billion, of which they spent $1.71 billion and saved $190 million. This process is illustrated in Table 6, which also shows what will happen on the third round. Notice that each round not only is larger than the preceding round but adds an increasing amount to the GNP. By the end of the third round the $1 billion increase in the annual rate of investment has caused an increase in the GNP of $5.61 billion.[5]

When will this process end? When the GNP reaches a new equilibrium. And that will happen only when the leakages from the circular flow equal the injections. Investment is an injection (it adds money to the circular flow), and saving is a leakage (it takes money out of circulation). In other words, *the GNP will reach an equilibrium*

[5] This is necessarily so because GNP ≡ C + S; that is, the total output of the economy must be identical to the value of the goods that *are* consumed plus the value of those goods that *are not* consumed. The change in consumption for the first three rounds is $5.049 billion, and the change in saving is $.561 billion; hence, the change in GNP is $5.610 billion, the total of the changes in consumption and saving.

TABLE 6 *Changes Resulting from an Increase in Investment Spending (in millions of dollars)**

Households

Businesses	CHANGE IN CONSUMPTION ΔC	CHANGE IN SAVING ΔS	GNP Δ(C + S)
1,000	900	100	1,000
1,000 900	900 810 1,710	100 90 190	1,900
1,000 900 810	900 810 729 2,439	100 90 81 271	2,710
			5,610

* *MPC* = 9/10; the assumed increase in rate of investment spending is $1 billion.

value when the change in the rate of saving matches the change in the rate of investment. In our example, the rate of investment increased by $1 billion per year. Hence, the GNP will continue to rise until its increase has generated a sufficient increase in the rate of saving to equal the increase in the rate of investment. That increase must, of course, be $1 billion. When the GNP has finally risen to the level that will induce households to save $1 billion a year more than they were saving prior to the increase in the rate of investment spending, the GNP will have reached its new, and higher, equilibrium level.

What increase in the GNP will be required to raise the annual rate of saving by $1 billion? Fortunately, we do not have to repeat the tedious process of following the circular flow until we reach the round in which the increase in the rate of saving totals $1 billion.

The ordinary algebraic formula for an infinite geometric progression will do the job for us. Translated into economic terms, the formula reads:

$$\Delta Y = \frac{1}{1 - c} \cdot \Delta E$$

(ΔY is the change in the GNP occasioned by the initial injection of spending into the circular flow; c is the fraction of each addition to income spent on consumption goods and services—that is, the MPC; and ΔE is the change in spending that initiated the disequilibrating forces causing the GNP to change.)

Thus, substituting in our formula:

$$Y = \frac{1}{1 - 9/10} \cdot \$1 \text{ billion}$$

$$= \frac{1}{1/10} \cdot \$1 \text{ billion}$$

$$= 10 \cdot \$1 \text{ billion}$$

$$= \$10 \text{ billion}$$

Therefore, we conclude that *if* households, in the aggregate, are disposed to spend nine-tenths of any addition to their incomes on consumer goods and services, the GNP will rise by $10 billion for every $1 billion in new spending. The new equilibrium level of the GNP is, thus, $310 billion, $9 billion *more* than the original increase in spending injected into the circular flow by the business sector. Keynes certainly used an apt expression when he termed this phenomenon the *multiplier effect*.

A THEORY FOR THE SHORT RUN

With this information in hand, we can now examine Keynes's disagreement with the classicals. Keynes accepted the self-correcting mechanism hypothesized by the classicals. He agreed that in the long run, the economy does automatically tend to a full-employment equilibrium level of the GNP. What, then, is the problem? It is succinctly put in an overquoted aphorism attributed to Lord Keynes: "In the long run, we are all dead." The corollary: It is the short run that hurts. Keynes argued that depressions should not be left to work themselves out, not because they will not do so eventually, but because society cannot afford to wait.

Our next question is: Why does not the economy tend to full employment in the *short* run? Because a major premise of the classicals, that of price flexibility, is faulty. Price flexibility may have been a valid assumption at one time; but in our time, argued Keynes, it does not obtain. Therefore, any theorizing based upon this invalid assumption must produce a misleading conclusion.

What happened to price flexibility? It was diminished by the forces discussed in Chapter 6. Monopolistic elements, whether in business, labor, or government, have some control over price. Prices do not respond freely to changes in market conditions. They show an especially stubborn resistance to downward movements. In times of slack demand for commodities, business firms may refuse to lower the prices of their goods. Laborers, especially those organized into unions, may refuse to accept cuts in wages. This will mean that some workers will be laid off, although for the senior members of the union[6] such a practice means income security. Governments enact minimum-wage legislation, which means that any employee who is not worth the minimum wage to his employer will be fired, since it is illegal to pay a worker less than the statutory minimum. The result is that the price flexibility required to produce full employment is not found in the modern capitalistic economy. Goods remain unsold because they are priced too high, and laborers, as a result of either uniform wage agreements or minimum-wage legislation are priced out of the labor market.

Similarly, the fall in interest rates may not induce businessmen to borrow the funds that households have saved. In a depression, there is often more than enough capacity to serve the economy; plants and equipment may be standing idle, and it will seem absurd to borrow funds to add more plant and equipment to their already idle facilities. Depressed periods bring with them great waves of gloom. Simple pessimism about the future may leave businessmen unwilling to borrow at virtually any rate of interest.

---

[6] Union rules generally provide that men be laid off in reverse of the order in which they were hired.

THE CREATION OF FULL-EMPLOYMENT
AGGREGATE DEMAND

Keynes took the world as he found it. Monopolistic economic units may be wrong morally and economically, but Keynes did not trouble himself with what the world *ought* to be like. He simply constructed a theory that would explain the existing economy.

Regardless of how you approach the matter, said Keynes, the only way to have prosperity is for people to receive incomes, and the only way to have incomes is to have spending. If we agree with Keynes that we must spend our way out of a depression, and that seems now to be a truism, the question is: From whom will the spending come? To answer this question, let us divide the economy into its three basic sectors: the consuming public, business firms, and government.

It is obvious that consumers will not spend more to get the economy out of a depression. If they would (or could), the economy probably would not have experienced the depression in the first place. Furthermore, many members of the public have nothing to spend, and this is really the essence of the problem.

Similarly, businesses are not likely to spend. As we have said, businessmen become depressed and pessimistic about the future. Their products are unsold, and their plants are idle. Why buy more plant and equipment and inventory when you have more than enough already?

We are left with government, the one spender unconcerned about saving for a rainy day or making a profit. The *federal* government can spend more than it takes in from taxes because it can deficit spend.

THE EVOLUTION OF THE GENERAL THEORY

During Britain's economic plight, Keynes was at the height of his prestige. Keynes's diagnosis at that time was that there was something wrong with the British monetary system and that, whatever was amiss, the British economy could not afford to wait to find the source of the illness. With characteristic impatience, he suggested that the government hire the unemployed for public-works projects.

In the late twenties, Keynes had not yet broken away from the classical concept of the interest-rate mechanism as a promoter of full employment. In 1929, when the United States joined the worldwide depression, he was overjoyed with what the entertainment-trade paper *Variety* called the "egg" laid by Wall Street. What cheered him were the low interest rates then obtainable. Keynes thought that the Great Crash had in it the seeds of the salvation of the American economy. He thought, along with all other orthodox economists, that now businesses would have a real motivation to borrow and would spend the money on new plant, equipment, and inventory, thereby putting people back to work.

Keynes—and everybody else—was wrong. The economic condition of the United States and the rest of the world worsened. By 1930, Keynes suspected that the depression was not going to cure itself in any acceptable length of time. Something was wrong with the then current explanations of the capitalistic economic order. By 1934, he was convinced that a theory holding that the economy has an automatic tendency to full employment had to be either faulty or misinterpreted, since for seventeen years the only observable tendency in the British economy was for unemployment and misery to grow worse. Two years later, Keynes delivered his new theory of the economy in his world-shaking *General Theory of Employment, Interest, and Money*.

Keynes theorized within the context of a *monetary* economy. This was a new approach, for money had been something of a side issue with the classical and neoclassical economists. They were *real* theorists—that is, they conceived of economic transactions as flows of actual goods and services. Money appeared in their theories only as a unit of account and a medium of exchange. As a unit of account, money is used to give goods money prices so that economists do not have to work with cumbersome barter terms of trade. As a medium of exchange, money facilitates the flow of goods and services so that consumers do not have to find someone with whom they may make a mutually advantageous trade of goods for goods. So, for the classicals and neoclassicals, money was only a convenience facilitating the basic, underlying functioning of the economy, which involved only actual resources, goods, and services.

Keynes saw that money could be troublesome, at least in the short run. Money is a store of purchasing power. This third function, to which the classicals paid scant attention, makes money troublesome.

Essentially, Keynes declared that if spenders choose to withdraw money from the circular flow by saving—that is, by storing some of their currently earned purchasing power until a later date—the flow of goods and services will be affected. The classicals, as we have seen, believed this not to be so because of price flexibility and the movement of the interest rate.

Unhappiness about the improper functioning of the economy is always most vocal when the economy is in a contractionary phase. After all, why should men and machines ever be unemployed when all over the world, among both the rich and the poor, countless wants— necessitous and luxurious—are unfulfilled. Unemployment is an inexcusable absurdity when thought about within the context of the economic problem. Why, when wants are insatiable, does man allow his productive capacity to stand idle? Keynes's answer to this question may seem more reasonable to laymen than the answer of the classicals because his answer involves money and possible aberrations in its use. Laymen's complaints about the economy are often focused upon supposed malfunctionings of money and the monetary system. When the economy fails to provide full employment for its members, despite the omnipresent economic problem, the two most frequently heard objections to the functioning of the monetary system are that there is not enough money and that, if there is enough, some people are bypassed in the flow of income.

The first complaint is not without interest, and there are a number of economists today who are extremely interested in the relation between the quantity of money in circulation and the aggregate behavior of the economy. But the second argument is the one Keynes investigated. It says, in effect, that even if a country is rich, or has the capacity to be rich, money does not get passed around from hand to hand in optimal fashion. Some money gets lost along the way, and, by the time the circular flow is complete, several players in the economic game have not been dealt a full hand. When the monetary flow diminishes, an additional injection of "new" money from some spender must occur if the economy is to be kept from slowing down. As we have seen, the federal government is the most likely and the most effective source of "new" money.

Keynes did not say flatly that the classicals were wrong. The trouble with the classicals' theory, he said, is that it is not perfectly general; it does not cover all possible cases. It is a correct explanation of *long-run* economic phenomena: In the long run, the economy does tend to the full use of its resources—Say's law does work. Given sufficient time, those wanting work for themselves and their resources will find it. This means that in the long run prices are flexible; eventually, the prices of resources, goods, and services must adjust themselves to the market determination of their worth, for actual goods and services are the ultimate reality of any economic system. Simple spending cannot bring forth production beyond the productive capacity of the economy. For an economy to exist and grow, there must be innovation, risk-bearing, investment in plant and equipment, and the performance of useful work in fulfillment of consumer demand. The basic circuit of the circular-flow model is correct. Economic activity consists of the flow of goods and services between households and the business sector. Over the long run, monetary functions must bow to the basic reality of economizing.

In the *short run*, however, Keynes pointed out, the rigidities in the economic system cause trouble. And we cannot wait for the short run to pass; the miseries of the short run are too severe to go unheeded. The long run may be very long indeed. As we noted in Chapter 6, Schumpeter indicated that although capitalism is incessantly changing, the changes may require years, perhaps centuries, to be effected. In the short run, then, rational men must take action, using the knowledge and tools at their disposal, to keep the economy from grinding to a halt. We shall explore shortly the question of whether these actions are consistent with a free-enterprise system.

The Implementation of Keynes's Theory

RESPONSE BY ACADEMIA. The Keynesian message was somewhat delayed in its impact because in 1936 there was no one to teach the economists of that day the new economics. Many economists, sneaking nervous looks at the *General Theory,* probably despaired of ever finding out what Keynes was talking about, for he used a new vocabulary and appeared to be somewhat intoxicated with his own language. Moreover, some older economists had a vested interest in the economics they had once learned, so they resisted the introduction of something they feared might reduce the value of their own store of knowledge. As younger faculty members turned to the study of Keynes and taught the *General Theory* to their own students, Keynes's message began to be heard in this country.

RESPONSE BY GOVERNMENT. Generally, the full implementation of Keynes's ideas by the government awaited the occupancy of federal offices by those exposed to Keynesian economics in college. Obviously, then, government responded slowly to the General Theory.

President Franklin D. Roosevelt was the first American president who could have come under the influence of Keynesian economics, for the General Theory was published during his administration and Keynes personally visited the President in Washington and wrote to him. Because Roosevelt's administration was marked by budgetary deficits and the use of what was then considered wholesale government intervention in the business sector, Roosevelt often has been referred to as a Keynesian, and the economic policies of the New Deal are sometimes believed to have been the first American expression of Keynesianism. This is not so. In his campaign for his first term, Roosevelt had criticized President Herbert Hoover for the large deficits that the latter had incurred. Roosevelt and Keynes did not understand each other. The President complained, probably with justification, that Keynes was unintelligible to him, and Keynes was convinced that Roosevelt was an economic illiterate. Roosevelt unbalanced his budgets reluctantly and in order to promote the social-welfare measures of the New Deal. Furthermore, his use of deficits to accomplish his welfare programs has caused many people to align Keynesian economics with the welfare state, while the achievement of a welfare state was never one of Keynes's objectives. In fact, he felt that one reason New Deal spending programs failed to stimulate the American economy was that there was too much social-reform and welfare legislation cluttering up a program that should have been single-mindedly confined to the achievement of economic recovery.

It is doubtful, in fact, whether Roosevelt ever accepted Keynesian economics. In his last letter to his Secretary of the Treasury, Henry Morgenthau, Jr., the President reaffirmed what must have been his constant conviction—that the soundest principle of government fiscal policy is a balanced budget.

ALLEGATIONS OF MARXISM. The least creditable charge against Keynesian economics comes from those who allege that it is tainted with Marxism. Those who contend that Keynes was a Marxist—even an unconscious one—betray a lack of knowledge of Keynes's purpose in writing the General Theory, which was the completely un-Marxist idea of making capitalism work. Keynes believed that capitalism *could* work and that it *should* work. True Marxists believe that capitalism cannot work and that it is a fool's errand to try to save it.

Both Keynes and the Marxists have, however, agreed that Keynes was *not* a Marxist. Keynes dismissed Marxism as "turbid nonsense." For their part, the Marxists have denounced Keynes as being indistinguishable from the rest of the "bourgeois economists" of the West. In the foreword to a Russian edition of Keynes's *General Theory,* the Soviet reading audience is warned against attaching any significance to Keynes's proposition that it is possible to save capitalism by eliminating its characteristic upheavals through deliberate government action. The foreword affirms that one of the chief tasks of Marxist economics is to destroy the illusion of Keynesianism.

Keynes believed in capitalism. In fact, he was critical of President Roosevelt for being antibusiness. Keynes advised Roosevelt to be more conciliatory toward business interests if he wanted to create an environment favorable to business recovery. The unfettered operation of the free-market economy was Keynes's ideal. He thought that the timely application of his remedial measures when the economy was bogged down would cause the economy to revive; after that, it would function according to the classical model.

The Vindication of Keynes's Ideas

Up to now, have we tacitly assumed that Keynesian economic policies did, or could, produce full employment? A common criticism of Keynesian economic policy is that it did nothing to stem the tide of the depression in the thirties and that credit for the return of prosperity must go to the Axis powers—the nations that started the Second World War. But is this not proof of the efficacy of Keynes's prescription? A great part of the purely economic effect of the war resulted from the impact of enormous government expenditures. We must agree with critics of Keynesian economic policy in their factual assertion that purposeful government spending to end the depression did not do so; but we must add that when the requirements of defense and war accelerated government spending, we *did* spend our way out of the depression. Prior to the war, Keynes had criticized the spending efforts of the New Deal as being too feeble. The then astronomical amounts advanced to finance the Second World War were "Keynesian sums." So, we may say that wartime spending did vindicate Keynesian economic policy. If it spends enough to put enough people to work, an economy in the doldrums *can* spend its way out of a depression.

THE LASTING IMPACT OF KEYNESIAN ECONOMICS

Before the Second World War ended, many individuals were fearful of postwar economic adjustments. Their fears were understandable, since the typical postwar experience was economic disruption. No one had forgotten the excesses of the 1920's and the awful experience of the Great Crash of 1929 and its aftermath.

What is our postwar economic record? There has been no repetition of the severe fluctuations that were typical of our prewar experience, and certainly there has been no economic catastrophe remotely resembling the depression of the thirties. We have not escaped from cyclical behavior entirely; there have been expansions and contractions. But since 1945 we have experienced none of the severe economic dislocations that were once thought to be the inevitable price of living in a highly developed capitalistic economy. Why not? It has taken time and the experience of war, and perhaps Lord Keynes's lesson is not yet perfectly learned; but the West has now arrived at a stage in which no responsible government will sit still while its economy disintegrates. Governments are no longer afraid to use fiscal and monetary measures to influence economic activity.

The United States did not wholeheartedly accept the tools of Keynesian economic policy until the Kennedy administration. The Kennedy administration itself appeared to follow the lead of the British, who had been rather tardy in their employment of fiscal and monetary medicines, considering that Britain was Keynes's homeland. Under the Conservative government of Harold Macmillan, however, the British finally made *intentional* budget deficits a part of their program for economic recovery. And the British, having belatedly adopted the Keynesian tools, chided their Yankee cousins for not following the same course.

John F. Kennedy was the first President to take Keynes's economics to heart, for he accepted the Keynesian thesis that government must play an important role in making capitalism work. At the same time that Americans had chosen a national administration conversant with

Keynesian economics, the business community was becoming less suspicious of the economic role that Keynes had assigned to government. However, some of the rapport that might have been established between business and government was frustrated when President Kennedy, rightly or wrongly, insisted that the steel industry not raise its prices in 1962. Although Kennedy obviously had support in some quarters, the business community as a whole was not warmed by this sort of Presidential attention, and what might have been a reconciliation between government and business was thwarted.

The importance to us of this confrontation is that the President's action in the steel crisis was not part of Keynesian economic policies. Keynes did not advocate the application of price controls, formal or informal, to specific firms and industries. He believed that government should exert its influence through *general* fiscal and monetary controls. Specifically, he felt that taxes should be raised and government spending decreased in periods of expansion to avoid "overheating" the economy, while he favored increasing public expenditures in depressed times and financing that increase through borrowing. In addition to these fiscal measures, he recommended the use of monetary controls. In times of contraction, an expansion of the money supply and a lowering of interest rates would encourage consumers and, particularly, businessmen to borrow and spend. In boom times, he recommended, the procedure should be reversed to achieve contraction. Thus, the government would affect the economy as a whole; it would not intervene in the decision-making processes of particular firms.

The administration of President Lyndon B. Johnson was the first that extensively employed from the outset the techniques of the new economics. The first few years of Johnson's Presidency were marked by an unusual rapport, almost unprecedented for a Democratic administration, with the leadership of the business community. There are probably at least three reasons for the change in attitude, at that time, on the part of the executives of major enterprises toward innovative government economic policy. First, most business leaders today are college graduates. Even if they were not exposed to Keynesian economics during college, their capacity for self-education has helped them to learn something about the new economics, and they have begun to recognize that it is an economics of, and for, a capitalistic economy.

Second, many practicing economists have come to regard economic growth, rather than full employment, as the primary goal of the American economy. This shift of concern continues to reflect the reactive nature of economics; for the economies of several foreign nations have shown some remarkable growth rates. As the leader of the free world, and as a model of what a largely free enterprise system can do, the United States cannot allow its growth rate to become sluggish. The objective of full employment has not been sacrificed; happily, growth and full employment are compatible goals. As the economy expands, the number of job and investment opportunities expands also. The realization that growth is a precondition of full employment has led many post-Keynesian economists to reject the possibility of keeping a population fully employed in a fairly static economy and convinced them that a desirable employment level will result from a proper growth rate. Accordingly, these economists have attempted to discover what the annual increase in our GNP ought to be to provide a desired level of employment. Growth is a goal naturally appealing to businessmen. It emphasizes more capacity, more sales, and more profits. It accords fully with the entrepreneurial spirit.

Finally, nothing succeeds like success. Businessmen could see the improvement that followed the cut in federal income-tax rates in 1963. Most impressive to the business community is the economic record of neo-Keynesian procedures. Gross national product has risen more than 40 percent; and, of more concern to businessmen, corporate profits have risen approximately 60 percent. To businessmen, these results are tangible; they can see the results in the increased business of their own firms. And they have seen that the period of prosperity has been coexistent with the length of time that neo-Keynesian policies have been applied.

EPILOGUE

The results of the interaction between the world of affairs and the economic thinkers we have just met are impressive. Adam Smith explained an entirely new economic system to its creators. Thomas Malthus described a population pattern that still plagues parts of the world and worries the rest of it. David Ricardo was instrumental in Great Britain's election of a free-trade policy when the time was ripe, and this policy not only transformed the British nation but had important implications for the development of the United States. From the writings of Karl Marx have come the most severe theoretical and practical challenges that capitalism faces. Alfred Marshall rebuilt the whole science of economics at a time when it was learning little from the world and consequently had little to say to the world. The economics of John Maynard Keynes born of the Great Depression, is very much a part of our own lives. A look at the record shows that the contributions of these men were largely shaped by the course of events during their productive years.

Is economics still a reactive science? It must be admitted that sometimes the impact of the world on current economic researches is hard to see, and in some cases it seems nonexistent. It seems true of all disciplines that, as they grow in sophistication, their scholars turn to work less immediately related to the external world. But, as has been repeatedly demonstrated, we can never tell when the results of pure scientific inquiry will have profound, even devastating, consequences for the world. The most spectacular, albeit grim, example of this is, of course, nuclear weaponry.

Moreover, for the most part, economics still *is* highly reactive in nature. At one time, a principal source of trouble in mature capitalistic economies was an apparently inherent deficiency of aggregate demand, creating a less-than-full-employment-equilibrium GNP. Thanks to the work of Keynes and the post-Keynesians, the specter of this type of economic problem is not as frightening as it once was. But has the lesson been learned too well? Now it seems that when we approach full employment, our economy has an irresistible tendency to inflation. In prosperous times, the cost of living keeps rising. In consequence of this current phenomenon, many economists have turned to a search for remedies for inflation. Some proposals call for tax increases to reduce aggregate demand, while other arguments call for changes in the methods of regulating the money supply as a means to combat inflation. Some economists feel that if the money supply grows no faster than the annual rate of increase in the GNP, the tendency to inflationary price rises will be significantly weakened. Whatever their positions, most economists agree that it is much harder to cool down an economy than it is to bring new life to a temporarily stagnant economic system. Much of the problem is political, not economic. Generally, anti-inflationary, anti-expansionary measures such as increased taxation and reduced government spending are not politically popular, and legislators whose jobs depend upon satisfying their narrowly self-interested constituents can perhaps not be blamed for their timidity in dealing with inflation.

The amazing postwar performance of the American economy has created a new set of problems—problems of the so-called affluent society. One of these problems is the growing disparity in economic status between the majority of the citizenry and a minority for whom economic progress seems to have brought increasing misery. In actuality, probably all members of Western economies are absolutely better off than were their counterparts of twenty and more years ago. Today's poor are not as *absolutely* deprived as were yesterday's low-income groups. But in the West, although, in the aggregate, people have moved upward on the scale of economic well-being, the rate of increase in real income has been markedly greater for the majority than the minority. As a result, the gap has widened between the "haves" and the absolutely better-off "have-nots" of society. A number of economists are concerning themselves with this problem, but much of the practical solution is not a matter of economic analysis or its application.

In addition to this problem of inequitable *distribution* of the national output, there is the problem of the *composition* of that output. Some economists, notably John Kenneth Galbraith (who is usually given credit for the phrase "the affluent society"), have charged that a free-market economy has an implicit bias favoring the production of private consumption goods. This is necessarily so, they contend, because individual consumers are responsible for much of the composition of production. Despite the efficiency with which the market economy satisfies the wants of individuals *as individuals,* these economists believe that the members of society have unsatisfied *collective* wants that they would prefer to see satisfied before some of their less urgent private consumer demands are fulfilled. For example, although people do want and are glad to have more stereos, cosmetics, and movie cameras, they would rather have more colleges, libraries, hospitals, medical research, and rapid-transit facilities. The problem is, say these economists, that the free-market mechanism is vastly more effective in registering individual preferences individually made than it is in reflecting the preferences of individuals as a community.

Furthermore, affluent societies must face the somber fact that they are surrounded by a majority of nations in which a majority of the world's peoples are destitute. Moralists often preach that the rich must share their blessings with the poor. But what is to be done when the poor are so numerous and their poverty so deep that a redistribution of income from the rich nations to the poor nations would have as little effect as trying to render the Atlantic Ocean less salty by emptying the Great Lakes into it?

The obvious answer, therefore, is to try to bring about economic development in the poor nations. This quest has opened a host of questions. The first is: "What has brought the affluent societies of the world to their level of development?" The economic historian has shown that the root system of the economic development of the West is deep and complex. Involved in it is the whole story of Western civilization. What can be done to bring about economic development in a society that does not have this heritage and cannot wait so long? Economists have given some partial answers: Underdeveloped nations should create and be helped to create an entrepreneurial class and a few basic nucleus industries and investment projects around which their economic systems can grow; their governments should promote "balanced growth" so that interdependent sectors will be in existence simultaneously; their administrators should learn techniques of economic planning; and, finally, there must be vast capital inflows to these countries from the developed nations.

While some economists are thus trying to unravel the causes of economic growth and apply them to the underdeveloped nations, other economists are concerned with the affluent nations themselves—for the rich, it seems, have problems of their own.

One of their greatest problems is a "liquidity crisis." There is insufficient money to finance the volume of trade caused by the enormous growth in the productivity of Western nations. The reason for this "money shortage" is that the ultimate international money is gold, and there has been an enormous outpouring of nongold wealth relative to the increase in the free world's gold stock. One severe manifestation of the liquidity crisis is the gold outflow from the United States. American international commitments, peaceful and military, the attractiveness of foreign countries as sites for capital investment by American business firms and private citizens, and the increasing competition of foreign goods have meant that the United States, for more than a decade, has been spending more abroad than she receives. As a result, foreigners possess large dollar balances. The United States treasury has pledged itself to redeem in gold dollars held by foreigners. There has been an increasing demand for the international money (gold) caused both by its shortage relative to nongold wealth and by doubts about the strength of the American economy. The result has been a severe drain of United States gold reserves—an outward and highly visible symptom of the trouble the nation is having with its balance of international payments. Free-world economists have been searching for an answer to the liquidity problem. Some solutions depend on finding a substitute for gold—perhaps by using so-called paper gold.

The economies of the developed nations are now so tightly knit together that the failing economic health of any one of them threatens the well-being of all. In the past, trade barriers of one kind or another were often used to insulate one nation from the economic actions of the rest of the world. Today's highly interdependent world economy forcefully reveals the ostrich-like nature of economic isolationism. The economists' emphasis on freer trade as a rational approach to international economics has borne fruit in such general agreements to reduce tariffs as the so-called Kennedy Round of trade negotiations and in such supranational organizations as the European Common Market.

Throughout this book, with the exception of the section on Marx, we have stressed the economics of primarily market-directed systems. Before we close, let us note that the reactive nature of economics asserts itself in centralist economies also. In the past few years, the leaders of the Soviet Union, beginning with Khrushchev, have become interested in learning more about the economizing processes of the free world. Apparently recognizing that economic centralism can be an impediment to growth and that economic incentives do seem to be responsible, in part, for the remarkable economic performance of the West, they have encouraged their economists to study Western orthodox economics and to apply what they learn to modifications of the Soviet system that can be accommodated by a very flexible Marxian dogma. Probably the most notable example of this change in communist policy is called Libermanism. Liberman, a Russian economist (and other Soviet economists, too) has advocated a greater use of economic incentives and decentralized economic processes in solving resource-allocation problems. Thus, the reactive nature of economics remains strong, not only in our own part of the world but in the world's major centralist economy.

As economic thinkers have been affected by the course of events, so they have produced ideas that have modified the environment that produced the initial stimuli. The recent experience of the Soviet Union is persuasive evidence in behalf of this viewpoint. Behind the assertion of reactivity lies the most important idea of this book—not the idea that the work of economists is more important than the work of other scholars, not even that economics must be seen as a reactive science, but the idea that thinkers, of whatever sort, affect our lives more strongly than any other force. John Maynard Keynes had something to say on this point:

> the ideas of economists and political philosophers, both when they are right and when they are wrong, are more powerful than is commonly understood. Indeed the world is ruled by little else. Practical men, who believe themselves to be quite exempt from any intellectual influences, are usually the slaves of some defunct economist. Madmen in authority, who hear voices in the air, are distilling their frenzy from some academic scribbler of a few years back. I am sure that the power of vested interests

is vastly exaggerated compared with the gradual encroachment of ideas. Not, indeed, immediately, but after a certain interval; for in the field of economic and political philosophy there are not many who are influenced by new theories after they are twenty-five or thirty years of age, so that the ideas which civil servants and even agitators apply to current events are not likely to be the newest. But, soon or late, it is ideas, not vested interests, which are dangerous for good or evil.[1]

This book may seem to have a narrow purpose. Actually, its goal is broader than teaching economics or even attempting to persuade the reader that economists' ideas are important and relevant. Any study of intellectual history—the history of ideas—should lead to the observation suggested by the quotation from Lord Keynes that no force of man exceeds the power of ideas to degrade or ennoble those who think them and those who are touched by them.

[1] John Maynard Keynes, The General Theory of Employment, Interest and Money (New York: Harcourt, Brace & World, 1936), pp. 383–84.

GLOSSARY

Absolute advantage. The situation in which one producer is more efficient in the production of certain goods than any other producer of the same goods. *See* Comparative advantage.

Capital. The produced means of production. A factor of production synonomous in economics with "capital goods." Capital goods are the inputs of one industry that are themselves the outputs of another industry. The income share paid to individuals to induce them to supply their funds to entrepreneurs for the purchase of capital equipment (rather than spend them on consumption goods or leave them idle) is called "interest."

Circular flow. The course of economic activity, which is necessarily a circular flow since transactions take place between buyers and sellers (i.e., what is an expenditure for one economic unit must be an income for some other economic unit and vice versa).

Comparative advantage. A situation in which a producer has a smaller absolute disadvantage (or a greater absolute advantage) over another producer in producing one good than he has in producing a different good. A comparative advantage, not an absolute advantage, is all that is necessary to make trade worthwhile. The principle of "comparative advantage" underlies any trading situation but is usually discussed in connection with international or interregional trade. *See* Absolute advantage.

Cost. Whatever must be given up to have a preferred alternative— best seen in the concept of "opportunity cost." The opportunity cost to an economy of having the goods it consumes is the things it must forego to have its current output mix. Thus, the opportunity cost of having a certain tonnage of wheat each year is the things the wheat-producing resources could have made had consumers not preferred to have the amount of wheat actually produced.

Curve. The visual, or graphical, depiction of the relation between two or more variables, only one of which is independent. Curves may be either linear (straight-line) or curvilinear. They are often used to depict tabular information. *See* Schedule.

Demand. The desire for a good coupled with the purchasing power needed to buy it. *Market demand* refers to the demand of all consumers in the market for a *specific* good or service. It is commonly represented by a negatively sloped demand curve (showing how much of a particular good consumers will buy in a given time period at each possible price). The negative slope illustrates the "law of demand," which holds that there is an *inverse* relationship between the price of a good and the quantity demanded. *Aggregate demand* refers to the total demand of all purchasers for all final goods and services.

Economic growth. An increase in an economy's ability to produce. Graphically, economic growth is shown by the rightward shift of an economy's production-possibility curve. Economic growth can occur as the consequence of an increase in the stock of capital, technological improvements (innovations), or an increase in the resource base of an economy.

Economizing. Choosing between alternative want-satisfiers in an economic situation. *See* Scarcity.

Entrepreneurship. The productive factor that assumes the risks of organizing and operating a business enterprise. The "entrepreneur," as distinguished from a "capitalist" (one who provides funds with which to buy capital equipment), sees the possibilities for establishing a firm to produce goods to satisfy wants, organizes the firm, combines the factors of production to produce the desired goods, attempts to maintain the firm as a viable entity, and assumes the risks attendant on these activities. The income share of the entrepreneur is called "profit."

Equilibrium. The condition that, once attained, will be maintained in the absence of the application of an external force. Alternatively, an equilibrium position is that to which any disequilibrium system must tend.

Factors of production. *See* Land, Labor, Capital, and Entrepreneurship.

Final goods. Either consumer or capital goods intended for their ultimate purchaser. Contrasted to "intermediate goods," which must undergo further transformation before being placed in the hands of their ultimate purchaser. Under different conditions, the same good may be either an intermediate or a final good. For example, to an automobile manufacturer, a spark plug is an intermediate good intended for installation in an automobile on the assembly line. The automobile is the final good. On the other hand, the same spark plug, if produced for the replacement market, is a final good. *See* GNP.

GNP. Gross national product. A nation's total output of *final* goods and services over a one-year period (which includes the value of the capital items that were used up in the production of the economy's total final output).

Goods. Anything that satisfies a want. Goods may be *tangible* or *intangible*. Intangible goods are often called services. An example of a tangible good is water; an example of an intangible good, or a service, is legal advice. Both tangible and intangible goods are classified as *free* or *economic* goods. A free good is one that requires no sacrifice, or cost, to obtain. An economic good is one that can be had only by giving up something (by incurring a cost) to have it. An example of a free good is the ordinary air we breathe. Air can be an economic good, however, if it is cooled, heated, dehumidified, or put under pressure, for such air can only be obtained at a cost. Economics is not concerned with free goods, as their acquisition poses no economic problem.

Inflation. A rapid rise in the *general* price level (as opposed to changes in the prices of specific goods occasioned by changing supply and demand conditions), or, alternatively, a decline in the purchasing power of money. Inflation stems from several possible sources—for example, an increase in the money supply unaccompanied by a matching increase in the aggregate supply of goods and services, an imbalance which causes money to become less valuable relative to nonmoney assets.

Innovation. The act of introducing into the economy a *new* product, service, process, or mode of operation. "Innovation" is not a synonym for "invention." A new product (invention) is not an innovation unless it is applied in the economic system.

Interest. See Capital.

Investment. The *actual purchase* of capital equipment by a business firm. (The technical meaning of the term differs from ordinary usage, in which "investment" usually means the purchase of bonds or shares of stock.)

Labor. All human exertion, mental or physical, performed in exchange for income. The income share paid to induce individuals to furnish their labor power to the productive process is called wages.

Laissez faire. Literally, "let do." The economic *policy* (as distinct from analysis) that no organ, particularly government should interfere with the free-market mechanism. The *analytical* base for laissez faire is the hypothesis, espoused by Adam Smith and most of the classicals, that a free-market system is fully self-regulating and that the good of all (the social welfare) is served most effectively if each individual pursues his own self-interest.

Land. Natural resources in their pristine form; for example, virgin soil, a lode of ore, a stream, an ocean, the climatic conditions of a particular geographical region. The payment made to owners of natural resources in return for the use of their property is called "rent."

Marginal propensity to consume (MPC). The ratio of a *change* in the consumption spending of an economy or an individual to a change in income—in other words, the proportion of any increase in income that will be spent on consumer goods. For example, a marginal propensity to consume of ¾ means that $3 out of every $4 increase in income will be spent on consumption and $1 will be saved. (Nonconsumption is defined as saving.) If this is the case, the *marginal propensity to save* must be ¼. Economists hypothesize that the value of the aggregate marginal propensity to consume is less than one—*i.e.,* that less than 100 percent of an increase in income will be spent on consumption. *See* Multiplier.

Market. The context in which the forces of supply and demand operate to establish the going price of a good or service; a collection of offers and counteroffers made by would-be sellers and buyers. The market price is established when the price at which goods are offered equals the price at which consumers demand them.

Maximizing principle. A fundamental assumption of economics about the nature of man. *For analytic purposes,* men are assumed to be maximizers. As consumers, they attempt to maximize the total utility they derive from the goods they consume subject to the limitations of income. As sellers of resources, individuals are assumed to act to maximize the total gain derived from the sale of their services, subject to such limitations as the desire for leisure, the need for rest, and so on.

Monopoly. Literally "single seller." Strictly speaking, the case in which there is a single seller of a product having no substitutes. Since most goods and services do have some kinds of substitutes, the working definition of a monopolist is a seller of a product for which there are no *close* substitutes. Most large monopolies are public utilities and, hence, are regulated by government.

Multiplier. The coefficient that indicates by how much the GNP will increase for a given increase in aggregate demand. Economists hypothesize that the value of the multiplier is greater than one. This being the case, an increase in autonomous spending will produce an increase in the GNP greater than itself. The numerical value of the multiplier is the reciprocal of the marginal propensity to save (1/MPS). *See* Marginal propensity to consume.

Nonprice competition. A form of market behavior in which rival sellers do not compete on the basis of price. Instead, competition, which may be quite severe, centers on quality, innovation, service, advertising, snob-appeal, product distinctiveness, brand names, and trademarks.

Normal profit. The profit that obtains when entrepreneurs are neither entering nor leaving an industry. Those entrepreneurs *already in* the industry are satisfied just to remain as they are. When such a situation obtains, an industry is said to be in long-run equilibrium. *See* Entrepreneurship, Profit.

Oligopoly. A market of few sellers, in which nonprice competition is usually dominant. Characteristic of the American economy. Examples are the tobacco, automobile, typewriter, fountain-pen, soap, steel, and motion-picture industries.

Perfect competition. A highly idealized theoretical construct in which there are so many firms so small in relation to the market that a single firm cannot affect the market price. The goods produced by the member firms of any one industry are homogeneous; there are no restrictions on exit from, or entry into, the market; and competitors have a perfect knowledge of the market. Actual market behavior and structures depart in varying degrees and in different respects from the ideal model.

Profit. *See* Entrepreneurship, Normal profit.

Rent. *See* Land.

Resources. The basic form of want-satisfiers. Business firms combine resources to form the finished goods and services demanded by consumers.

Scarcity. The basic fact of economics. Scarcity exists whenever wants exceed the means of satisfying them. The existence of scarcity produces an "economic situation." In an economic situation, consumers are *forced* to choose between alternative want-satisfiers because they cannot satisfy all their wants at the same time.

Schedule. A tabular expression of the relation between several variables. Customarily, one variable is independent and the others change in relation to it. An example is a demand schedule, in which the independent variable is price and the dependent variable is quantity demanded per time period. *See* Curve.

Shortage. A phenomenon that obtains when the price of a good is held *below* the free-market equilibrium price, causing the quantity of a good that would-be buyers demand to exceed the amount that producers are willing to put on the market. The opposite of shortage is surplus, which exists when the price of a good is held *above* the free-market equilibrium price. In a free market, there are no impediments to the full functioning of the forces of supply and demand; hence, shortages and surpluses are temporary phenomena that will be quickly eliminated as the automatic mechanism of the market establishes the equilibrium price—the price at which the quantity demanded of a good equals the quantity supplied.

Supply. In the sense of *market supply,* the amount of a specific good or service that producers will put on the market in a given time period at any possible price. *Aggregate supply* refers to the totality of all goods and services produced by an economy during a specified time period (usually one year). *See* GNP.

Surplus. As presently used in economics, an unnecessary payment. A payment to a factor owner is considered to be *economically unnecessary* when it is not needed to provide the incentive for the factor owner to furnish a flow of productive services. Some economists (*e.g.,* physiocrats) prior to the development of the Ricardian rent theory defined surplus as a return to human effort in excess of the value of that effort. The source of the surplus was believed to be Nature. In Marxian economics, surplus retains the general Ricardian meaning of an unnecessary payment, but Marx, in the phrase "surplus value," characteristically applied the term to the income of the capitalist class. For another important use of the term surplus, *see* Shortage.

Unemployment. The situation that exists when any resource, or productive factor (not just people), is not used and, at the same time, the economy is foregoing goods and services that it could have *without undergoing any sacrifice, or cost,* by using the unemployed resources.

Utility. The ability of a good or service to satisfy a human want. Economic theory assumes that rational individuals strive, subject to the limitations imposed by their purchasing power, to acquire the amount and combination of goods and services that will maximize their total utility.

Value. The power of one good or service to command other goods and services in exchange. *Price* is the monetary expression of the value of a good.

Wages. See Labor.

Wages fund. An invalid theory of the classical economists, holding that there is only a certain amount of wealth (output) in an economy that can be used to pay workers. A logical consequence of the theory is that any activity on the part of laborers to raise their wages is futile, since the totality of wages is limited to the extent of the wages fund.

Wants. The basic desires for goods and services.

Wealth. In present usage, a nation's *stock* of tangible economic goods. In the past, usage was less precise. For example, Adam Smith used wealth in the sense that we use income (as a *flow* of goods and services over a given time period.) Thus, Smith's "wealth" of nations was something more nearly like our concept of GNP. The mercantilists defined wealth largely as a nation's stock of precious metals.

INDEX

Marxian economics (*cont.*)
nomics and, 223–24; definition of
property in, 134; and revolution, 151,
154–55; socialism and, 131–32; "socially necessary" labor theory of value
and, 136; source of surplus value in,
138–44; in Soviet Union, 233; vision
of future, 151–58; welfarism and, 154
(*see also* Dialectical materialism;
specific entries)
Maximizing principle, 55–56
Mercantilism, 27–36; appraised, 31–34;
colonialism and, 30–31; death of, 35–
36; balance-of-trade doctrine of, 32–
34; monetary theory of, 34–35; premises of, 29–31; Smithian disavowal of,
72; trade, obsession with, 35–36;
wealth as power in, 31–32
Methodenstreit, 165–66
Mill, John Stuart, 12, 86*n,* 133, 164–
65
Money: Aristotle's view of, 25; in
economic analysis, 28; in Keynesian
economics, 220–21; in mercantilist
theory, 34–35; production and, 34–
35; quantity theory of, 34; role of,
17–18; scholastics' view of, 25
Monopolies: dynamic view of, 195–97;
Marxian view of capitalism and, 150–
51; nature of, 191; oligopolies and,
192–93; in Smithian economics, 69–
70, 78
Monopolistic competition, 191–93
Moral restraint, in Malthusian population principle, 86
MPC (marginal propensity to consume), 213
MPS (marginal propensity to save),
213
Multiplier effect, 212–17
Mun, Thomas, 30–31, 36

Natural liberty, system of, 56–58
Neoclassical economics, 170–99 (*see
also specific entries*)
Neo-Malthusians, 86*n*
New economics, 203
Noncompetitive markets, problems of,
193–95
Nonprice competition, 61
Normal profit, 106

Oligopolies, 192–93; dynamic view of,
195–97; interdependence of, 193–94
Opportunity cost, 6*n,* 17
Optimal solutions, 199
Oversaving, Malthusian thesis of, 125–
27

Parsimony, in Smithian economics, 74–
76 (*see also* Saving)
Partial-equilibrium analysis, 95, 197;
in consumer-demand study, 174
Perfect competition, 60–62
Petty, William, 36
Physiocratic economics, 36, 126; and
agriculture, 37, 38; and circular flow
of income, 39–42, *40;* class divisions
in, 37; and extractive industries, 37;
laissez faire economics and, 39; role of
nature in, 37, 38–39; Smithian disavowal of, 72; solution for taxation
problem, 38
Pitt, William, 87
Political economics, 162
Political economy, 28
Population, principle of (*see* Malthu-
sian economics)
Poverty, 80–81, 230–32
Price, market, determination of, 182–
84, *183*
Price flexibility, 218
Price level, general, 34
Price-taking firms, 189–91
Production: cost of, 140–44, 198–99;
factors of, 10; laws of (Mill), 165;
money and, in mercantilist theory, 34–
35
Production-possibility curve, 14–17, *15;*
in mercantilist economics, 32; ques-
tions raised by, 18–19
Profit, 11, 190*n;* normal, 106; in
Ricardian system, 109–13
Progress, Marxian definition of, 146*n*
Progressive businesses, 195

Quantity theory of the value of money,
34
Quesnay, Francois, 39, 52

Rationality, 31
Rent, 11; differential, theory of, 93–

'3ð.9